D0078276

A Simple Path to Sustainability

Case Production Operating Manager: Carrie Yasemin Paykoc

Project Managers: Elizabeth Long and Maribeth Neelis

Technical Editors: Becky English and Sarah E. Thompson

Research Team:

Fred Andreas	*David Jacobs*
Stephen R. Bernard	*Elizabeth Long*
Kenneth Bettenhausen	*Liz Lowry*
Elizabeth R. Brost	*Clint McCarver*
Clay Chase	*K. J. McCorry*
Elizabeth S. Cooperman	*Jennifer Mich*
Jamie M. Dandar	*Maribeth Neelis*
Sharen A. Durst-Aldridge	*Carrie Yasemin Paykoc*
Blair Gifford	*Maria Elena Price*
Natasha Gleichmann	*Alan Romero*
Pamela Goodrich-Yohe	*Graham Russell*
Robin Groppi	*Christopher Thorp*

A Simple Path to Sustainability

Green Business Strategies for Small and Medium-Sized Businesses

Fred Andreas, Elizabeth S. Cooperman,
Blair Gifford, and Graham Russell, Editors

Property of
Baker College
of Allen Park

AN IMPRINT OF ABC-CLIO, LLC
Santa Barbara, California • Denver, Colorado • Oxford, England

Copyright 2011 by ABC-CLIO, LLC

All rights reserved. No part of this publication may be reproduced, stored in a retrieval system, or transmitted, in any form or by any means, electronic, mechanical, photocopying, recording, or otherwise, except for the inclusion of brief quotations in a review, without prior permission in writing from the publisher.

Library of Congress Cataloging-in-Publication Data

A simple path to sustainability : green business strategies for small and medium-sized businesses / Fred Andreas . . . [et al.], editors.
   p. cm.
 Includes bibliographical references and index.
 ISBN 978-0-313-38269-7 (hard copy : alk. paper) — ISBN 978-0-313-38270-3 (ebook) 1. Small business—Environmental aspects. 2. Sustainable development. 3. Social responsibility of business. I. Andreas, Fred, 1952– II. Title.

  HD2341.S553   2011
  658.4'083—dc22   2010051248

ISBN: 978-0-313-38269-7
EISBN: 978-0-313-38270-3

15   14   13   12   11   1 2 3 4 5

This book is also available on the World Wide Web as an eBook.
Visit www.abc-clio.com for details.

ABC-CLIO, LLC
130 Cremona Drive, P.O. Box 1911
Santa Barbara, California 93116-1911

This book is printed on acid-free paper ∞

Manufactured in the United States of America

*To the outstanding sustainability leaders presented
here, and to the change agents of the future.*

Contents

Zero-Waste Hospitality

PART III: OVERALL LESSONS

Preface

Fred Andreas

Mr. Keller's freshman class at Hampton High sat atop a hillside in the rolling suburban hills north of Pittsburgh overlooking the vista below. The lush green carpeted valleys awash with the late summer mist teemed with birds darting and bugs buzzing in every direction. With a characteristic Robert Goulet voice and a sweep of his arm, Mr. Keller proclaimed, "This . . . is Ecology!" That first day of high school met the freshmen's expectations, with the school's icon of science proclaiming a new paradigm, sending the students scrambling for their pencils and the word again . . . E-what? How do you spell that? Pencils at the ready . . . "Ecology!" he boomed a second time with a sweep of his arm and a smirk on his face. It was late August, 1967. That salvo and others like it in the 1960s signified the birth of the modern sustainability movement as part of the mainstream. It was my high school; you can't get more mainstream than that!

Almost a half-century later, BP's disastrous oil spill in the Gulf of Mexico kick-started the summer of 2010 with a deadly reminder that the extraction industry, even while supplying a thirsty U.S. economy, still disconnects stewardship and responsibility from corporate profits. Here in the 21st century, the century of sustainability, with the word on every school child's lips, we have collectively experienced the shame of one of the largest man made disasters in human history. Thus we see how far our corporate culture *hasn't* come from the days of the Industrial Revolution. As a metaphorical last gasp, this disaster may well elucidate an unprecedented and universal awakening on a national scale. This disaster, created as a direct result of our thirst for cheap oil, remains our collective responsibility and may form the impetus to cap the mantra of "drill, baby, drill." According to the U.S. Energy Information Agency, the United States uses almost one-fourth of the world's energy for only 5 percent of the world's population. We drunkards, high on oil and energy as proclaimed by President George W. Bush, began sobering up some time ago on a new sustainability paradigm.

Hard lessons continue over the decades as the result of unbridled, unsustainable economic development. Many include environmental disasters. Most poignantly, the West still suffers the effects of over foresting and clear-cutting from the building of our 19th-century cities, contributing to the pine bark beetle's destruction of the Rocky Mountain pine and fir forests. Clear-cutting and subsequent regrowth of lodgepole pine pioneer species set the stage for the devastation of entire swaths of pine forests. That artificially created monoculture allowed opportunistic pests to devastate the entirety of the high-altitude forests more than a century after the original environmental devastation. Many U.S. Forest Service predictions include the complete devastation of those forests within the next 10 years, changing the Western landscape for centuries to come. These disasters serve merely as bellwethers of the larger problem: the focus on the bottom line at the expense of all else, the ultimate valuation of profits above everything, a monolithic approach to business success. Without consideration of sustainable principles in business, today's actions will create equally devastating and lasting effects for our children's and grandchildren's futures.

The current financial and market crisis coupled with the ongoing Great Recession of 2008–2010, remain an enigma of the U.S. business model. Not since the Great Depression of the 1930s have the fundamentals of U.S. business been so called into question. The conundrum of this collapse forms baseline questions, asking for new sustainable models to provide answers about how to sustain an economy of this size over the long term. Coupled with United Nations (UN) predictions of China's potential doubling and India's tripling of U.S. Gross Domestic Product by the end of the century, these predictions create both daunting prospects and tremendous opportunities. Statistics from the U.S. Department of Energy indicate that energy and carbon remain stubbornly attached to economic development, increasing on an almost one-to-one basis. We all know that things must change. But how?

The term *sustainability* relating to business and development, coined by the Prime Minister of Norway, began with the 1987 UN World Commission on the Environment. Sustainability included the requirement to "meet present needs without compromising the ability of future generations to meet their needs." Being sustainable meant "using methods, systems and materials that won't deplete resources or harm natural cycles."[1] Now, almost a quarter-century later, by today's standards, these definitions seem insufficient and limited. As time goes on, sustainability includes new ideals that permeate previously unimaginable parts of our lives. The concept evolved with the motto of the "triple bottom line," including the concepts of "people, planet, and profits," highlighting a growing movement of business *not* as usual.

The triple bottom line of sustainability, through the combination of social, environmental, and economic factors, evolved through use to indicate separate yet equal silos of interests. All three values, individually important, sadly remained in many ways disconnected from one another. The Environmental Protection Agency transposed the triple bottom line concept into "P3: People, Prosperity and the Planet" at almost the same moment the construct became passé. Too bad. It had a nice ring to it. But wait a minute! Expanding the P3 concept to include fundamental interconnections, collaborations, and integration dismantles the separate silo concept of the triple bottom line, refocusing the underlying principles and suggesting cooperation and inclusion as the very foundation of sustainability.

The new paradigm expanded to include wide-ranging principles of ethics and stewardship, defining a new path for sustainability in the 21st century. That path encompassed a broader definition, moving beyond the boundaries of the triple bottom line. Sustainability now permeates all aspects of our collective existence. Broader principles of ethics and stewardship now form new foundations for our future with small business maintaining the flexibility and focus necessary to support these new principles. If sustainability runs throughout the entire culture, seemingly separate concepts such as diversity, time, and money translate into a more integrated approach to business. *Sustainability then defines a path—a journey of inclusion and stewardship—and not merely the result, the bottom line.* A diverse approach to a business plan, participants, services, products, financing, employees, shareholders, the public, and environmentalism all create far-reaching opportunities and responsibilities. Small business, as the backbone of the U.S. economy, affords great opportunities to nurture a sustainable future.

Indeed, the impetus for this book sprang from fundamental cooperation between individual disciplines. The new Integrative Graduate Education and Research Traineeship Program known as IGERT at the University of Colorado Denver (UCD) partnered with the Connected Organizations for a

Responsible Economy (CORE), a business nonprofit association dedicated to promoting environmentally and socially responsible business practices. Together the team focused on a cooperative and integrative approach to this project. The College of Architecture and Planning as well as the Business School at UCD worked with CORE to create this book showcasing sustainable business practices through a dozen successful and diverse small business models. A number of graduate students from both disciplines participated directly in this book, performing research and, in many cases, authoring drafts and final chapters. The dozen businesses showcased in this book—many not focusing on traditional sustainable products or services—exemplify the breadth and strength of sustainable business practices. Sustainability, while not presented as a solution, is offered as a path, a *Simple Path to Sustainability* in each of these business models.

The concept of sustainability may best be described as an expansion into global thinking. Not the cliché of the 1970s of thinking big and acting small, as in "think globally and act locally." Again, the moniker remains too limited. Thinking globally and acting globally nurtures and develops today's complicated and interconnected world based on the integration of P3: People, Prosperity and the Planet through social, economic, and environmental values. These connections define an expansive $P3^3$ concept that ties these disciplines together into a network of interrelated, integrated, and cooperative approaches. Employee environment and attitude, as well as company environmental policy, expand the notion of the bottom line into a series of webs. $P3^3$ expands our horizons, exemplified by the chess game of our fathers versus the chess game of Star Trek, where every move exists in three dimensions, thinking in 3-D.

The words *sustainable* and *green,* voted by a National Public Radio survey as the most overused words of 2008, may yet develop into a universal political, economic, and social movement.[2] How will these concepts translate into practice? With an expanded understanding of the triple bottom line, these new principles translate into new directions in sustainable business. Sustainability as a concept, initiated in the last decades of the 20th century, may dramatically affect our future. These concepts run through the foundations of the business, environmental, and social worlds. Small business as the largest private-sector employer, may offer the best opportunity for sustainable economic vitality and approaches. Our sustainable future rests within the expansion of business into a new and innovative approach through the global, expansive thinking of $P3^3$, based in the principles of integration, cooperation, and inclusion. These concepts form the basis for this book.

Today, many businesses, governments, and organizations embrace sustainability through multiple facets of sustainable integration. These words and approaches are almost ubiquitous within federal, state, and local governments as well as universities committed to a myriad of programs supporting everything from sustainable development and investment to resource programs for their constituents and employees. The U.S. Green Building Council and Leadership in Energy and Environmental Design (LEED) continues to redefine the entire building industry by setting the bar for minimum green standards, putting the idea of sustainable development on everyone's lips. Human resources throughout the culture integrate "best practices" that support growth and empowerment in workers' daily activities. Sustainability no longer remains a static concept of "do no harm." It's expanded into a web of integrated solutions that supports global thinking in a geometric fashion.

A Simple Path to Sustainability examines a dozen success stories in one of the nation's hotbeds of sustainability, the Front Range of Colorado. These stories reflect a diverse approach to sustainability through a wide range of business types. No one solution solves these companies' sustainability challenges. A full spectrum of solutions provides many colorful sustainable business opportunities. The businesses in the book include architects and developers, places where you'd expect sustainability. The book also includes other businesses not commonly thought of as sustainable, such as a bank, a brewery, a manufacturer, a hospital, a hotel, a machine shop, a printing company, a trash and recycling company, and a financial investment company, all providing a template for sustainable business practice success.

From the examples in this book, you'll find an investment company and a bank revamping their approaches to support more sustainable businesses and loans. You'll discover how architects and developers fulfill their mission of providing green and sustainable design while supporting sustainable investment and employee empowerment. You'll find an industry changing its manufacturing practices by focusing on an environmental component while supporting opportunities for its workers. A brewery utilizing 100 percent renewable power and recycled content supports its employees through an employee ownership model and direct management. A trash and recycling company concerned with overseas dumping of unusable waste now supports one of the highest local recycling rates in the country and an employee-friendly environment. A hotel utilizing energy management and pollution prevention methods manages to include community support programs within its core values. A machine shop founded and nurtured on the principles of ethical longevity supports a team concept that values diversity and support for all employees. All showcased companies provide public transportation, educational opportunities, and sustainability programs for their workers for green career advancement. Every company views sustainability as a multifaceted, integrated foundation to its business success.

Returning to the roots of sustainability in the mid-1960s . . . Mr. Keller's freshman class on the hillside of those misty green hills of Pittsburgh discussing ecology, stewardship, and a sustained future may have preceded the coining of the concept of sustainability by two decades, but those discussions and others like them formed the foundations of sustainability as a fundamental value of our modern culture over the last half-century.

Global-level thinking in sustainability, a paradigm based on connections, helps define the baseline concept not merely by the results but by its path to the future. Every company has a story. *A Simple Path to Sustainability* illustrates the close relationships among ethics, stewardship, and integration for walking that path. From the initial inspiration to success focused on the future, these mainstream businesses lay foundations for sustainable practices, creating longevity, influence, and ultimately sustainable success. Through these examples, a new understanding of sustainability emerges— one with broad application, with sustainable business practices focused on concepts such as sustainable purpose, ethics, and stewardship, creating a shift to the new global century through innovative global thinking.

NOTES

1. *Defining Sustainability,* Washington State University, School of Architecture and Construction Management, Seattle, WA. 2009 http://www.arch.wsu.edu/09%20publications/sustain/defnsust.htm

2. Inskeep, S. (Narrator). "List: Stop Using Overused Words Like Bailout," *Morning Edition* [Radio broadcast]. Washington, DC: National Public Radio, 2008.

Chapter Summaries by Industry Focus

ARCHITECTURE

Chapter 4: Barrett Studio Architects

For the past 28 years, Barrett Studio Architects has provided sustainable designs for customers worldwide, operating as a full-service environmental design architectural firm. Its LEED-certified architects focus on green architecture combined with contemporary design sensibilities, receiving awards and early on fulfilling a unique market niche.

Chapter 5: Forest City

Starting in 1920 as a family lumber supply company, Forest City Enterprises became a publicly traded diversified real estate company that acquires, develops, owns, and manages commercial and residential real estate properties throughout the United States. In 1999, Forest City became a sustainable company with its successful Stapleton project in Denver, Colorado, with green practices benefiting both the environment and the marketing of Forest City's projects, and sustainability added to the firm's list of core values across the country.

BANKING

Chapter 8: Boulder Valley Credit Union

Starting small, Boulder Valley Credit Union (BVCU) installed a solar electric system and energy-efficient lighting and windows to reduce its energy costs and its carbon footprint. To celebrate, it decided to provide customers with environment-friendly gifts and lower loan rates for home solar electric systems and fuel-efficient cars. To BVCU's surprise, it became known as an industry leader in sustainability and so decided to include the environment in all its decisions, from a green supply chain to paperless operations and providing public education on sustainability—all of which benefited the credit union's reputation.

BREWING COMPANIES

Chapter 9: New Belgium Brewery

New Belgium Brewery is the third largest craft brewery nationally and a leader in sustainable business, believing in corporate social responsibility not only for the environment, but also for the brewery's employees and community. In 1998, New Belgium became the first wind-powered brewery in the United States, thanks to a unanimous vote by the employee-owners, and the firm demonstrated that cultivating a culture of sustainability can enable a business to become profitable, successful, and an industry leader.

ENVIRONMENTAL PRODUCTS

Chapter 3: Eco-Products

Eco-Products started out as an inspired idea to distribute paper products made from post-consumer recycled content as a father and son climbed Longs Peak in the summer of 1990. Operating initially from a family garage, the company grew steadily over 16 years to generate yearly revenues of $50 million, with its own brand of compostable food service products distributed to some of the largest food service distributors in the country, including Disney theme parks, Busch Gardens, SeaWorld, and Major League Baseball stadiums, while remaining a carbon-neutral company.

HOSPITALS

Chapter 6: Boulder Community Hospital

Boulder Community Hospital started out with grassroots efforts to be environmentally responsible, which led to an environmental stewardship as part of the hospital's culture, which was formalized with policies to guide environmental efforts in 1995. The hospital achieved a LEED Silver certification designation, reaping many sustainable management awards, considerable cost savings, and greater customer and employee satisfaction and a stronger sense of community.

HOTELS

Chapter 13: Boulder Outlook Hotel

In 2002, an investment team purchased a flailing Ramada Inn in Boulder, Colorado, and created the Boulder Outlook Hotel, which became a nationally renowned sustainably managed hotel that engages in energy-reduction, pollution-prevention, and community support programs. The hotel treats customers with a truly environmentally friendly experience during their stay; rooms are entered with recycled-content key cards, illuminated by compact fluorescent light bulbs, cleaned with Green Seal certified products, and have amenities such as a chlorine-free pool, rentable reusable water containers, continental breakfast with organic selections, and educational recycling stations.

MACHINERY REBUILDING AND REPAIRING

Chapter 11: Denver Machine Shop

The Denver Machine Shop, Inc., a family-owned firm founded in 1916, provides a valuable success story in ethical longevity passed down through generations, including a team approach that values employees and diversity. The award-winning company uses its extensive expertise in equipment repair, rebuild, and reuse to extend equipment life and helps other companies find alternatives to the wasteful dispose-and-replace mode of equipment use that is so common today.

PRINTING

Chapter 7: The Digital Frontier

With increasing scrutiny by green-minded customers, The Digital Frontier, a Denver-based printing company, got a jumpstart on its competition when the firm converted to an environmentally friendly line of printers and printing chemicals. Later the firm extended its commitment to sustainability by infusing this ethic throughout its operations, educating its customers as well on the importance of sustainability in printing purchasing decisions.

RECYCLING

Chapter 10: Guaranteed Recycling Xperts

In 2004, network engineer Mike Wright purchased GRX, a small electronics recycling company. He initially addressed many of the issues common to recycling complicated materials, such as the typical practice of shipping products that can't be scrapped to countries where they ultimately create socially and environmentally dire consequences. Under his leadership and commitment to a sustainable model that goes beyond U.S. laws and regulations, Guaranteed Recycling Xperts now claims an impressive 94 percent recyclability rate, a companywide commitment to sustainable business practices, an employee-friendly work environment, and an increased intake from 30,000 to 800,000 pounds per month.

SOCIALLY RESPONSIBLE INVESTING

Chapter 12: First Affirmative Financial Network, LLC

First Affirmative Financial Network, a financial services firm headquartered in Colorado Springs, has been dedicated to the double bottom line since its inception in 1987, having done much along the way to debunk the myth of a trade-off between portfolio returns and socially responsible investing. Starting with $1 million in start-up capital, the firm currently has over $700,000 of assets under management and over 4,000 accounts with a mission of combining competitive investment returns and impacting social change that has resonated with customers.

Chapter 2: Measuring Costs and Benefits

As with any strategy, measuring the success of its components is critical for long-term success. This chapter provides an overview of revenue benefits and cost savings associated with sustainable management strategies and methods used by small and medium-sized firms to report and benchmark their progress, along with resources available to small and medium-sized firms for measuring their carbon footprints and partnerships that can be made with firms that provide help in measuring and purchasing offsets to assist the investment in new proenvironment energy sources and projects. The chapter also discusses the use of a more sophisticated life-cycle analysis for manufacturing firms and provides examples of the type of reports to stakeholders used by some of the small and medium-sized organizations presented in the book's cases.

PART I

Overview

ONE

Introduction

Graham Russell

The most frequently cited definition of sustainability is that used in a report by the Brundtland Commission to a 1987 United Nations conference. It defined sustainable developments as those that "meet present needs without compromising the ability of future generations to meet their needs." Various attempts have been made since then to elaborate this original effort to incorporate the idea that any economic or business system operates within a site, which contains natural and human resources on which the system depends for its viability and on which the system will continue to depend in the future. A reasonable working definition of a sustainable system might now be:

> A sustainable system is one that fulfills present and future needs while using, *and not harming,* renewable resources and unique human-environmental resources of a site: air, land, water, energy, mineral resources, and human ecology and/or those of other (off-site) sustainable systems.

The upsurge of interest in "greening" our economy in recent years seems to demonstrate that the United States has begun to wake up to the excessive demands being placed on the world's resources by the existing global economic model. This belated awakening (the Europeans and Japanese have been aware of these issues for many years) has been driven in large part by the rising cost of energy, most notably the rising price of oil, which ravaged Americans' pocketbooks in the form of $4 (and more) per gallon of gasoline in many states for several months in 2008 (still, however, far below the heavily taxed price in most European countries).

While rising energy prices are the most obvious and immediate manifestation of rapidly rising demand-side pressures on global resources, the overwhelming evidence is that we will soon see similar resources challenges in water, land use, forest products, and a number of minerals. Indeed, during 2008, we saw sharp increases in the prices of many foods around the globe, partly the result of escalating fertilizer costs (itself partly a consequence of the rising cost of oil and natural gas), but also partly the result of changing dietary preferences in the world's major developing economies (China, India, Brazil, etc.), where people are increasingly demanding higher-protein meat and fish diets. The rising demands on world resources from the need to raise increasing numbers of pigs, cows, and poultry were also responsible for a good portion of the rising cost of food around the world in 2008.

Another example of the impact of rapidly rising demand-side pressure on natural resources has been the dramatic increase in the price of iron ore, which has risen from just over $20 per ton in 2000 to around $200 per ton in 2010. This escalation has been very largely due to the explosive growth of building and infrastructure projects in China (has anyone counted the number of tower cranes within a 15-mile radius of downtown Beijing or Shanghai recently?), which produced more steel in 2009 than the United States, Europe, and Japan combined. Prices charged to Chinese steel mills by the world's iron ore mining companies doubled in some years in the middle of the past decade. This evolving situation has so far gone largely unnoticed in the United States, because the use of steel is no longer something that drives the U.S. economy in the way it did 100 years ago in the age of railroad construction and the rapid expansion of the United States' big cities. Sooner or later, however, increased costs of commodities like iron ore, potash (a key ingredient of fertilizers), lumber, and others will feed through into the economies of the developed world with potentially very disruptive consequences.

While the global economic downturn after mid-2008 caused many of the demand-side pressures to abate somewhat, the Chinese economy is growing rapidly once again (10% annualized or higher in several recent quarters in 2010), and there are signs that the devastated U.S. and European economies will achieve modest growth rates in 2010 and for the next several years. The price of a barrel of oil has already recovered from a low in the high $30 range in early 2009 to nearly $90 at the end of 2010. The share prices of most of the world's major commodity producers have risen sharply in anticipation that, as a full global economic recovery kicks in, we shall see a return to the kinds of pressures on many global resources we saw in the period leading up to the summer of 2008. Vale, based in Brazil, is the world's largest iron ore mining corporation and, despite being virtually unknown in the United States, now has a market capitalization about the same as that of Chevron, the second-largest American oil company.

A basic premise of this book is that, in the coming decades, anything that grows in the earth or is extracted from the earth—in short, the vast majority of the resources that sustain our global economy—is facing demand-side pressures across the globe that will drive steep price increases or possibly even cause the world eventually to run out of certain resources altogether (e.g., oil). If we do not find more efficient ways to use these critical natural resources on which we depend, our existing global economic model may face very severe disruption, possibly—in the worst case scenario—to the point where political stability will break down, leading to wars as the competition for scarce resources intensifies. We call this situation the global sustainability challenge.

We did not embark on this book from the standpoint of whether it's right or wrong for humans to spoil the planet on which they live to the point where it may eventually become uninhabitable in the way we understand it today. Indeed, this is fundamentally a book about business and financial opportunity. On the other hand, we have talked to many mainstream, unsentimental business people who have told us they sometimes wonder whether their children and grandchildren will have a quality of life as good as that which we enjoy in the United States and Europe today. Or whether they will face rising costs of everything, more limited lifestyle choices, less mobility, and, in general, a lower standard of living. We also have talked to people who wonder whether it's okay to continue to expand our existing economic model with little regard for the billions of people in the world who live on $1 per day or less.

As we've said, this is *not* a book about the morality of the existing global economic model. However, it seems intuitively obvious that the vast majority of humans would support the idea of preserving the planet for future generations and working toward a situation in which the vast numbers of the world's poor people were elevated to a higher quality of life.

So, what if we could create a tidal wave of thought change in our comfortable Western economy that would enable us to do the following:

1. Improve the efficiency with which we use and reuse the world's finite resources so that they will still be available for use by future generations? And, by the way, at the same time reduce the environmental degradation that results from some of the existing ways in which we use those same resources?
2. Engage the imagination and innovative talents of every business in our economy—yes, we mean *every* business—to see how they could benefit from revamping their products, services, and operations in such a way that they would not only be making a contribution to solving the global sustainability challenge but would be simultaneously improving their competitive position and their financial results?
3. Draw into the mainstream of the global economy the billions of people who currently struggle just to survive in such a way that they were making a real contribution to the global economy and improving the quality of their own lives at the same time?

Economic thought leaders have understood the developing resource constraints in our existing global economic model for many years, as well as the increasingly troubling social dimensions of the problem. They also understand clearly that governments alone will not be able to resolve the global sustainability challenge. Even though there is an urgent need for policy action on a global scale, in the end, we will have to engage the ingenuity and massive resources of the global business community to get the job done.

Whether we live in the comfortable, developed economies of the United States, Europe, and Japan; in the massive, aspiring economies of China, India, Brazil, Russia, and Indonesia; or whether we live in the struggling economies in parts of Asia and Africa, it is no longer acceptable for businesses to pursue their operations without consideration of their impact on the global environment, the communities in which they operate, and the generations that will follow them in the business world. Increasingly, the world demands that the business community find solutions to the global sustainability challenge.

While we feel comfortable in saying the global sustainability challenge is one of the greatest challenges humankind has ever faced, we also feel confident in asserting that it is also one of the greatest financial and economic opportunities that has ever been presented to the world of commerce. Those companies that rise to the challenge of making the global economy more sustainable will be the winning companies; they will gain the trust of customers and society in general, and they will be the ones that generate the best financial returns for their shareholders. Those that continue to do business as usual in disregard of the global sustainability challenge will lose their competitive advantage and will be punished by customers and investors alike. We call this the global sustainable business opportunity.

Most big companies with thoughtful and progressive leadership—especially those with a global presence—understand the global sustainability challenge and the opportunity it represents. Much has been written about how the world's major corporations are redefining their business strategies to ensure that the environmental and social impacts of their operations are major driving forces of the way they operate as well as the more traditional financial considerations. Increasingly, these reports are demonstrating the financial and competitive benefits of pursuing a strategy that is rooted in the principles of sustainable business management (Nidumolou et al., 2009; Economist Intelligence Unit Report, 2009).

For some businesses, this means simply maintaining their license to operate. For example, many of the world's major mining and oil and gas companies are obliged to address the environmental and social needs of the communities in which they work simply to do business in many parts of the world. For others, it means aggressive cost reduction programs based on doing things in a more environmentally and socially sound manner. DuPont has reduced its operating costs by many billions of dollars over the past decade through more responsible use of chemicals and improved reuse and waste disposal practices.

For other firms, sustainable business management means designing new products and services that address the resource constraints and other eco-demands of their customers. Sun Microsystems' development of more energy-efficient servers was prompted by the massive electric power demands of Google and others in their huge data centers—demands that were becoming a serious constraint on the growth potential of these companies; General Electric's famous energy-efficient locomotives have found a market all over the world; and, of course, there are the makers of eco-friendly clothing and other consumer products such as Patagonia and WhiteWave Foods Company that have built their entire business around customers' demands for more eco-friendly products.

What is also clear, however, is that, despite the upsurge of interest in and commitment to more sustainable operations among larger organizations, the vast majority of smaller business leaders have yet to embrace this type of thinking. There are many reasons for this:

1. The "tyranny of the urgent" that afflicts most small organizations and the imperative to focus on things like cash flow and staff availability that allow them to survive from one month to the next. These concerns preoccupy the leaders of smaller organizations in such a way that they do not have the time to think through what can be accomplished by embedding sustainability into their strategic thinking.
2. A perception that establishing more sustainable practices requires huge investment resources and that this is a luxury only larger corporations can afford or that it will reduce operating margins and cost the company money.
3. A belief that perhaps it's someone else's job to address the global sustainability challenge or that "I can make my fortune the old way before it affects me and my business too much."

Given that smaller business enterprises account for the greater part of gross domestic product and employment in most countries, our contention is that we must engage the imagination and resources of the small and medium-sized business community if we are to be successful in the effort to create a more sustainable global economy. Eventually, we need to reach a situation in which every business organization around the world—regardless of its location, size, and the nature of its business—understands that it will not survive and prosper unless it builds the principles of sustainable business management into its strategic thinking.

THE PROJECT

The development of this book project brought together three separate groups that are involved in sustainability education: Connected Organizations for a Responsible Economy (CORE), the University of Colorado Denver Business School's sustainable management program, and the University of Colorado's College of Architecture and Planning. CORE is a nonprofit business association based in Denver whose mission is to help smaller businesses understand how they can benefit and achieve competitive advantage through sustainable business strategies. CORE's activities bring it into contact with a wide range of organizations, and it became obvious in early 2008 that there are, in fact, many smaller businesses that do understand the advantages of a strategy based on the principles of sustainability and have achieved demonstrable competitive advantage in their markets by changing the way they operate and the products and services they sell. The University of Colorado Denver has been actively engaged in sustainability and was one of six universities in the United States that was awarded a National Science Foundation award for sustainability education, including the creation of an integrated interdisciplinary PhD in sustainability. The College of Architecture and Planning has been actively engaged in sustainability for the past three decades, and its students have won top green building awards, including four of the five awards in the United States Green Building Council's Natural Building Competition for the Western Region for three years. The Business School began a new MBA degree in managing for sustainability and an MS management specialization in 2007 to provide students with the tools they need to become change agents in business and within communities. For 2009 to 2010, the MBA program was ranked by the Aspen Institute among the global top 100 Beyond Grey Pinstripes MBA programs for preparing MBAs for social and environmental stewardship.

The project partnership between CORE, the Business School and the College of Architecture and Planning aims to bring excellent and needed case study resources of small and medium-sized business successes in sustainability to the business community as well as the classroom. We felt that if we could highlight the stories of these companies and bring them to the attention of other small business owners, we could help spread the gospel of the advantages of sustainability to the small and medium-sized business community. We also understand that the generation of students contemplating a career in business is demanding more real-world examples of successful sustainable business strategies as part of their overall education.

We, therefore, had several objectives in conducting this research and writing this book:

1. To fill the gap in the literature and in general educational resources for smaller businesses to help their leaders understand that adopting more sustainable business management practices is a recipe for improved financial results as well as for making a contribution to a better economic model for future generations.

2. To use the material gathered to develop a series of educational courses on sustainable business for delivery to small business leaders via extended educational programs at local and regional universities.

3. To show that any business can achieve superior economic and financial performance by building sustainability thinking into its strategic

planning and day-to-day operations, regardless of its size, geography, or the nature of services and products delivered.

4. To present workable sustainability ideas to businesses. These ideas are drawn from the 12 case studies described in this book. Some of the questions this book answers include: How can small business take advantage of the sustainability movement? What will sustainability mean to your organization's image and its ability to compete in its marketplace? Will sustainability help in recruiting and retaining the best employees? Will your company be able to use sustainability thinking as means to create a strong, productive corporate culture that provides employees with a compelling reason to come to work beyond the basic need to earn a living?

SUSTAINABILITY AND CLEANTECH

The current frenzy of interest in "cleantech," while reflective of the perceived need to make better use of the world's resources, has to some extent obscured the much wider message encompassed by the sustainability concept. The best definition of cleantech is that provided by the Cleantech Group (Cleantech Group LLC, 2010), which coined the term about 10 years ago:

Cleantech represents a diverse range of products, services, and processes, all intended to:

- Provide superior performance at lower costs, while
- Greatly reducing or eliminating negative ecological impact, at the same time as
- Improving the productive and responsible use of natural resources.

It is a common misperception that, for a company to be sustainable, it must have a product or service that essentially meets the cleantech definition above and that is intrinsically eco-friendly. Thus, renewable energy companies, energy efficiency technology companies, and those with waste minimization or water-related technologies are perceived to be, by definition, sustainable, whereas companies that do not deliver green or cleantech products or services fall outside the sustainable definition.

There are several things wrong with this perception. First, plenty of companies with a cleantech product or service do *not* have a sustainable business model (e.g., biofuels companies with operations that adversely impact local agriculture or water supplies). Second, the definition of cleantech entirely ignores the critical social definition of sustainability; preservation of human capital is as much a part of a sustainable system as the protection of natural resources. And, finally, as noted above, *every* company—not just cleantech companies—has a role to play and can achieve a competitive advantage from the process of creating a more sustainable business model.

While some of the companies featured in this book do, in fact, have intrinsically eco-friendly or socially responsible products or services, many of them do not, and we were able to confirm that every company can take steps to make its operations and activities more sustainable regardless of the nature of its products or services.

DRIVERS OF A SUSTAINABILITY-BASED STRATEGY

Our research enabled us to confirm many of the beliefs we'd always held about sustainability in business, but we also learned some new things. For instance, we were surprised at the wide range of factors that caused the small companies to embark on a sustainability journey in the first place. As expected, it was often the personal philosophy of the owner or founder to use his or her business not only to make a living but also to contribute to the wider good of society and the community. In others, the impetus toward a more sustainable business model came from a severe environmental regulatory problem that was threatening the viability of the enterprise or the need to break out of a market stalemate by developing new products designed to build a brand image around eco-friendliness or social responsibility. In one case, the actions of a couple of midlevel employees kicked off a corporatewide drive toward sustainability.

In almost all cases, we found that companies started off with small, typically inexpensive initiatives, achieved some measurable successes, and then moved on to more ambitious steps once they realized that sustainability works, even for a small business. We also confirmed that sustainability is as much about the preservation of human capital as it is about being green. All of the companies realized that they could use sustainability as a focus for building a strong, productive people environment that engaged the commitment of employees over and above the basic need to earn a paycheck.

We found that the leaders of our target companies were intensely proud of their sustainability efforts, not just because they felt it had helped them to build a more financially successful business but also because they felt they were making a real contribution to the welfare and well-being of the community and society in which they operate. They were more than willing to share their thoughts and ideas on sustainability in small businesses and have committed to support our continuing educational efforts in the future by making themselves available for teaching and presentational assignments.

SUSTAINABILITY—A UNIVERSAL BUSINESS SUCCESS FACTOR

Although our research was done on smaller companies in the greater Denver area, this is not a book about Colorado; similar successful small companies can be found across the United States and around the world that have built their success using a strategy that uses a commitment to environmental and social responsibility as a driver for innovation and competitive advantage. Rather, this is a call to action to the millions of other small companies that have yet to discover the benefits of developing a truly sustainable business model.

LESSONS LEARNED

(1) "Those companies that rise to the challenge of making the global economy more sustainable will be the winning companies; they will gain the trust of customers and society in general, and they will be the ones that generate the best financial returns to their shareholders."

(2) "Every company—not just clean-tech companies—has a role to play and can achieve a competitive advantage from the process of creating a more sustainable economic model."

(3) "In almost all cases, companies started off with small, typically inexpensive initiatives, achieved some measurable successes, and then moved on to more ambitious steps once they realized that sustainability works, even for a small business."

(4) "All of our companies realized that they could use sustainability as a focus for building a strong, productive people environment that engaged the commitment of employees over and above the basic need to earn a paycheck."

REFERENCES

Cleantech Group LLC, "Cleantech Definition," 2010, http://cleantech.com/about/cleantechdefinition.cfm

Economist Intelligence Unit, *Management Magnified: Sustainability and Corporate Growth,* November 2009, http://graphics.eiu.com/upload/eb/SAS_Sustainability_WEB.pdf. A report on how sustainability delivers superior growth performance sponsored by SAS.

Nidumolu, Ram, C.K. Prahalad, and M.R. Rangaswami. "Why Sustainability Is Now the Key Driver of Innovation," *Harvard Business Review,* September 2009, pp. 1–10, http://graphics8.nytimes.com/images/blogs/greeninc/harvardstudy.pdf. An excellent article on sustainability as the driver of corporate innovation.

TWO

Measuring Costs and Benefits

Elizabeth S. Cooperman and Elizabeth R. Brost

> Being a good steward of the environment and our communities and being an efficient and profitable business are not mutually exclusive. In fact they are one and the same.
>
> —Lee Scott, CEO, Walmart 2005

INTRODUCTION

Doing well by doing good is a motto widely used by managers adopting sustainable management strategies, suggesting financial as well as social and environmental benefits. Estimating sustainability-oriented costs and revenues is valuable for capital budgeting to determine whether the capital investment for a sustainability strategy will be worthwhile.

However, managers often fail to include the financial costs and revenues of sustainability ventures in strategy discussions. Costs and revenues for sustainability strategies are important key assumptions for deciding on the best strategy, benchmarking progress, and reporting a strategy's return on investment to investors. Measuring costs for new environmentally friendly products or services provides valuable information for pricing the new products as well, with customers often willing to pay a premium over other products and services. Sustainability reports that include tangible financial measures and other intangible measures can also help to inform stakeholders how a firm is doing from a triple bottom line perspective (economic, social, and environmental performance).

Measures of costs, revenues, and environmental and social benefits of sustainability strategies are also an integral part of doing business in terms of engaging customers and motivating employees to continue in their sustainability efforts.[1] Measuring a firm's carbon footprint is of key importance for benchmarking a firm's impact on the environment and for estimating financial and environmental savings that result from sustainability strategies. For firms engaged in manufacturing, a life-cycle analysis (LCA) measures and analyzes the environmental and social impact of a product or business process, which can help a firm identify opportunities for improvements in the design or manufacturing process to reduce environmental impacts and costs.

SUSTAINABILITY ANNUAL REPORTS

Corporate social responsibility environmental and sustainability reports are commonplace now for large firms and are often posted on company Web sites. ProLogis, Alcoa, Walmart, Target, Toyota, Ford Motors, and Starbucks, among thousands of other companies, post sustainability reports that provide great detail on a company's activities and environmental impact. In sustainability reports, large companies often use the 79 indicators provided by the Global Reporting Initiative (GRI; www.globalreporting.org). The GRI includes general indicators for economic, social, and environmental reporting with protocols to explain each indicator, methodology, and the intention for the scope of an indicator. The GRI also provides sector supplements for particular industry sectors, such as the mining industry (see Alcoa's Web site sustainability section at www.alcoa.com). For small to medium-sized firms, these Web sites often provide help and resources as well as examples of different types of reports. Other methods for measuring and reporting greenhouse gas inventory include the Greenhouse Gas Protocol (www.ghgprotocol.org) and the Climate Registry (www.theclimateregis try.org).

In 2006, about 34 large S&P 100 firms and 1,000 other organizations utilized the GRI framework and reported sustainability measures (Epstein, 2008, pp. 224–226). By 2008, this number ballooned to over 2,500 companies, with over 50 percent of the largest companies reporting globally (Hausman, 2008, p. 1). A 2008 survey by KPMG (www.kpmg.com) and SustainAbility (www.sustainability.com) on annual sustainability reports, commissioned by the GRI, found that 60 percent of readers for sustainability reports were businesses, including prospective customers and investors, and about 40 percent of readers were consultants and government employees. Firms issuing sustainability reports note that their reports helped them to establish positive reputations, develop new customers, and find new investors. Readers pointed out that firms should include difficulties as well as successes in implementing strategies to lend the reports credibility. Firms achieved greater credibility if they integrated sustainability strategies within the firm's overall mission and strategies (Blajchman, 2008).

Epstein (2008, p. 137) and Epstein and Wisner (2006) summarize the different dimensions that can be used to create a balanced scorecard for reporting results as follows:

- *A financial dimension* (sales revenues from sustainable products and efforts and energy cost savings, including the avoidance of future regulatory costs);
- *An internal business process dimension* (supplier certification, toxic or hazardous waste reduction, reductions in packaging volume, and product recalls);
- *A stakeholder dimension* (increased employee, customer, and community satisfaction; awards received for green/sustainability practices; charitable donations to community, environmental, or social organizations); and
- *A learning and growth dimension* (diversity in the workforce, sustainability-trained employees, hours volunteered for community projects by employees).

Epstein (2008, pp. 138–142) points out that, in addition to reporting to external stakeholders, organizations need to measure and report sustainability efforts to employees, with incentives included to encourage improvement to meet goals for each dimension.

Jeff Gardner and Fred Cohen (2008) note in a PricewaterhouseCoopers short article that 56 percent of firms with revenues over $20 billion realize the financial benefits and urgency of strategies and are committed to environmental issues. Environmental, social, and governance (ESG) indicators help to address the needs of key stakeholders. Reporting ESG milestones helps organizations meet their goals and quantify the investment value for sustainability strategies.

FINANCIAL, SOCIAL, AND ENVIRONMENTAL
BENEFITS OF SUSTAINABILITY PROGRAMS

Exactly what should be reported and how performance should be reported depends on a firm's particular strategies, industry, and use for measures. Sources of revenues from sustainability programs include revenue increases associated with:

- Better branding and creation of a distinctive market niche;
- Additional socially and environmentally aware customer bases;
- New products and services, including technological innovations;
- Increased sales, market share, and other competitive advantages; and
- Sales of renewable energy to utility companies and municipalities.

Sources of cost reductions include:

- Reduced energy costs as the result of greater cost efficiency;
- Reduced packaging materials and costs;
- Lower waste and waste management costs;
- Declines in training costs and employee turnover;
- Government tax rebates and other energy rebates;
- Reduced energy bills and other carbon offsets; and
- Conservation savings and benefits.

Additional economic gains may be less tangible, such as:

- Gains in reputation and community goodwill;
- Attraction of better, more dedicated employees; and
- Risk reduction from environmental, regulatory, and social responsibility exposure (such as avoiding regulatory sanctions, being allowed to operate in countries with stringent environmental regulations, avoiding lawsuits, consumer boycotts, and loss of reputation or other costs for environmental or social damages).

Some benefits and costs are intangible, such as reputation gains, but by making a list or inventory of the costs and benefits, managers can be more cognizant of progress toward qualitative goals and become aware of what areas need improvement. Managers also can use this inventory to generate new ideas to meet an organization's sustainability goals.

METRICS

Although it is challenging to measure social, environmental, and financial costs and benefits, many small to medium-sized firms are using metrics to measure both social and financial costs and benefits ranging from simple measures for performance standards to more complex financial estimates as proxies for expected tangible and intangible benefits. Cases for small to medium-sized companies highlighted in this book provide good examples in a variety of industries, including Boulder Community Hospital (BCH), Boulder Valley Credit Union (BVCU), New Belgium Brewery, Eco-Products, and Boulder Outlook Hotel.

Boulder Community Hospital

As a zero-waste hospital, BCH developed clear, concrete measures of performance under its sustainability initiative, including quantifying pounds of paper and containers recycled, pounds of compost diverted from land-fills, other landfill diversions, gallons of water and kilowatt-hours of elec-tricity saved, number of trees saved, and number of electronic equipment components recycled. BCH put these savings into financial terms. In addi-tion, BCH recognizes intangible reputation measures. A summary of BCH's progress since implementation of its initiatives in 2000 to 2007 includes both intangible and tangible measures (Abelkis, 2007):

Intangible Reputation Measures

- Gold Award from the state of Colorado for environmental leadership, recognizing the reduction of hazardous and solid waste, fuel and energy reduction, and preservation of open space in the foothills.
- Selection as a pilot hospital to study pharmaceutical disposal practices to assist in designing statewide regulations in health care settings.
- Recognition as one of the top 10 green hospitals in the United States.
- LEED Silver certification for the Boulder Community Hospital Foothills Campus in Boulder, Colorado, in 2003—the first health care project in the nation to receive LEED Silver certification.

- Recognition as a zero-waste hospital from Eco-Cycle, including improvements in water efficiency, environmentally preferable purchasing, and utilizing alternative energy, eliminating mercury, working on latex and PVC elimination, and promoting alternative transportation.
- Other environmental awards, including the Rotary Our World Award, the Bronze Award in Colorado Environmental Leadership, the Colorado Recycles Award—Overall Recycler of the Year, the Hospitals for a Healthy Environment Environmental Leadership Award, and the Making-Medicine-Mercury-Free Award.
- Surveys of employees and patients indicating morale benefits of activities.

BCH Tangible Measures of Savings

Recycling

- 424,927 pounds recycled in terms of paper, containers, and compost diverted from landfills
- 38 percent annual diversion rate
- 982 tons recycled since 2000

Resource Conservation since the Program's Inception

- 5,091,317 gallons of water savings
- 3,411,805 kilowatt-hours of electricity savings
- 44,408 cubic yards of landfill diversions
- 12,365 trees saved
- Diversions from landfills, including landscaping waste composted, construction waste diverted, electronic equipment recycled in the United States, medical equipment and supplies sent to be reused as part of the Mante Medical Mission and Project C.U.R.E.,[2] batteries recycled, and furniture repurposed, resulting in 3 million pounds of materials diverted from landfills since the program's inception in 2000.

Annual Cost Savings

- $600,000 total savings

  - $120,000 surgical wrap reduction
  - $95,000 reprocessing instruments reduction
  - $90,000 to $125,000 shredding service elimination

- $45,000 in trash hauling reduction
- $35,000 lighting efficiency operating savings
- $150,000 environmental services (EVS) cost savings
- $25,000 water efficiency operating savings

To obtain the quantifiable items, careful accounting had to be done throughout the hospital to determine savings. Developing the metrics first enabled management to determine the most important benchmarks based on strategic objectives and action plans. Then managers determined the most appropriate measures and the means to collect data on these measures.

Boulder Valley Credit Union

BVCU is a small, nonprofit credit union that took a somewhat different approach for reporting its sustainability to members. BVCU maintains real-time reporting of energy generated and greenhouse gases avoided due to its rooftop solar photovoltaic system that quantifies energy generation on a daily, weekly, yearly, monthly, and lifetime basis on its Web site (www.we carecolorado.com/monitoring.html).

In addition, BVCU's Web site provides sustainability reports on its eco-partners and social and environmental efforts (www.wecarecolorado.com/ efforts.html). Although many benefits are nonquantifiable, the reports provide excellent information on proenvironmental efforts as well as renewable energy benefits to stakeholders. As detailed in the Boulder Valley Credit Union chapter of this book, BVCU estimated total costs for its implementation of a solar-powered panel system and other efforts to become a zero-waste credit union at about $90,000 since the beginning of its efforts in 2007. Being frank with members—about future financial benefits with fixed energy costs and having a zero-carbon footprint—provides stakeholders with a realistic mental model for assessing BVCU's sustainability initiative, where benefits including reduced, fixed energy costs will be achieved over the next 15 to 20 years. In addition, BVCU provides detailed information on its partnerships to protect the environment with other firms and other environmental education events for its customers and community.

New Belgium Brewing Company

New Belgium Brewing Company, as a larger regional business, has a more elaborate presentation to its stakeholders on its Web site (www.new belgium.com/files/shared/07SustainabilityReportlow.pdf). This includes a formal sustainability report and a life-cycle analysis. New Belgium's sustainability report includes details of different aspects of the firm's environmental performance, including the creation of a sustainability management system (SMS), the firm's carbon footprint, a product life-cycle analysis, and intangible information on its cultural and social performance efforts.

From December 2006 to August 2007, New Belgium carefully developed a sustainability management system to estimate its carbon footprint using 2 consultants and 16 volunteers from all parts of the company. The SMS helps New Belgium to determine its current environmental impact, identify targets for improvements and plans to achieve the targets, and keep the cycle of improvement moving along. The system includes four major tools: (1) carbon footprint reduction, (2) water stewardship, (3) closing loops, and (4) advocacy. These tools are used to help with decision making for purchasing, design, capital portfolio management, and strategic planning. New Belgium's *2007 Sustainability Report* is an outcome of the system. In 2007, New Belgium's SMS team created a goal to reduce the firm's carbon footprint by 50 percent per barrel.

Although the company had been involved in estimating its carbon footprint since 2006 as a member of the Chicago Climate Exchange (www.chi cagoclimateexchange.com), managers only had verifiable data in 2007 for some areas of its operations. To help perform the LCA, managers set up a partnership with the Climate Conservancy (www.climateconservancy.org) to complete an LCA of its greenhouse gas emissions.[3] As noted in New Belgium's *2007 Sustainability Report*), raw and packaging material including the transportation to the brewery amounted to 48 percent of the overall footprint, with the brewery making up 5 percent and the downstream impacts 47 percent of the total. Retail contributed 60 percent of the downstream impacts, and, of the retailer's contribution to the overall footprint, retail refrigeration accounted for 93 percent. Hence, New Belgium's managers realized that the retail side of the business was creating the largest environmental impact.

With the LCA information, New Belgium's managers researched how the footprint would change under different proposed scenarios. New Belgium's sustainability report includes energy and water treatment plant process analysis and efforts to reduce packaging and increase recycling. The report also discusses more intangible items, including the results of an employee satisfaction survey; wellness activities to improve employee health; and recognitions, including an award from *Outside Magazine* (www.outsideon line.com) as the best place to work in America. The detailed carbon footprint report, presented jointly with the Climate Conservancy, appears on the New

Belgium Web site (www.newbelgium.com/files/shared/the-carbon-foot print-of-fat-tire-amber-ale-2008-public-dis-rfs.pdf).

Eco-Products

In contrast, Eco-Products is a firm that creates environmental products that reduce waste for its customers. Eco-Products has a Web site (www.ecopro ducts.com) that included in 2010 an About Us section with a history of Eco-Products and what the firm does. The site also includes a Footprint section that discusses the efforts of Eco-Products to measure and limit its carbon footprint, including instituting an environmental management system that allows Eco-Products to benchmark and quantify its resource consumption associated with energy, water, waste, and track improvements. A Life-Cycle Analysis section discusses an LCA performed for different products. A Carbon Offsets section provides information about Eco-Products' partnership with Renewable Choice Energy in Boulder (www.renewablechoice. com) whereby Eco-Products calculates its total greenhouse gas emissions at the end of each quarter and purchases a corresponding number of verified emission reductions (VERs), a commodity sold to finance U.S. methane capture projects. A VER represents a reduction of one metric ton of carbon dioxide (CO_2) or its equivalent. Eco-Products also provides on its Web site case studies of its customers and their sustainability achievements.

Boulder Outlook Hotel

As an alternative for reporting on sustainable strategies, Boulder Outlook Hotel, as a zero-waste hotel, provides a video on its Web site that describes how it engages in its environmental activities and how the hotel manages its recycling operations (www.boulderoutlookhotel.com/ecovid.html). The video also portrays how the owners determined the costs of doing business and their decision to become a zero-waste hotel. From the start, the owners felt that they would need to absorb the costs to become a zero-waste hotel, but, to their surprise, they found that they had a large increase in new customers in their new sustainable niche, which increased revenues to absorb the costs. In turn, hotel guests learn new ideas for reducing their own carbon footprints. Costs were approximately $600 per month to move the hotel to zero waste, with a documented rise in revenues of at least $10,000 per month.

Hence, sustainability reports and measurements differ widely. They can be a simple and informal overview, such those performed by Eco-Products and Boulder Valley Credit Union, or they can include detailed tangible and intangible measures, such as Boulder Community Hospital's. They can contain detailed reports, such as New Belgium's LCA, carbon footprint report, and sustainability report. The metrics can vary considerably depending on the size of the organization and its products, services, industry, and goals and can include nonfinancial measures.

SOURCES OF INFORMATION ON METRICS FOR SUSTAINABLE STRATEGIES

In addition to GRI guidelines, trade associations offer guidelines for the best measures to use for firms in particular industries. An industry of consultants on performance metrics has also developed. An example is Natural Logic Sustainability Strategy Feedback Assessment Metrics (www.natlogic. com), which provides evaluation, training, and key performance indicator systems to streamline the collection of environmental performance data. For firms wishing to use enterprise resource planning, dashboards are also available to track and drive performance and sustainability reporting. Sustainable Measures, another private consulting firm, offers workshops, training, and a database of indicators and other resources for companies desiring effective metrics to measure their progress.

Prior to its acquisition by Oracle, Sun Microsystems joined with Natural Logic (www.natlogic.com) to develop a forum for community discussion of metrics and other issues that is currently under development at www.open. eco.org. The sustainability reports of public companies, such as Alcoa, Walmart, General Electric, Baxter, BP, Unilever, and ProLogis, among others, provide good examples of types of measures used by firms in various industries. Nonprofit organizations offer assistance as well. Business and Sustainable Development Global offers case studies on its Web site focusing on different industries (www.bsdglobal.com). University centers for sustainability, such as the Center for Sustainability at Aquinas College in Grand Rapids, Michigan, offer information and links to sustainability topics, including sustainability metrics (www.centerforsustainability.org). Sustainability Reporting Programs, a Canadian nonprofit organization, provides business case studies, indices and metrics for measuring sustainability, external links, and other useful information. The Pioneers Group provides a best-practice forum to help firms develop and implement sustainable development strategies in different sectors, including a set of indicators to use for individual operating units. Online magazines also provide advice, such as *Environmental Leader: The Executive's Daily Green Briefing* (www.environmentalleader.com) and *Sustainable Life Media* (www. sustainablelifemedia.com), and many others.

For environmental programs, firms often rely on the International Organization for Standardization (ISO) 14001, environmental management system. SA 8000 provides metrics for human rights. A softer guide, the ISO 2600, is in development to help identify, measure, and certify a firm's obligations in the area of social responsibility. On November 1, 2010, the ISO launched the ISO 26000 Guidance on Social Responsibility providing guidance to all types of organizations regardless of their size, location, or whether they are for-profit or non-profit. The ISO 26000 is designed more for small and medium-sized firms providing voluntary guidance standards versus a certification and includes concepts, background, principles and practices, and core subjects on social responsibility. The ISO 26000 provides advice on the integration, implementation, and promotion of socially responsible behavior throughout an organization, the identification and engagement of stakeholders, and communication of performance, commitments, and other social responsibility dimensions (see www.iso.org/iso/socialresponsibility_2006-en.pdf for a summary overview and www.iso.org for up to date information).

The Organisation for Economic Co-operation and Development and the International Labor Organization also provide menus of standards and guidelines. Organizations have also worked with the International Institute for Sustainable Development (IISD), which provides guidance on corporate reporting practices, including case studies on business and sustainable development (www.bsdglobal.com). The European Union's Eco-Management and Audit Scheme provides help in understanding pertinent environmental laws.

Environmental consultants in the new sustainable metric industry can measure firms' carbon emissions and overall carbon footprints. The Climate Conservancy and other sustainability consultants can partner with firms to complete life-cycle analyses. Regional nonprofit firms, such as Eco-Cycle in Boulder, Colorado (www.ecocycle.org), provide assistance and expertise on recycling, and zero-waste certification. For assistance in measuring greenhouse gas emissions and purchasing carbon offsets, regional and national firms such as Renewable Choice Energy, also in Boulder (www.renewablechoice.com), can be partners. Similarly, state-sponsored organizations for sustainable development, such as Greenprint Denver (http://www.greenprintdenver.org), will partner with organizations. Nonprofit firms promoting business sustainability, such as Colorado Connected Organizations for a Responsible Economy (www.corecolorado.org), has offered (in association with Deloitte), GRI sustainability reporting training courses. The courses are taught by LEAD Canada, a not-for-profit corporation that provides training, projects, and networking to further the goals of environmental, social, and economic sustainability (www.leadcanada.

net) and Sustainalytics, a global provider of environmental, social, and governance research and analysis (www.jantzisustainalytics.com).

ADVICE ON METRICS

Hausman (2008) suggests that it is important for companies to focus on simple but important impacts that are relevant to their own situations versus an enormous phonebook of measures, which is all-too-common for many companies' sustainability reports.

"Focus on material impacts, provide quantifiable targets, and then next year tell us your progress against that metric," says Hausman. By using trend data, firms can see their progress over time and allocate resources to appropriate areas in the future. In choosing a sustainable initiative, it is important that the strategy is aligned with a company's overall mission and strategies and that it is appropriate for the firm.

Epstein (2008) similarly notes that metrics should come from a firm's particular strategies and goals and should be identifiable over time. For example, trends in greenhouse gas emissions over time can be a useful measure for environmental goals and can help to identify where emissions can be reduced. Stakeholders need to be identified, which helps a firm to decide on it its sustainability strategies, goals, and objectives and how relevant progress can be measured. Companies can select the best strategies before making investments through identification and measurement of financial, environmental, and social costs and potential revenues to be generated for different projects. Goals and measures should convey a firm's values. Sometimes, simpler and shorter is better, as long as the firm can measure its performance over time, focusing on the firm's strategy and particular strengths. By having clear, focused, and easily understood measures, a firm's goals and performance can be clearly communicated to its stakeholders, and progress over time can be accurately evaluated.

CARBON FOOTPRINT CALCULATORS

There are a number of different sources for carbon calculators, with some entities on the Internet providing free calculators for simple cases or for companies that can provide partnerships to offset carbon footprints. The standard unit of measure for CO_2 is a metric ton, which is 2,204.62 pounds. Direct emissions, known as Scope 1, are based on company-owned and -controlled operations. Indirect Scope 2 emissions are those involved with the purchase of energy, such as the purchase of electricity from an electric utility company. Indirect Scope 3 emissions are other indirect emissions associated with business travel, employee commuting, waste disposal, and other outsourced activities.

A free carbon footprint calculator can be found at www.carbonfootprint. com/carbonfootprint.html. CarbonFootprint.com also provides a link for tips for reducing an organization's carbon footprint and explains that a carbon footprint measures the impact of activities on the environment in terms of the amount of greenhouse gases produced with the use of fossil fuels for electricity and transportation. A primary footprint shows direct emissions of CO_2 from these activities, and a secondary footprint includes the indirect CO_2 emissions based on the entire life cycle of products used. Similarly, Carbon-Partner.com (www.carbonpartner.com) provides a CO_2 emissions calculator that provides monthly emissions for travel by different types of cars (small fuel efficient, average, or SUV), electricity usage (kilowatt-hours per month), natural gas consumption (cubic feet per month), fuel oil heating (gallons per month), air and train travel (miles per month), general food and waste (number of people in household who eat meat). The application yields a calculation of approximate annual and monthly emissions and the number of trees necessary to be planted each month or each year or other actions needed to offset these emissions. Cities, state energy offices, and nonprofit and for-profit firms provide partnerships for carbon offsets to reduce a company's environmental impact.

Some environmental organizations provide carbon footprint calculators via helpful spreadsheets. For example, the Time for Change Web site (time forchange.org) provides a downloadable carbon footprint calculator as an Excel spreadsheet (timeforchange.org/offline-carbon-footprint-calculator). Similar free or low-cost calculators can be found at Shareup.com (www. shareup.com/Carbon_Footprint_Calculator-download-50109.html), the Nature Conservancy's Carbon Footprint Calculator (www.nature.org/initia tives/climatechange/calculator), Renewable Choice Energy (www.renew ablechoice.com/impact-calculator), and on the Web sites of state energy conservation offices, such as the Texas State Energy Conservation Office (www.infinitepower.org/calculators.htm).

COMPANY GREENHOUSE GAS INVENTORY AND ENVIRONMENTAL PROTECTION AGENCY WEB SITE ASSISTANCE

A greenhouse gas inventory accounts for how much greenhouse gases are produced or removed from the atmosphere over a particular time period, such as a year, and provides information on the activities that create emissions and removals and the background for the methods that are used for calculations (see Environmental Protection Agency, 2010). The United States Environmental Protection Agency (EPA) provides an online calculator for estimating personal emissions and some technical guidance on corporate greenhouse gas inventories and small business tools. A link at www. epa.gov/stateply/smallbiz/footprint.html provides information on "How To Calculate Your Carbon Footprint." Included are steps for selecting an operational or financial approach and defining an organization's boundaries, helpful documents for small businesses, low-emitter guides to greenhouse gas management, a glossary of terms needed to develop a firm's greenhouse gas inventory, a simplified emissions calculator in Excel, and a simplified inventory management plan in Microsoft Word. In addition, small business managers can e-mail questions, attend free training webinars, and join the Climate Leaders Small Business Network to set goals, share best practices with other small firms, and receive recognition for successes. Tutorials and case studies are provided as well.

LIFE-CYCLE ANALYSIS

Although difficult for a firm just initiating a sustainable management strategy, at some point, a life-cycle analysis can be very useful, such as the LCA that New Belgium Brewery performed for its Fat Tire beer in 2007. LCA provides a detailed assessment of the total impact of a product, including consideration of both wholesale and retail operations and the supply chain of materials and transportation used to create the product. LCA involves a measure of the environmental and social impact of a process. Managers analyze the LCA results to identify opportunities for improvements in the design or process of a product. LCA measures the material and energy flows involved in the entire life cycle of a product or service and assesses the impacts of those flows and materials. Weidema and colleagues (2008) point out that LCA is more involved and more difficult to calculate than carbon footprinting, but it provides a more complete assessment of the full environmental effects of a company's operations, which is particularly important for manufacturing companies. Often partners are useful in helping with an assessment, such as New Belgium's partnership with the Climate Conservancy.

Several types of life-cycle analysis may be performed on a product, including: *cradle-to-grave* (from manufacture to end of life), *cradle-to-gate* (from manufacture to distribution), *cradle-to-cradle* (for products expected to be recycled at the end of their useful life), *gate-to-gate* (working only on value-added processes), *well-to-wheel* (focusing on the transportation of a product), and *economic input-output* (estimating the materials and energy required for an activity and the resulting environmental emissions). Each variant has a different assessment score. A firm needs to decide which scope to include that is most relevant to stakeholders and provide assessments that will enable the greatest potential efficiency and emission improvements.

Because the measurement of greenhouse gas emissions associated with a specific product is constantly evolving, and because official standards are still being developed, industry standards are often used. Choices include ISO 14000, a widely accepted assessment model first published in 1996 that specifies the actual requirements for an environmental management system applying to environmental aspects that an organization has control over and can influence (see http://www.iso14000-iso14001-environmental-man agement.com/) and the Climate Conservancy[4] assessment, which concentrates only on greenhouse gas emissions and is thus a narrower assessment. Alternatively, a company may perform its own assessment, which is done by experts within a company's different areas. A firm needs to choose its LCA route carefully to ensure collection of the most relevant information on its product and customers. Any LCA process includes decisions on the scope, gathering environmental impact data, mapping the current process, identifying impact areas, and analyzing the data to assist in decision making. With standards and measurements and impact assumptions being constantly modified and improved upon, LCA is improving. There are limitations, however. One limitation is that previous assessments become obsolete with improvements. Another limitation is that most LCA software used in the United States is based on assumptions and measurements provided by the EPA or the U.S. Department of Energy, but these standards may not apply to foreign-based companies or overseas branches of domestic companies. LCA practices also do not identify or measure the social impacts of a product.

A business can conduct an LCA on its products in one of three ways: it can create its own process and measurements based on in-house experts, it can use a consultancy that assesses products based on ISO 14000 standards, or it can use an outside group that has created its own standards and measurement methods. Each option carries certain advantages and drawbacks.

Self-assessment is the most independent method that does not necessarily have to conform to ISO standards. However, internal experts in the company need to have intimate knowledge of the firm's product, customers, uses of and environmental impact of each component part, and the manufacturing, distribution, and disposal processes involved. Questions of legitimacy

Property of
Baker College
of Allen Park

from peers and consumers without the certification of a reputable third party may arise. Because the ISO is an expansive nongovernmental organization with 161 member countries, utilizing ISO 14000 standards can lend greater credibility to LCAs and create uniformity across countries for businesses with out-of-country operations. Many countries operate under different environmental and business standards. Thus, governments often adopt ISO standards for easy communication across countries. Because the ISO is recognized as a compilation of best practices, companies can save the costs of having to hire experts to create special company standards. ISO best practices are continuously evolving.

The ISO 14040 and 14044 standards list four major steps for carrying out LCAs:

- *Determining the goal and scope of the project* (deciding and justifying which processes will be included, establishing parameters, and justifying choices to support the overall goal of the study, including describing the methodology and impact categories included);
- *Undertaking a life-cycle inventory of the product* (data collection and verification stage, including data on all greenhouse gas emission measurements and chemical usage in the production process);
- *Impact assessment* (information is evaluated to determine the environmental impact based on emissions over the product's life);
- *Interpretation of the LCA* (identifying areas of greatest impact, deciding on impact reduction strategies to be implemented, if any, often including an independent review and comparison to best industry practices and competitors).

The Climate Conservancy developed a methodology for measuring the environmental impact of manufactured goods based on its own research and on the standards set forth in the Greenhouse Gas Protocol. Greenhouse gases emitted are analyzed during the making, use, and disposal of a product using a cradle-to-grave analysis for manufacturing companies. This analysis begins with the raw material acquisition and ends with the waste generated by a company. The assessment method is similar to that recommended by the ISO, and the information sources are well known in the sustainable business world. The Climate Conservancy, as a smaller nonprofit assessment service, is not as well known as the ISO, so businesses may have to spend extra time educating stakeholders on their analysis. However, a Climate Conservancy partnership reduces the complexity of the LCA, reducing the costs and time to perform the assessment. Also, a "Climate Conscious" label can be used on products that meet Climate Conservancy emissions requirements, providing incentives for assessing a product as part of an overall marketing strategy.

CONCLUDING REMARKS

When undertaking a sustainability initiative, it is important to measure the costs, savings and revenues, and other benefits to get all stakeholders (board members, owners, employees, customers) on board. Measurements do not have to be complex, but they should be honest and strive to measure accurately the impact of initiatives and the financial return (if any) and intangible benefits that will be received from the initiative. The initiative should be consistent and integrated with a firm's overall mission and strategies. Internally, these metrics serve as benchmarks for future improvements and help the organization's managers see where the firm has been to help determine its best strategies for the future.

LESSONS LEARNED

(1) "Costs and revenues for sustainability strategies are important key assumptions for deciding on the best strategy, benchmarking progress, and reporting a strategy's return on investment to investors."

(2) "Measuring a firm's carbon footprint is of key importance for benchmarking a firm's impact on the environment and for estimating financial and environmental savings that result from sustainability strategies."

(3) "For firms engaged in manufacturing, a life-cycle analysis measures and analyzes the environmental and social impact of a product or business process, which can help a firm identify opportunities for improvements in the design or manufacturing process to reduce environmental impacts and costs."

(4) A variety of measures can be used for reporting progress on sustainability efforts to stakeholders—from detailed quantified savings to a short report on intangibles gained or savings in energy costs to a sophisticated life-cycle analysis—with a variety of public resources and partners to help a firm with measures and offsets.

NOTES

1. See Acumen Corporate Content Consultant as an example of a consulting firm that helps companies with sustainability report writing: http://www.acumencommunications.co.za/sustainability-report-writing.html.

2. Boulder-Mante Sister Cities Project, http://boulder-mante.org/MedicalMission.html; Project C.U.R.E., http://www.projectcure.org.

3. This LCA was performed for a six-pack of one of New Belgium's most popular products, Fat Tire beer. For a six-pack of Fat Tire, the LCA estimated total CO_2 emissions at 3,189 grams. This measure would be used as a benchmark for examining future emission reductions. See the full report at http://www.newbelgium.com/files/shared/07SustainabiltyReportlow.pdf.

4. The Climate Conservancy is a group consisting of university, business and engineering professionals, and graduate students that developed its own standards. The ISO standards are not required in the United States.

REFERENCES

Abelkis, Kai, Sustainability Coordinator. "Boulder Community Hospital Initiatives," PowerPoint presentation, 2007. Also see *Boulder Community Hospital Sustainability: Interview with Kai Abelkis* by Carrie Paykoc on YouTube, http://www.youtube.com/watch?v=DKfeS_FJntk (Part 1) and http://www.youtube.com/watch?v=5RXvwAQgtxQ (Part 2).

Blajchman, Amiel. "Sustainability Reports: Who Reads Them, and Why?" *The Inspired Economist,* October 28, 2008, 1–3, http://inspiredeconomist.com/2008/10/28/sustainability-reports-who-reads-them-and-why/.

Epstein, Marc J. *Making Sustainability Work: Best Practices in Managing and Measuring Corporate Social, Environmental, and Economic Impacts.* Sheffield, England: Greenleaf Publishing; San Francisco: BK Publishers, 2008.

Epstein, Marc J., and P. S. Wisner. "Actions and Measures To Improve Sustainability," in M. J. Epstein and K. O. Hanson, eds., *The Accountable Corporation,* Vol. 3, Westport, CT: Praeger, 2006, 207–234.

Gardner, Jeff, and Fred Cohen. "Business Reputations at Stake," PriceWaterhouse Coopers short article, http://www.pwc.com. Adapted from "Warming up to Climate Change, *View,* Summer 2008, www.pwc.com/view.

Hausman, Alex. "The 3 Keys to CSR Reporting Are Materiality, Materiality, and Materiality," *Environmental Leader: The Executive's Daily Green Briefing,* June 3, 2008, www.environmentalleader.com.

International Organization for Standardization Web site, http://www.iso.org.
United States Environmental Protection Agency, *Greenhouse Gas Emissions,* 2010, www.epa.gov/climatechange/emissions/index.html.
Weidema, Bo P., Mikkel Thrane, Per Christensen, Jannick Schmidt, and Soren Lokke. "Carbon Footprint—A Catalyst for Life Cycle Assessment?" *Journal of Industrial Ecology,* March 21, 2008, Vol. 12(1), 3–6.

PART II

Sustainability Cases for Small to Medium-Sized Firms

THREE

Eco-Products

Christopher Thorp and Sharen A. Durst-Aldridge

All quotes and information not otherwise cited in this chapter come from extensive interviews with Steve Savage, 2008–2009.

A CONCEPT IS BORN

The long shadows of the early morning sun stretch up along the ascending slope of Longs Peak. High above the long horizon, Steve Savage and his father, Kent, approach the end of an expansive field of rocks and crags, clambering over and around jagged boulders the size of small automobiles. The bright orange light of the morning sun inspires a moment of pause from their ascent to the top of the 14,259-foot peak, a journey that began hours before by starlight. The view along the eastern horizon reveals much of the continuously developed grid of cities, suburbs, and agricultural land from Fort Collins in the north to Denver in the south. Steve had just graduated from the University of Kansas with a degree in economics. While he planned to spend the majority of the summer of 1990 at a family cottage in Michigan, Steve returned to his hometown of Boulder for a visit in June, where he and his father decided to trek into the nearby mountains for the ambitious hike.

As the sun continues to slowly rise, the topic of Steve's future plans is brought up in conversation. Steve reveals his interest in pursuing a graduate degree in international finance after taking the year off to travel through

Logo for Eco-Products. (Courtesy of Eco-Products.)

Russia. With the economic and political reforms sweeping the newly disbanded Soviet Union, Kent acknowledges his son's attraction to the potential business opportunities within Eastern Europe's emerging free-market economies. However, he presents his son with another business idea that had been bouncing around in his head, one that would tap into an emerging market a little closer to home. In the interest of promoting ecological stewardship and environmental conservation, Kent proposes to create a company that would encourage and facilitate other businesses to become more environmentally responsible.

Kent Savage is not new to ecological issues. Born William Kent Savage in 1930, Kent was named after his great uncle, the celebrated California conservationist William Kent, who, in 1908, endowed nearly 300 acres of prime sequoia redwood forest to the national government under President Theodore Roosevelt, creating the Muir Woods National Monument. After serving as an Air Force fighter pilot in the Korean War, Kent earned his business degree from the University of Cincinnati. He worked in the technology sector for much of his career, including more than a decade with

IBM. In the early 1980s, Kent and his family moved from the Chicago suburbs to Boulder, Colorado, where he worked as a management and marketing consultant and assisted Small Business Administration applicants in marketing research and growth management.

Kent later became involved in the growth and success of Boulder's Eco-Cycle, serving as chairman of the board from 1992 to 1996. As a nonprofit recycling processor, Eco-Cycle's mission is to encourage and facilitate not only recycling but also a zero-waste society. However, its success relies in part on market forces to provide useful and desirable products manufactured from recycled content as well as the means to distribute and make the products available to consumers.

The idea of bolstering the market for recycled-content products is at the core of Kent's concept for this new business. In the interest of completing the loop, he proposes to create a company that would serve as a "convenient, attractive, and cost-effective source for a wide variety of products made from recycled products."

The shadow of Longs Peak stretches for miles over rugged peaks and moraines as Steve and Kent traverse around to the west-facing slope of the mountain. As they continue to climb, they discuss Kent's idea. What is the target market? What types of products could be sold? What is the source of the products? Who is the main competition? The idea achieves a certain momentum in Steve's mind by the time he and Kent reach the summit.

As one of the tallest mountains in Colorado, the view from the top of Longs Peak is extensive in every direction. Kent and Steve quietly survey the vast surroundings, taking in the magnitude of their accomplishment. A humbling sense of the natural grandeur serves to further legitimize the mission and purpose behind Kent's ambitious business proposal. In three months' time, Kent will have secured grants to write a business plan and develop the first catalog for the company he and Steve will call Eco-Products, Inc. For three years, the business will slowly grow out of Kent's garage and into expanded facilities and warehouses. Within 15 years, Eco-Products will greatly expand its market share by investing in the manufacture of compostable plastic products derived from corn and sugarcane, a venture that will propel the company to reach sales figures as high as $40 million in a year. Eighteen years after the initial concept was discussed on the side of Longs Peak, and after steadily growing into the leading wholesale supplier of compostable and environmentally friendly products, Eco-Products will create a new spin-off company called Ellie's Eco Home Store, making a wide variety of environmentally friendly products and services available to the general public.

Photo of Kent Savage. (Courtesy of Eco-Products.)

STARTING OUT

Eco-Products strives to make a positive impact on the global community by offering a wide selection of high quality, environmentally friendly products at competitive prices.

—Company Mission Statement

Kent and Steve officially began Eco-Products on October 1, 1990. The original business plan described a burgeoning market opportunity to "capitalize on both the reality and the perception among consumers and businesses that it is crucial to both recycle and purchase recycled products." Consumer surveys citing people's attitudes and concerns with regard to recycling and the environment were used to support Eco-Product's assertions, as well as Environmental Protection Agency findings on the high cost of building new landfills. The business plan organized the growth of the company into three progressive phases. Phase I described the company as a "recycled paper products distributorship." Phase II envisioned a "retail store in Boulder, CO, selling products made from recycled paper, plastic and metal." Given the success of the first two phases, the third phase sought simply to "expand the number of retail outlets."

Eco-Products slowly evolved out of the first phase, focusing initially on the business-to-business wholesale distribution of products made from recycled paper. Steve remembered making his initial sales calls to anyone who might use a lot of paper, including local businesses, churches, preschools, fraternities, and sororities, offering such products as computer and copy paper, toilet paper, and paper towels. In the early years, Steve made deliveries around town in an old Subaru. "My dad was always extremely conservative, growing the business with cash flow," Steve recalled, "so we grew very slowly, but we learned a lot and we stayed in business, as opposed to dumping a lot of money into a business and going into debt." This was particularly challenging early on, as sales of office paper products yielded fairly low margins due to relatively high competition from established stores and mail-order companies, most of which had their own recycled-content offerings. With stagnant sales and little growth, it appeared Steve would soon be returning to school to pursue his postgraduate ambitions.

The focus of Eco-Products shifted from office paper products to food service and janitorial supplies with the company's first large account from the Denver-based company Peaberry Coffee. "Peaberry kind of put my plans of going to graduate school on hold, because Eco-Products started growing." For the first 15 years, Eco-Products continued to build its business with its own capital. "We didn't pay ourselves much, but revenue always grew, and we've never had an unprofitable year," explained Steve. He and his father moved out of the garage in 1993 and into a 3,500-square-foot facility in Boulder, where they remained for five years. In addition to food service and paper products, Eco-Products expanded its line in 1996 to include a growing variety of building products, many of which contain a high level of postconsumer recycled content. The company also relocated its offices to another Boulder location and added a 20,000-square-foot warehouse in Lafayette, Colorado.

During this time, Kent, who had participated in the day-to-day operations of the company from the start, allowed Steve to take a more active role in running the business while he gradually reduced his own involvement. Kent continued to provide valuable leadership and direction to Eco-Products until his death in 2003. The company he started with his son had steadily grown into one of the leading distributors of environmentally friendly products in the world. Before long, however, Steve would lead Eco-Products into new territory. The company expanded its market share by adding the manufacture and marketing of its own products to an already successful formula.

Photo of Eco-Products Cups. (Courtesy of Eco-Products.)

TRANSITION

From Plants to Products to Plants.

—Company Slogan

Until 2005, the company's business model was to assemble an array of recycled-content products from a variety of companies, including International Paper, Weyerhauser, Solo Cup Company, and Georgia Pacific. As a distributor and reseller, Eco-Products served these manufacturers by making their products available to businesses and individuals. What made Eco-Products unique was how it exclusively provided a full line of environmentally friendly products while other companies offered only a few "green" items as a specialized segment of their mainstream product line.

In 2005, Eco-Products introduced a pioneering innovation to this model: rather than acting strictly as a distributor of other companies' merchandise, Eco-Products invested in the manufacturing of its own products using a new technology that created 100 percent compostable plastic resin from corn and sugarcane. "We found out that to become a sustainable business, you really need to brand yourself," Steve explained. He seized the unique opportunity of doing so with this new technology, citing four important characteristics seldom found within a single product group: "These products are made from natural resources, they're compostable, they're equal in quality [to petroleum-based plastic], and they're also competitive in price." Eco-Products expanded upon the model of providing products to the food-service industry by branding its own line of compostable plastic hot cups, cold cups, cutlery, clamshells, plates, bowls, and other single-use items. All products are certified by the Biodegradable Products Institute, the "primary governing body in the U.S. for compostability certification" (www.bpiworld.org/BPI-Public). This ensures that the products will biodegrade within 60 days of being added to a "commercial composting environment."

Between 2005 and 2009, the company drastically grew in size and revenue due in large part to this expansion. Before 2005, Steve explained how the company "really didn't have a plan other than to grow revenue and bring environmental products to local Boulder and Denver businesses . . . it hadn't been until the last several years that we have really known who Eco-Products is, what we're doing, and how we're going to get there." Steve credits two other people in the company for having played a significant role in the ambitious expansion: Luke Vernon, who is now the chief operating officer, and Jim Lamancusa, who is Eco-Products' former director of sales. "I could never have done it without their help," admitted Steve. "The three of us worked as an incredible team to first identify this opportunity and then to execute the vision." Luke and Jim were both hired in 2004 and quickly demonstrated their enthusiasm for the company's ecological mission. With Luke's management of product development and Jim's leadership in sales, the team began the expansion in 2005 and started selling the new products in 2006.

When planning to launch the expansion, Eco-Products chose to produce the majority of its new products in Asia. While Steve would have preferred a domestic option for manufacturing, he was pleased to find the compostable technology in Asia to be "well ahead" of the domestic producers. This allows Eco-Products to distinguish itself from its competition in several important ways. While other companies such as International Paper, Fabri-Kal, and Wilkinson have a limited offering of similar products, Eco-Products offers a full line of compostable single-use food service products under the Eco-Products GreenStripe trademark. The company can also boast of having the highest heat tolerance in its hot food and beverage products, which, at 135° Fahrenheit, is a full 30° higher than the nearest competition. "We were able to not only brand, but to reduce costs, and to develop superior products," Steve explained.

The GreenStripe trademark not only creates an important brand, but the eye-catching stripe and logo serves as reminder that the product is compostable. This is particularly important in the interest of directing the discarded product to the appropriate composting facility. Because the products look and perform like plastic derived from petroleum, compostable items can potentially contaminate the recyclable plastic supply if mistakenly mixed in with a user's recyclables. Eco-Products provides information on where customers can find appropriate facilities in their area as well as other tips on how to minimize their environmental footprint. If a suitable composter is unavailable, the company still encourages the use of its products, which allows customers to "reduce their environmental impact by using products that are made from rapidly renewing resources" (see Eco-Products, www.ecoproducts.com).

The recent success of Eco-Products can be attributed to several important factors, including intelligent product development, innovative marketing, and, to a significant degree, timing. According to an article in the *Wall Street Journal,* the volatile price of oil has made sustainable products more attractive to consumers. "It's great for us," Steve is quoted as saying. "Our products are made from a corn derivative, and our competition uses petroleum. They are having price increases where our prices are stable" (Dale, 2008). Add to this the perception that "having a zero-waste convention, football game, birthday party, county fair or music festival is fast becoming the status-quo" (Snider, 2008), and Eco-Products is poised for continued growth and success. Eco-Products is the exclusive supplier of compostable food service products to a growing list of major companies, including Hilton Resorts, NBC, Busch Entertainment Group (Busch Gardens and SeaWorld), and Major League Baseball (in over half of the stadiums by the end of 2009). Since 2005, the company has grown from around 10 employees to over 60 and has established a network of national distribution centers with warehouse facilities in Aurora, Colorado, Stockton, California (both opened in 2007), and Harrisburg, Pennsylvania (opened July 2008). From annual sales of $3.2 million in 2005, revenue steadily grew to $5.6 million in 2006, $11 million in 2007, $36 million in 2008, and $47 million in 2009. The company's revenue is expected to reach $62 million in 2010, with 2011 projections as high as $74 million. Eco Products was recognized on *Inc.* magazine's Inc. 5000, a list that "celebrates the fastest-growing private companies in America," ranking 834 in 2008, 270 in 2009, and 297 in 2010 (Inc. 5000).

Photo of Steve Savage. (Courtesy of Eco-Products.)

WALKING THE TALK

Our business philosophy is protective of the environment and mindful of the impact it has on the lives of our employees and their communities. We are committed to returning profits to our investors and ensuring a strong future for our employees. Our goal is to be a leader in the sustainability movement.

—Eco-Products Company Sustainability Policy Statement

When Steve and Kent Savage started Eco-Products in 1990, environmental stewardship was at the heart of their mission. As a for-profit company, they were certainly interested in making money by tapping into the burgeoning market of ecologically sound products and services. At the same time, they were also passionate about how the success of their business could have a positive impact on the environment and their community. As described in the original business plan, "this is a for-profit, capitalistic business serving a worthy cause . . . everything Eco-Products, Inc. does will convey environmental consciousness" (Eco-Products Business Plan, p. 22).

"For the first ten years, Eco-Products was just trying to survive," said Steve, when asked about what environmentally friendly measures were adopted early on. "Of course we always recycled . . . to me that's just one of those things you always do." In addition, Steve mentioned how Eco-Products became one of the first companies in the mid-1990s to purchase wind energy credits. "That was probably our first step in really doing something different than a normal business—other than biking to work."

Today, Eco-Products is involved in a wide variety of strategies, programs, sponsorships, and incentives that not only convey an image of environmental stewardship but have a genuine impact on conserving resources, saving dollars, and maintaining a culture among employees of social responsibility. "We are a zero-waste business," Steve explained. "We compost or recycle all waste produced at our facility. In addition, we allow our customers to drop off their compostables if they don't have access to a compost facility." Other measures include a 49-kilowatt solar array that was installed on the roof of the company's main office to "help reduce global warming and also help offset the 'carbon' cost of doing business" (Eco-Products Company Environmental Practices). The system produces over 50 percent of the main office's energy needs and provides real-time and historic data on the company's Web site, where customers and employees can view how much energy is being saved. "We are a carbon-neutral company," explained Steve, which is significant given the distance many of the products have to travel. Eco-Products works with about 7 to 10 manufacturers in Asia to produce its line of compostable products, which are shipped to the United States and distributed through the company's supply network.

Eco-Products offsets all transportation by purchasing carbon credits from the Boulder-based company Renewable Choice Energy. Renewable Choice, in turn, invests in projects that "prevent the same amount of greenhouse gases from entering the environment." Eco-Products' fleet of trucks are also doing their part. They are powered either by clean-burning natural gas or biodiesel. "By doing this, we've saved thousands of gallons of gasoline and reduced the amount of pollution created by our trucks" (Eco-Products Company Environmental Practices). Employees are also encouraged to use alternative forms of transportation and are rewarded with an extra $100 per month for doing so three or more times a week.

The innovative compostable products manufactured by Eco-Products can also be credited for reducing carbon and conserving natural resources. The products are made possible by the biopolymer provided by NatureWorks LLC, a joint venture between Cargill and Teijin Limited of Japan. When compared to the petroleum-based alternative, this "biopolymer currently uses 65 percent less fuel resources to produce, and reduces greenhouse emissions by 80–90 percent compared to traditional petroleum-based polymers" (NatureWorks, 2010). According to the Eco-Products Web site, the positive effects of using these compostable products are quantifiable. Because the products are made from rapidly renewable and sustainable resources rather than those derived from petroleum, in one year, Eco-Products' customers can be credited as having saved the equivalent of "742,414 gallons of gasoline (enough to drive around the earth 673 times), 13,478,914 pounds of greenhouse gases, or 8,629,476 kilowatt-hours of energy (enough to power the average American home for 810 years)" (Eco-Products Green Facts).

Eco-Products sponsors various sustainable events and programs throughout the year. Eco-Cycle, "one of the largest non-profit recyclers in the USA," is an important partner with Eco-Products in an effort to encourage companies and individuals and communities to become truly zero waste (Eco-Cycle, 2010). One of the most significant distinctions bestowed upon Eco-Products is the recognition it received by the Colorado Department of Public Health and Environment's Environmental Leadership Program. The program offers "benefits and incentives to members that voluntarily go beyond compliance with state and federal regulations and are committed to continual environmental improvement" (Colorado Department of Public Health and Environment, 2008 and 2010). Eco-Products was elevated in 2008 from its previous Bronze Achiever status to Gold Leader, continuing in 2010, the highest level of recognition possible.

LOOKING AHEAD

As all things green are enjoying mainstream appeal, the timing is right for a one-stop shop in Boulder selling natural and organic products at competitive prices.
—Ellie's Eco Home Store Promotional Advertisement

From Eco-Products' inception, Steve and Kent Savage planned to open a store to provide environmentally friendly products to the public. "We were supposed to roll out a retail store when we were about $10,000 per month in revenue," Steve recalled. Now, 18 years and "$50 million a year later," the company will finally make this plan a reality. The groundwork for the new retail store was laid in 1996, when Eco-Products launched a building supply division to complement the many wholesale products already available. When the company became increasingly recognized as the leading supplier of compostable food service products after 2005, there was some confusion about where one segment of the business stopped and the other began. In December 2007, Eco-Products decided to spin off the building supply division into a new retail company. "We had to come up with a name for it," Steve recalled. "We went through 'Natural-This,' or 'Eco-That.'" Eventually, he named the company after his daughter, Ellie. "It gives a personal feel to the store, and the tagline can still be 'Organic Home Center.'"

Steve and his board of directors have a much broader vision for Ellie's than to carry only building supplies. "It's everything for your home that is not food," explained Steve. The primary strategic concept behind Ellie's

**Photo of Ellie's Eco Home Store.
(Courtesy of Eco-Products.)**

is that the store will complement natural food stores like Whole Foods or Sunflower Markets. "The idea is to be right next door . . . so you can go buy your organic bananas from one store and then come in and buy everything else for your home at another." Ellie's has already established a presence both online and in a small store at the company headquarters in Boulder. In 2007, this division contributed $1.7 million to Eco-Products' revenue. The first stand-alone Ellie's Eco Home Store opened in November 2008 next to a Sunflower Market in Boulder. "The plan is to make the first store a success, and then to open several more stores in the next three years," said Steve, targeting such markets as Cambridge, Massachusetts; Santa Cruz, California; Bend, Oregon; and Seattle, Washington.

Ellie's is the first of several potential offshoots, start-ups, or acquisitions that Eco-Products may potentially explore as it continues to grow. "It's very possible that Eco-Products is going to own other businesses," comments Steve. "Ellie's is one of them. We could get into—and this is a big could—but solar, hydrogen fuel cells, water cleaning technologies." Steve used General Electric as an example of a company that has been involved in making anything from lightbulbs to locomotives and jet engines.

SOURING ECONOMY

Never before in modern times has so much of the world been simultaneously hit by a confluence of economic and financial turmoil such as we are now living through.

—Treasury Secretary Timothy Geithner,
April 2009 (Knowlton, 2009)

In the midst of the global economic downturn that toppled many of Wall Street's largest financial institutions, Steve admitted that he had to revise his company's revenue projections. "Before, we thought we'd triple sales. Now we think we're just going to double."

The adjusted 2009 projection of $48 million is a significant increase from the $36 million in 2008. "$50 million is still not out of the question," expounded an optimistic Steve. As for the company's recent venture into retail, the newly opened Ellie's is still pulling in break-even numbers. "Based on those numbers we're already looking for a store number two," explained Steve. Eco-Products also expanded the reach of its Green-Stripe compostable products by selling them through King Soopers/City Market. Other retailers are expected to follow.

Despite the slowing economy, the continued growth of Eco-Products is a testament to a successful business model, visionary leadership, and a simple concept. The scope of the company as a world-class leader of environmentally friendly products and services is significant when considering how Steve and his father started back in 1990. The fundamental objective, however, remains true to the original idea that was initially proposed by Kent Savage on the side of Longs Peak 20 years ago. Looking toward the future, Eco-Products is poised to make an even larger impact on the environmental movement by making it even more mainstream. "That is now my desire," explained Steve, "to not only change the food service industry, but let's change other industries as well!"

LESSONS LEARNED

(1) Growing slowly and financing a new business with cash flow can be advantageous in terms of learning a great deal and staying in business versus putting a great deal of money into a new firm or going into debt.

(2) Finding an idea for a sustainable business can come from what's needed in the marketplace, with Eco-Products creating useful products for recycled paper, plastic, and metal.

(3) Movement from low-margin products to higher-margin products can be valuable, such as Eco-Products' shift from being a wholesale distributor for products made from recycled paper to food service and janitorial supplies, followed by expansion into a growing variety of building products and later investing in the manufacture of its own products using a new technology.

(4) "What made Eco-Products unique was how it exclusively provided a full line of environmentally friendly products while other companies offered only a few "green" items as a specialized segment of their mainstream product line. Eco-Products expanded upon the model of providing products to the food-service industry by branding its own line of compostable plastic hot cups, cold cups, cutlery, clamshells, plates, bowls, and other single-use items."

REFERENCES

Biodegradable Products Institute, http://www.bpiworld.org/BPI-Public.
Colorado Department of Public Health and Environment, 2008 and 2010, *Environmental Leadership Program Overview,* http://www.cdphe.

state.co.us/oeis/elp/index.html   and   http://www.cdphe.state.co.us/oeis/elp/documents/2010membprofiles.pdf.

Eco-Cycle. *About Us,* http://www.ecocycle.org/Aboutus/index.cfm.

Eco-Products Business Plan, provided by Steve Savage at Eco-Products.

Eco-Products. *Eco-Products Company Description: Go Green,* http://www.ecoproducts.com/companypercent20pages/howpercent20topercent20gopercent20green.htm.

Eco-Products. *Eco-Products Company Environmental Practices,* http://www.ecoproducts.com/companypercent20pages/environmentalpercent20practices.htm.

Eco-Products. *Eco-Products Company Sustainability Policy Statement,* http://www.ecoproducts.com/va-cms/sustainability.html.

Eco-Products. *Eco-Products Green Facts,* http://www.ecoproducts.com/companypercent20pages/greenpercent20facts.htm.

Inc. 5000 '08. *No. 834 Eco-Products Boulder CO,* http://www.inc.com/inc5000/2008/company-profile.html?id=200808340.

Inc. 5000 '09. *No. 270 Eco-Products Boulder CO,* http://www.inc.com/inc5000/2009/company-profile.html?id=200902700.

Inc. 5000 '10. *No. 297 Eco-Products Boulder CO,* http://www.inc.com/inc5000/profile/eco-products.

Knowlton, Brian. "Global Economy Called Worst Since 1945," *The New York Times,* April 22, 2009, http://www.nytimes.com/2009/04/23/business/economy/23outlook.html.

NatureWorks. *Turning Corn into Plastic,* http://www.cargill.com/corporate-responsibility/environmental-innovation/pioneering-new-businesses/corn-plastic/index.jsp.

Snider, Laura. "Boulder's Eco-Products Set To Explode," *Boulder Daily Camera,* September 3, 2008, http://www.dailycamera.com/news/2008/Sep/03/boulders-eco-products-set-explode/.

FOUR

Barrett Studio Architects, Boulder, Colorado

Fred Andreas
Contributing Research by Clay Chase, Pamela Goodrich-Yohe,
David Jacobs, and Christopher Thorp

One morning, David Barrett sat in his kitchen next to a window angled open just enough to let in a breeze that pushed the steam over his coffee mug. Reading the newspaper on the kitchen table, he noticed a headline: "Windows That Open Are the Latest Office Amenity." He read the title a few times just to make sure he wasn't missing some important other detail to the story—the hook, something to make him read on. This was a full, *front-page* spread in the *Wall Street Journal* (Templin, 1998). The thought crossed his mind: this is incredibly underwhelming. The 20th century was all but over—a century in which sustainability ebbed and flowed many times—only to end with this underwhelming mantra. At the time, he knew little about the sustainability of large commercial buildings. Nonetheless, the idea of it seemed incredibly odd . . . something as simple as windows that open creates a meaningful future . . . a literal metaphor of open ideas for closed and sealed buildings.

Every business and industry is affected by concerns for sustainability, just as each of us is affected everyday by the choices we make, the products we use, and the way we live our lives. Unlike other industries, architecture is placed at the forefront of the sustainable movement. It bears the image of sustainability, because architecture means to build, sculpt, and manipulate space, which ultimately means using materials and energy to change what came before. Those choices make projects that, in the developed world, use huge amounts of environmentally degrading energy until the day they are demolished. This is not to say that sustainability is more important to architecture than it is to any other industry. Rather, architecture is a particularly physical and tangible manifestation of either consumption or sustainability compared to other industries, whose thinking, processes, and values around sustainability are not visibly experienced and occupied.

Examining sustainability in architecture means rethinking what, where, why, and how we build and, ultimately, live most of our lives. Sustainable solutions in the architectural industry are diverse and vary greatly by design process, building type, materials, and systems. The approach taken by Boulder, Colorado–based Barrett Studio Architects is an excellent example of sustainable solutions as a unique and refreshing approach to sustainability in business. Barrett Studio is not mainstream. The firm's work is eclectic and certainly not considered greenwashing. Clients and employees past and present, as well as other architects and builders in the area automatically associate sustainability with Barrett Studio Architects. Yet, one will not find

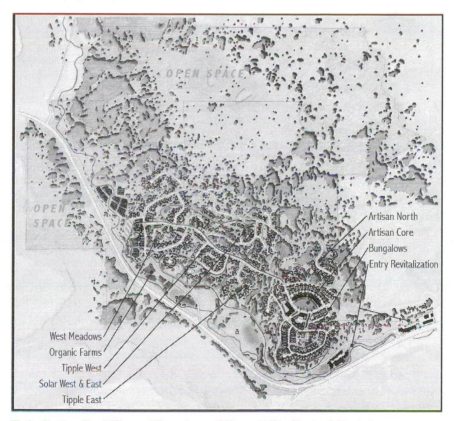

Twin Buttes EcoVillage. (Courtesy of Barrett Studio Architects.)

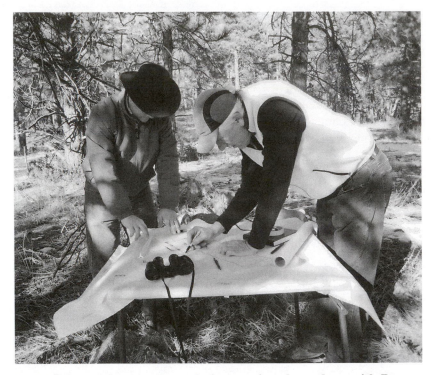

David Barrett always starts a design on site, shown here with Barrett Studio Architects employee Sam Nishek. (Courtesy of Barrett Studio Architects.)

a checklist or prescribed metric of sustainable elements or approaches in the office.

Although sustainability is both budgeted into each project and presented to every client, Barrett Studio's reputation stems from its foundational integrated approach. This approach brings the firm local, regional, and international business. David Barrett, founding principal, admits he sometimes has the opportunity to be selective about clientele, a coveted place to be in the architectural field. Does this translate into sustainability for the elite? Not for David. With over 30 years of architectural practice focusing on energy-efficient and sustainable design strategies, David Barrett remains increasingly interested in expanding his experience and philosophy from single, stand-alone homes, schools, and places of worship to entire communities of interrelated systems working together in support of the health, efficiency, and vitality of the community.

HISTORY

In 1970, Richard Nixon was president, and college students were protesting all over the United States. In Ohio at Kent State University, David Barrett was finishing his undergraduate degree in architecture. In May, the Ohio National Guard shot and killed four young Kent State students. That tragedy and the cultural division in the United States inspired David to question architecture's role in serving humanity. How can we make holistic design available to all? How can we protect the environment? He and other students believed that architecture had a profound responsibility to effect a positive change in the lives of others.

After graduating from Kent State in 1971 with a professional bachelor's degree in architecture and serving as an intern for several firms in Pittsburgh, David began working on an environmentally friendly student center at Florida A&M University. The design resulted in a partially underground building that utilized passive cooling systems. The project aligned with David's ideals and won an AIA Florida (a chapter of the American Institute of Architects) design award.

David felt that the practice of architecture—mired in tradition—was too slow to respond to social and environmental concerns. He was searching for a place in the world of architecture, a place that reflected his vision of joyful and responsible design. Once he became licensed, he entered the graduate program at University of Colorado, Boulder, where he had opportunities to explore his interests in passive heating, cooling, solar energy, and social responsibility.

This education, coming at a time of an oil embargo and a new public consciousness around energy conservation, spurred David to band together with fellow students to challenge the norms of the dominant industry culture. David's master's thesis was an animated film titled *Regenesis: The Rebirth of the American City*. The basis for David's eventual private practice was beginning to take shape. Moved by the cross-disciplinary approach of Charles and Ray Eames, David began working for Carl Worthington and Associates in Boulder. Similar to the Eames's, Worthington's firm combined a multidisciplinary studio approach that included architecture, landscape architecture, land planning, interiors, and multimedia production.

In 1977, David decided that it was time to pursue his own vision of a practice that merged his environmental and social values with a holistic approach to design. His firm, Sunflower, named for the heliotropic relationship of biology and the sun, was launched with the aid of grants from the Solar Energy Research Institute and the success of winning various competitions.

David built a clientele designing small, passive solar residential projects that came to form from a process David calls "deep listening" and his concurrent development of a design model called "ecomorphic principles." He felt that he needed to prove that an environmental design approach was more than a fad. Were there clients willing to break with convention and embrace these values and sometimes provocative theories? Could architect and client work together as societal change agents?

The breakthrough came when he won a commission from a philanthropic initiative of American Honda Motor Company to develop the Eagle Rock School and Professional Development Center to serve at-risk children. During his presentation, it became evident that David's commitment focused on changing the conventional approach to design. His track record of innovation and exploration and his development and use of ecomorphic principles convinced Honda that it had found its architect. Honda's commitment to changing the way children are educated began by hiring David's design firm, Sunflower, which had a commitment to changing society's relationship with the built environment.

The Eagle Rock project positioned Sunflower as an authority on sustainable design and as a firm with a social conscience. Sunflower eventually became Barrett Studio Architects, and, after 30 years of designing, it has become a leader in sustainable design and an important part of the established mainstream design community.

The ultimate success of Honda's Eagle Rock School and Professional Development Center gave Barrett the traction he needed to find other clients with a passion for change. With projects such as the Abbey of Saint Walburga, the Casa Viento EcoLodge in Venezuela, the Holiday Urban Neighborhood, and the Friendship Center in Dushanbe, Tajikistan—all projects with clients who shared these values and delighted in the environment—David's business grew. In 1997, Barrett Studio was selected as the AIA Colorado Firm of the Year, and, in 2002, David Barrett was honored as the AIA Colorado Architect of the Year. After 35 years, Barrett Studio remains a model of a sustainable architectural practice that will continue to innovate into the new green economy.

BARRETT STUDIO'S MISSION

Barrett Studio Architects is a highly motivated professional design group dedicated to the practice of architecture, community and urban design, and interiors. Its approach to design is holistic, viewing the environment as a totality. This ecologically oriented perspective explores the relationships involved in a project, the interconnections that influence design decisions, and the opportunities to produce projects of meaning, excellence, and, always, beauty. The firm believes that sustainability must remain integral to all business practices. The triple bottom line is just a start. Employees share and practice core values of sustainability both at work and at home. Managers care about making a difference and taking action.

More than ever, this process cannot be the isolated realm of the expert. It is their experience that meaningful solutions will stand the test of time creating the result of co-creativity. Through the rigors of an integrated team approach, they find both the joy in making and the satisfaction of being a part of something larger than themselves. With each project, they first create a process that uniquely considers the potentials of the site, the climate, the client, the use, and of course, the budget. The tangible results stem from a product of passion, communication, creativity, integrity, and commitment to see an idea through. "This is what we do. This is who we are." (Barrett Studio Architects Web site)

Staff members outside the Barrett Studio in Boulder, Colorado. (Courtesy of Barrett Studio Architects.)

SUSTAINABLE BUSINESS PRACTICES

David Barrett has seen an increasing number of businesses adopt varying versions of a sustainable business model. He believes that sustainability must become an integrated mind-set in the business and not just a line item on the expense sheet. When times get tough, businesses shouldn't say, "Oh, sorry, times are tough this month so, no more green strategies allowed."

Barrett Studio maintains the enviable position of clients seeking out its services. Because the firm has the reputation of incorporating sustainable design principles as well as sustainable practices within the office, it attracts clients who have already embraced green ideals. Barrett's legacy of sustainable design established the studio as a responsible and highly reputable firm. This enables the firm to choose projects that reflect its ideals yet remain flexible enough to work with clients' budgets and requirements.

Barrett Studio's standards are continually evolving, informed by David's experience. It may seem counterintuitive, but the business team values the absence of checklists and other static measures. Due to the constant evolution of technologies and the diversity of projects, a standard checklist would quickly become obsolete. Instead, projects utilize montages and EcoVisions that act as touchstones throughout the design process. Clients track the implementation of the sustainable measures and love the results.

GETTING STARTED WITH A SUSTAINABLE
BUSINESS STRATEGY

Barrett Studio's commitment to sustainability goes back a number of decades. Ever since the social and environmental changes of the 1960s and 1970s, sustainability remained on David's radar. As far back as the late 1970s, when David was at the University of Colorado, Boulder, his graduate studies introduced him to a group of like-minded students with a focus on solar technologies and sustainability. Even his original business venture, Sunflower, modeled on heliotropic principles, focused toward bio-awareness. From these early beginnings, David created an evolutionary approach to his business practice.

Every year during the staff retreat, we'd brainstorm about ways to become more sustainable and more effective. At the yearly Staff Retreat we'd re-vision our goals addressing the Studio at large. It was used as a way to check in on our individual lives and outlooks on the world, determining where we're headed so we can move forward with a cohesive vision. We worked from focused intentions, that manifests as a completely organic process. Sustainable planning is one of the keys to sustainable success. (David Barrett, interview by research team, 2009)

Not everything in the sustainable architecture business is easy. Forward thinking often flies in the face of conservative traditions in academia, among the general public, and in the architectural community. Many of David's original ideas born in the solar movement, remained marginalized by the A list of architects represented by the mainstream firms. Recognizing its specialty niche in the market, Barrett Studio seeks clients with similar beliefs or interests and embraces its role as a community and client educator. Its reputation in green principles has remained the hallmark of the studio for 35 years. That unique and consistent conveyance of the company's mission translates into a powerful marketing tool. Because of its position in the field, Barrett Studio attracts private clients interested in learning more about sustainability and the built environment. It applies a careful consideration process to larger public requests for proposals, evaluating them critically and responding only to those that it feels best suited for and those that enable the company to make a difference. This selectivity fosters a perception in the community of a high-quality, ethically based studio. A strong and long-standing reputation in sustainability represents yet another key to success.

MARKETING

Building on the firm's reputation, Barrett Studio's marketing plan focuses first on conveying a clear and consistent message to its market. The organization's long-standing membership in eco-conscious groups and its reputation for sustainability serves to differentiate the firm from its competitors. This difference is showcased in industry and consumer publications, presentations at conferences, public workshops, award nominations, and targeted advertising in eco-design publications.

Staying ahead of the competition remains part of the company's secret to success. Barrett Studio consistently researches new technologies to advance sustainability not only in its projects but also in its own office. The key is staying abreast of the newest technologies and systems and then implementing and integrating them into both the business and the lives of employees. If the studio wants to investigate new products, it researches, tests, evaluates, utilizes, and recycles them, supporting a holistic mind-set. For example, unrecyclable plastic binders from an office cleaning were recycled through Craigslist; they disappeared from the alley the next day. For Barrett Studio, sustainability is not about preset assumptions or predefined parameters. Sustainability develops from a conscious effort based on underlying principles and an eye toward innovation and flexibility.

Remaining competitive requires staying up to date with the latest developments. Whenever new products or ideas become available, the entire studio learns about them in any number of eco-based journals and publications or lunch presentations by local distributors. Evolving technologies and products researched in these venues and involvement in industry conferences and workshops provide an understanding of the latest developments. Some technical eco-based periodicals that Barrett Studio consults include *Ecospecifier, Environmental Building News, Green Building News, Eco-structure, and Pharos.* Other interesting reading and ideas are often found in more consumer-oriented magazines such as *Metropolis, Abitare,* and *Dwell.*

Likewise, belonging to local green business groups creates opportunities for valuable connections. Groups such as the Boulder Green Building Guild, United States Green Building Council, and Colorado Straw Bale Association help the business stay abreast of news in the local green market. Long-standing memberships and active involvement in such organizations help to reaffirm the firm's credibility. Maintaining a presence in the local green community helps to differentiate the firm in an increasingly crowded field. Attending charitable events, contributing to silent auctions, providing pro bono or discounted services to local nonprofits, and participating in lighthearted community events all illustrate alternative methods for staying active in and supporting the local community. The company also donates 10 percent of its annual profits to local nonprofits with a housing or sustainability focus, supporting sustainable local communities in the area. Community and stewardship then becomes another key to success.

STAKEHOLDER INVOLVEMENT

Barrett Studio keeps its business model simple. The sole proprietorship has no shareholders and no board of directors; however, it is modeled after a cooperative. David engages all employees, requesting their input and supporting their involvement. The company maintains an open-book accounting policy with profit/loss information shared with all employees on a monthly basis. Decisions on spending and benefits often include a larger circle beyond David and business director Maggie Flickinger. Their fair-share profit distribution program is particularly effective because of this continued sharing of information, creating a loyal, informed, and vested employee base.

A SUSTAINABLE BUSINESS MODEL

Without consciously espousing it as a business model, we follow the triple bottom line: People, the Planet and Profit.

—Maggie Flickinger, Barrett Studio business director

The P3 movement—people, the planet, and profit—covers all aspects of sustainability. Recycling materials, composting at the office, buying locally, supporting local green businesses such as Eco-Products and Ellie's Eco Home Store, using and specifying local manufacturers, utilizing remanufacturing for office supplies such as ink cartridges, using 100 percent recycled paper, installing drivers to support double-sided printing, and contracting with a local green cleaning company all represent Barrett Studio's P3 business commitments. Other initiatives include collecting and recycling items through the city's Center for Hard to Recycle Materials; replacing incandescent office lighting with efficient xenon, CFL, and LED fixtures; and purchasing wind power to offset energy provided by the local utility, Xcel, which still generates most of its electricity from the burning of coal.

FIRM CULTURE

One of the greatest attributes of sustainability in any business, but especially in a service business, is sustainable policy that supports the firm's own people, its most valuable asset. Barrett Studio supports a sustainable workforce through a variety of policies on flex time, telework, and promoting membership in local organizations. Many architectural firms' cultures support onerous overtime schedules that have become the norm, with a typical work week of 50 to 60 hours. At Barrett Studio, a 40-hour work week remains optimal—in terms of optimal performance and optimal attitude. The firm found that the team is as productive working 40-hour weeks as it is working longer hours. The enjoyment of a balanced lifestyle is integral to team spirit and a sustainable business model.

With a strong core value of sustainability behind the studio's designs, business director Maggie Flickinger focuses on sustainably running the business as well, through carefully addressing of financial, staffing, and human resources challenges, evolving the studio culture through an economic and human perspective. She coordinates marketing efforts and visual communications that reinforce the studio's values and philosophy. She strives to bring Barrett Studio's business practice into alignment with the firm's design practices. With Maggie focusing on sustainable business development, practice, and policy, David is free to focus on the evolution of the studio's design practice and its position in the community.

Sustainable best practices create a sustainable business culture based on a team approach. Employees earn a minimum of two weeks vacation annually, but, under the Priority Program, they may make an annual election to reduce their compensation—while retaining all other benefits—in order to accrue an additional week of paid time off. When overtime does accrue, compensatory paid time off is offered. Other employee benefits include 100 percent employer-paid health and dental plans, simple plan retirement matching, regional transit passes, socializing at monthly employee dinners held at rotating employee homes, meeting for beers after work, and annual retreats, which last year included a trip to Gold Lake in the mountains above Boulder, featuring both business and pleasure. The firm believes in continuing education for its employees, regularly subsidizing seminars, retreats, and conferences. All of these benefits are available to every employee from day one of employment. These sustainable business practices focus on enhancing the individual and the team in their day-to-day business and personal lives, bolstering their careers and their life balance as part of the P3 commitment.

SUSTAINABILITY CULTURE IN THE COMPANY

The employees fully participate in these sustainable choices both at work and at home. The "people" part of the sustainability program includes everyone in the office. It's not so much an incentive program to convince people to participate as it is that Barrett Studio attracts employees who are already interested in integrating sustainability into their lifestyle. As an example, approximately 70 percent of the employees regularly ride a bike or the bus to work; the studio's employees won the 2007 Business Challenge for Ride Smart Thursdays, a program of the Denver Regional Council of Governments.

The firm creates a sustainable business plan focusing on pay, performance, management and benefits by:

Maintaining a moderate work week and respecting employees by not overworking them

Encouraging the use of alternate and public transportation

Creating financial incentives establishing a sustainable investment in the firm

These unique precedents in the architecture industry support the firm's employees and maintain the organization's P3 commitment.

FIRM EFFICIENCY

The efficiency of Barrett Studio Architects and its individual employees is tracked on a monthly basis for comparing projected and goal efficiencies. The billable hours for work on paying projects determine the relative efficiency of each employee's efforts. Billable hours include time spent working directly on a contracted project. The target employee efficiencies vary depending on the employee's role. An associate with greater business experience and prospect development maintains a lower billable hour's goal than a lower-level job captain or intern primarily focused on drafting. The lower target frees the leaders of the firm to work on nonbillable, essential work such as marketing and client contact. With employee billable goals ranging from 12.5 percent to 90 percent, the collective studio goal averages approximately 67 percent. Internal hours include marketing, request for proposal response, office and administrative functions, education, technology, organization, and other functions. All employees become aware of their individual goals with the aid of a software program that allows them to track their billable percentage in real time. The entire staff remains involved in the fiscal structure of the firm as well as the financial impact of working below or above their goals. This awareness and feedback translates into a motivated workforce invested in generating billable work and sustaining profitability.

TECHNOLOGY

Increasingly, businesses utilize technology to control travel and other expenses for projects located in distant locations. For Barrett Studio, this includes utilizing digital technology such as video conferencing, Web posting, and digital remote transmission for construction administration photos, documentation, specifications, and changes. Videoconferencing and telecommuting saves both human and synthetically generated energy and may be one of the most sustainable strategies, saving substantial time and money, creating an additive approach to the sustainability of a project.

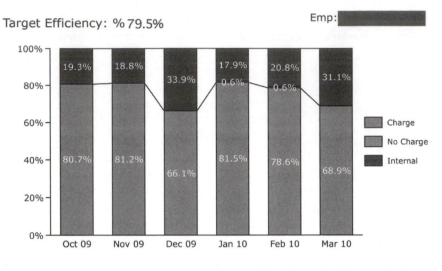

Target Efficiency: %79.5%   Emp:

As of Thu, 25 March, 2010 at 11:21 AM

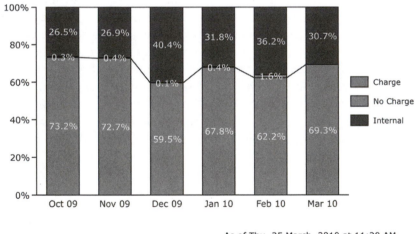

Target Efficiency: % Studio Wide

As of Thu, 25 March, 2010 at 11:20 AM

Target Efficiency Graphs. (Courtesy of Barrett Studio Architects.)

Such business decisions, affecting simple yet expensive business operations, address the lowest-hanging fruit, producing effective and affordable results. The Twin Buttes EcoVillage in Durango required weekly meetings, resulting in weekly WebEx and Skype meetings with consultants and client alike, saving substantial time, money, energy and carbon in comparison to travel-mediated business. Sustainability mission accomplished!

COMPETITION

More and more businesses understand that an integrated mind-set and business philosophy create success, and competition gets tougher every day in the green architecture business. Virtually every architectural firm classifies itself as green and sustainable. It's splashed over every Web site and advertisement; it seems everyone has become green. Maintaining Barrett Studio as the green and sustainable firm of choice in the minds of its clients remains a key focus for the studio. The fact that the architectural industry is moving in a new direction helps create a new mainstream, one based in sustainable principles. The trend today, however, is that firms with no green experience or passion are jumping on the bandwagon and calling themselves green. Ultimately, these firms simply attempt to establish a green division or appoint a sustainability director in an attempt to expand their markets and their workloads. Often, the only green produced is money. Barrett Studio's history of working consistently in the green field with an integrated commitment supports its long-standing reputation. It intends to continue its recognized expertise based on its 30-year legacy, carrying that reputation forward and branding its sustainable expertise more effectively than others in the market. Expertise and reputation has become another key to success.

TRACKING BUILDING PERFORMANCE

A key challenge for the business community in general and in the architectural industry specifically is insufficient feedback in obtaining quantified results from sustainable activities. Architecture is increasingly complex, and sustainable design is an even more complicated undertaking. A sustainable approach to projects must focus on tracking activity and quantifying success. Measuring and comparing energy performance and correlating those metrics to any single business decision remains a difficult task. Even determining the carbon footprint of buildings and businesses remains extremely difficult without extensive analysis. Programs produce wildly varying results and conclusions based on differing assumptions, leading sometimes to "analysis paralysis."

Substantial time and effort go into simple day-to-day activities, so the simplest solutions may provide opportunities for the greatest sustainability.

Encouraging employees to either ride the bus or bike to work can dramatically affect any office's energy use and carbon footprint, representing a very simple solution. Sustainable opportunities include educating the public and clients on the basics of sustainable best practices. These opportunities translate into increased performance with quantified sustainability, energy consumption, and savings. A motivated and vested workforce focused on a team effort will create sustainable solutions beyond any single sustainable strategy directed by top management. Simple solutions translate into sustainable business success. Knowing to turn off the lights; to walk, bike, or ride to work; to recycle; and to create more efficient office strategies because everyone cares—taken together, such best practices may yield surprisingly high performance results when a team is focused on success. The simplest solutions may be the most effective.

CREATING CORE SUSTAINABILITY VALUES

Maggie and David's advice for new or existing small companies interested in making the transition toward sustainability is to create a set of sustainable core values integral to the business practice and the ideals shared by all employees. They suggest creating a core belief system held by each individual within the company. This sustainable principle could be applied to any business in any industry, focusing on the people aspect of the P3 equation. While larger companies may educate their workers to change to a more sustainable attitude, a smaller company is more effective starting from a shared sustainability ideal. It makes no sense for someone who doesn't recycle at home to run a company whose focus is sustainability. In contrast, when individual commitment matches the business commitment, credibility and authenticity remain reinforced in the minds of both clients and colleagues.

TWIN BUTTES CASE STUDY

In the rugged landscape just west of Durango, Colorado, a new paradigm for living is taking shape. Architect David Barrett and associate Amy Kirtland have thoughtfully conceived of a "living community" designed as an interconnected system of built environments, cultivated food-producing plots, and significant tracts of open space. Acting as master planner, Barrett Studio, along with Durango residents who actively participated, designed elements of the community inspired by the integrated systems of a living organism. Buildings are carefully placed within the landscape for low energy consumption and for the cooperative social and civic involvement of its residents. The community of Twin Buttes is designed to exist in concert with nature while honoring the historic and cultural character of the region.

Located two miles west of downtown Durango, the Twin Buttes EcoVillage will set a new standard for how communities are created, allowing residents to live, work, and play with minimal ecological impact. David Barrett developed an entirely new vision—an *EcoVision*—for the Twin Buttes development when he was brought on to the project in 2007. The first step was to decrease the presumed developed area of the 600-acre property and increase the preserved natural open space to 80 percent. David designed an "elegant density" in which a variety of sizes and types of residential and mixed-use buildings exist, forming layers of complexity and creating a sense of community and diversity. This also allows services and amenities to be offered within a primarily residential community. The financial accessibility and socioeconomic diversity of the community are supported by ensuring that affordable units remain available for lower-income residents. Sixteen percent of the residential units will be "affordable/attainable," seamlessly embedded throughout each cluster community.

Clustering the development also supports the walkability of the neighborhoods, easing reliance on automobiles. An eight-mile system of interconnected trails, bike lanes, and sidewalks is designed to allow residents easy access to any point within the development as well as a direct connection to downtown Durango, with no more than 15 minutes from any point in the project by bicycle. As a result of a comprehensive transportation demand management plan, the necessity of single-occupancy vehicle trips to and from Twin Buttes is expected to realize a 30 percent reduction in comparison to typical Durango use.

With over five acres of permaculturally planned farmland and community gardens, including cattle, fishing, and apiaries, the residents of Twin Buttes will have opportunities for an intimate connection to the earth and to the local production of homegrown food.

With over 30 years of architectural practice focusing on energy-efficient and sustainable design strategies, David Barrett has become increasingly interested in how to expand his experience and philosophy from single, stand-alone homes, schools, and places of worship to entire communities of interrelated systems working together in support of the health, efficiency, and vitality of the community.

The *EcoVision,* an original document written by David, outlined the big ideas for the development of Twin Buttes. These ideas identified patterns useful in the planning of any sustainable community and include the following:

Harvesting the sun. Early site analysis revealed excellent solar exposure that could be available to all lots through studied protective measures such as thoughtful site planning and solar fences, enabling daylighting design features and solar energy.

Resource awareness. The developer committed to reduce energy use by 50 percent compared to required energy standards and created a locally tuned green building checklist.

Elegant density: The design featured diversity in lot size, building type, and amenities, a qualitative textural mix that most people greatly appreciate.

Connectivity. The development team consulted with engineers and multimodal experts to produce easy access and diversity of transportation means.

Affordable living. Barrett Studio developed diverse, affordable housing offerings embedded in market rate areas—one size doesn't fit all!

Sense of place. The firm conducted historical research to honor the mining, homesteading, and ranching past of the area and held town hall–style meetings to involve the community in a dreams and fears process around development issues.

Twin Buttes EcoVillage's 600 units of housing prepares the over 1,000 residents for a radical sustainable lifestyle change. This lifestyle change includes concepts of community with gardening, walking and biking to work, reducing energy use, and increasing awareness of resource conservation—all techniques currently used by Barrett Studio to dramatically increase the sustainability of its architectural practice and its employees' personal lifestyles.

HOLISTIC SUCCESS

Utilizing the "walk the talk" motto, the holistic success of Barrett Studio illustrates the application of sustainability to the philosophy of redefining community. Communities where sustainability best practices can be successfully deployed include an eco-village or an office. While Barrett

Studio's work focuses on sustainable architecture and solutions defining a new paradigm for the 21st century, its business practices likewise focus on sustainable solutions. The ideals of P3—people, the planet, and profit— apply equally to the projects, the firm, employees, clients, and business profits, and the associated principles create an authentically sustainable business model. For Barrett Studio Architects, profitability never focuses exclusively on money, but rather on a broader 21st-century concept of sustainable rewards. Those rewards include a fundamental focus on lifestyle, ethics, and stewardship of the local area, the region, and the planet, as well as the studio's clientele and employees. These successes translate directly into an abundance mentality and a truly sustainable profit.

LESSONS LEARNED

(1) Barrett Studios "conceived of a 'living community' designed as an interconnected system of built environments, cultivated food-producing plots, and significant tracts of open space." Buildings are carefully placed within the landscape for low energy consumption and for the cooperative social and civic involvement of its residents. The community of Twin Buttes is designed to exist in concert with nature, while honoring the historic and cultural character of the region.

(2) David designed an "elegant density" in which a variety of sizes and types of residential and mixed-use buildings exist, forming layers of complexity and creating a sense of community and diversity. This also allows services and amenities to be offered within a primarily residential community.

(3) Sticking to your vision is key—in this case, a vision of a practice that merged his environmental and social values with a holistic approach to design is important and will over time be recognized. The organization's long-standing membership in eco-conscious groups and its reputation for sustainability serves to differentiate it from its competitors.

(4) "For Barrett Studio Architects, profitability never focuses exclusively on money, but rather on a broader 21st-century concept of sustainable rewards. Those rewards include a fundamental focus

> on lifestyle, ethics, and stewardship of the local area, the region, and the planet, as well as the studio's clientele and employees. These successes translate directly into an abundance mentality and a truly sustainable profit."

REFERENCES

Templin, Neal. "Windows That Open Are the Latest Office Amenity," *Wall Street Journal,* August 26, 1998.

Twin Buttes, Durango, CO, twinbuttesofdurango.com/thevision.html.

FIVE

Forest City: The Evolution of Sustainability in Forest City's Development of Stapleton

Fred Andreas
Prime Contributing Author Pamela Goodrich-Yohe
Contributing Researcher and Author Robin Groppi

HISTORY OF FOREST CITY ENTERPRISES

According to the Ratner House, original founders of Forest City in the 1930s, the company traces its roots in the United States to the first decade of the 20th century, when members of the their family immigrated to the United States from Bialystok, in what was then Russia (now Poland). Frieda Ratner was the first to come to America in 1904, followed by other family members in successive years. Through the years, the Ratners invested in and ran many different businesses. Two of these individual businesses, Forest City Material and Buckeye, combined in 1929 under the Forest City name. Their success led to the construction of garages and eventually single-family homes in the Cleveland area. Becoming their own supplier for residential development gave the Ratners a financial advantage. During the Great Depression, the Ratners, known for their generous and liberal credit policies, allowed struggling families to build their own affordable housing. As a result, Forest City became a major lumber supplier and real estate developer in the Ohio market (Funding Universe). Their development work continued successfully into the last half of the 20th century with a number of nationally recognized mixed-use developments.

In Colorado in 1995, the new Denver International Airport was relocated northeast of Denver, leaving the old Stapleton International Airport as an abandoned Brownfield on the eastern edge of the city surrounded by residential neighborhoods and easy access to a major thoroughfares and downtown.

The City of Denver through the Stapleton Development Cooperation (SDC) entered into a selection process for a master developer. The SDC was a private sector, nonprofit entity created by Mayor Wellington E. Webb and the Denver City Council in 1995 to oversee the disposition of the former Stapleton International Airport (Stapleton Development Corporation, 1995). By November 1998, it had selected Forest City, now a large, nationally known private-sector firm with strong management and ownership ties to the Ratners. According to Tom Gleason, Forest City's public relations manager, local Colorado residents understand and value the importance of maintaining the quality of life and options for future generations. He describes the push from the City of Denver to include sustainability for the Stapleton redevelopment:

> I want to make it clear that we were implementing the vision of the community and, of course people in Colorado understand the importance of protecting our environment. As a matter of fact, Forest City, a

Neighborhood construction. (Courtesy of Forest City Stapleton, Inc.)

company that has been around for over 80 years, has a set of core values, integrity and commitment to community and things of that sort; we did not add sustainability as a core value until we became the master developer at Stapleton. (Gleason, 2008)

FINANCIAL CREATIVITY

The ambitious scope of the redevelopment of the former Stapleton International Airport produced a range of creative financing mechanisms. The project represents a true example of public-private partnerships. The Denver Urban Renewal Authority (DURA) issued bonds for the front-end financing for Stapleton's infrastructure with repayment through tax increment financing (TIF). TIF, tied directly to retail sales tax revenue, is retired through the sales taxes generated within the project. As a result of TIF challenges, a unique partnership evolved between Forest City, the City of Denver, and DURA, allowing for the financing necessary to fuel the continued development within Stapleton. In other cases, Forest City as master developer provided front-end financing not tied to TIF bonds and the tax sourced repayment. The Park Creek Metropolitan district oversaw the development of infrastructure, regional roads, and utilities that connect Stapleton to the surrounding area. With its many years of development and financing experience, Forest City developed the buildings and sites for the commercial and residential projects, affording them unique access to new and innovative financing mechanisms.

STRATEGY

Melissa Knott, a graduate student and daughter of a developer, was finishing her MBA in sustainability at the University of Colorado's School of Business. Her internship included developing a new resource, the *Green Book,* a sustainability plan for Stapleton to educate the public and influence the development. The development plan outlined in the *Green Book* included seeds of the concept that economy and sustainability must go hand in hand. Knott, hired by Forest City on a temporary contract, initially became a consultant to manage the writing of Stapleton's sustainability strategy. Even though Forest City adopted the *Green Book* as a sustainability guideline, the specifics were not explicit. Eventually hired as Forest City sustainability director, Knott became integrally involved in developing specific sustainability approaches and policies at Forest City and the Stapleton Development.

In the beginning, Forest City had little in the way of a sustainability strategy. It was new territory for Forest City, yet the company remained committed to a new sustainability philosophy. The company's sustainability efforts ebb and flow with each individual project. Forest City realizes that the building of credible relationships remains one of the key cornerstones of success throughout the company and its projects.

If your project managers all understand sustainability and how that applies to your business, then you know you are already light years ahead. You can hire a sustainability consultant, but it is never as successful as when you have an architect that really understands what to do. Sustainability became a core value for our company both here and nationally. (Knott, 2008)

Initially Forest City worked with the Rocky Mountain Institute (RMI), reviewing sustainability measurements and strategies. RMI, an innovator in Leadership in Energy and Environmental Design (LEED) and green building, was interested in establishing new criteria for sustainability within the Stapleton Development. Forest City, however, found numerous established and successful standards primarily through LEED that provided appropriate measurements for green without having to develop entirely new criteria. Forest City eventually determined that allocating resources toward helping builders and contractors meet the current LEED standards created the most effective approach rather than developing new metrics. The process featured an inclusive approach that allowed the developer's designers and builders to determine the priorities and timing of various strategies. Experience eventually determined the appropriate areas to focus on, producing the best sustainable results for the time and money invested.

Through the process, Forest City maintained a successful relationship with Calthrope and Associates of California. Known nationally as preeminent urban designers of New Urbanism communities, their philosophy corresponded to Forest City's rising interest in sustainable neo-traditional neighborhoods. Forest City's goal for Stapleton included the development of walkable neighborhoods supporting a valued sense of community with lower vehicle miles traveled.

RELATIONSHIPS AND NETWORKING

Through the process, the Forest City leadership found that clear values, networking, a sense of humor, and good basic business practices produced a successful business model. Their role as master developers included supporting people to achieve Stapleton's green objectives rather than pushing the process along. They found that if you work together and build a good team through give and take, you will go further in reaching your sustainability goals. Eventually Forest City's performance in the residential market dramatically increased with an inclusive process involving everyone from executives to builders.

Forest City also learned that another path to a successful outcome in sustainable development included the incorporation of the latest green and sustainable technologies. Up-to-date knowledge of innovations and sustainable strategies in ecological building practices set their projects apart in a tight residential market. With the proliferation of new technologies and strategies in sustainability, Forest City relied on experts in different industries. For example, as members of Denver mayor John Hickenlooper's Greenprint Council, focusing on relationships, acquiring information, implementing new sustainability strategies became an integral part of their success. Forest City supported an open approach to sharing knowledge, encouraging builders to share their expertise and experience with new players, and partnerships within and throughout the project. Presentation was the key! The entire approach worked well for the builders with green research presented in a positive manner.

CHANGING CHALLENGES AND ROLES

Forest City found the interdisciplinary approaches to business and projects challenging and the constant problem solving and brainstorming exciting. With sustainability developing into a mainstream approach, Forest City encouraged meaningful and open dialogue among all players. The Forest City team constantly focused on sustainable and life-cycle aspects of the project, supporting maintenance while not compromising value, avoiding typical slash and cut "value engineering." Planning became an essential component of the process. Forest City found that the recent changes to the real estate market required supporting sustainable practices to an even greater extent. A thorough understanding of the balance between the initial cost and the long-term paybacks remained essential to supporting the investment in sustainable practices.

Forest City continues to measure its progress against a constant set of established sustainability standards. Working with mainstream organizations such as the Department of Energy and the Environmental Protection Agency (EPA), they continue to utilize the Energy Star Rating System, allowing builders to track their results as compared to sustainability standards. This approach not only produces results; these strategies become copy for marketing the project. For example, across the board, Forest City's builders have an Energy Star rating higher than the Energy Star standard. They not only save energy and money but also market those results. Providing clear and quantified results based on the cost and efficiency of each strategy enables Forest City to evaluate each sustainable practice.

Forest City's approach of implementing sustainable concepts with cost-saving strategies assigns a cost just for sustainability. When the project is completed, a complete review of the actual expenses provides the exact cost of sustainability. Forest City found that LEED Silver Certified building costs remained minimal if it incorporated smart planning. Those projects take advantage of low-hanging fruit such as Brownfield site reclamation. Charlie Nicola, vice president of design and construction for Forest City Stapleton, believes that the cost for LEED Certification remains too high and must come down. For example, fundamental commissioning for mechanical systems, which requires post-construction inspection and adjustment, costs around $80,000 per project. Additionally, architects charge around $50,000 for the certification of a typical suburban office building. With LEED-based green building strategies becoming commonplace, those costs should come down (Nicola, 2008).

Nicola admits Forest City largely eliminated LEED Certification of Stapleton's affordable housing due to the costly commissioning and certification process. "Our goal is to do the right thing, whether the project ends up with a LEED Certification is secondary" (Nicola, 2008). Despite the cost, Forest City recently completed two commercial LEED Certified projects; one Silver, the other Gold. Forest City plans to remain flexible when determining the use of LEED Certification when weighed against the financial constraints of any project.

WORKING WITH WHAT YOU HAVE

The City of Denver's overall plan for Stapleton became the driving force behind recycling the old airport. Forest City's innovative program of recycling materials such as concrete and asphalt from the former Stapleton airport runway supplied the development with "enough aggregate to build the Hoover Dam!" Nicola exclaimed. Recycled Materials Company, Inc., of Arvada, Colorado (http://www.rmci-usa.com), completed the demolition and removal of 6.5 million tons of concrete and asphalt, providing crushed aggregate for walkways, landscaping, and fresh concrete. "The important thing to remember . . . if recycling had not been implemented, all of this material would have gone into a landfill with new material for hard-scapes being mined and shipped" (Nicola, 2008).

Forest City incorporated as much natural-looking "Staplestone" in their projects as possible, manufactured from recycled concrete blocks from the demolition of old Stapleton airport's retaining walls, infrastructure, pipe beddings, road base, and landscaping. Forest City continues to work with Denver Recycles. Forest City enjoys the highest recycling rate in the city and helped to develop the pilot program for compost pickup. Forest City continues to redefine its goals as the Stapleton Development project continues.

An additional innovation includes the reuse of water. "Denver Water required us to flush all the water lines for clear water tests. During the drought of 2007, we did not want to waste water, so we would capture it in tanks and use it for irrigation and construction site dewatering" (Nicola, 2008).

GREEN COUNCIL

Forest City found that a successful sustainable policy depends on the company's universal implementation of innovations across the human resources spectrum as well. Managers must take the lead, but ultimately everybody must participate equally. Early on, the leadership of Forest City started an internal effort to help employees promote sustainable practices within the office. Employees throughout Forest City, regardless of pay or authority, share ideas locally and nationally. The employees constantly work on different sustainable initiatives, such as educating people on the value of double-sided printing or using water coolers and reusable water bottles rather than bottled water. The Stapleton team avoided formal goals but created a variety of projects supporting a sustainable office environment. "We try not to have people spend too much of their time on the projects that come out of the employee meetings. We simply weigh an idea, and if it has a strong positive, we try it" (Knott, 2008).

Today, Forest City Stapleton maintains sustainable strategies embedded in the day-to-day practices of the company's operations, with all employees working to promote sustainable business practices. Employees become more motivated when empowered to initiate their own sustainable ideas. The office now supports a long list of projects with enthusiasm as exemplified by the community newspaper, *The Front Porch*. That paper, started by Forest City, not only includes neighborhood news, but also utilizes 40 percent recycled paper as suggested by its employees. Policies provide employees with the tools to become sustainable experts on their own projects and in their own lives.

CONNECTION TO THE COMMUNITY

Forest City's core values of integrity and commitment to a sustainable community and neighborhood make Stapleton Development one of the country's top sustainability projects, with the company winning numerous national and international sustainability awards since 2004. The amenities designed into Stapleton's neighborhood include farmers markets, access to exercise classes, local shops, restaurants, recreation facilities, retail, banks, award-winning charter schools, and 30 percent of land dedicated to open space. *The Front Porch,* published by two Stapleton residents, continues to enjoy a wide circulation throughout northeast Denver, keeping tenants and homeowners apprised of local news.

A child playing at Founder's Green in Stapleton. (Courtesy of Forest City Stapleton, Inc.)

EDUCATION AS MARKETING TOOL

Forest City originally attempted to convince the builders at Stapleton that building green was in their best interest with Charlie Nicola endorsing the financial benefits of using sustainable design guidelines. Despite his best efforts, he found that the builders remained apprehensive in the beginning. The market, however, spoke very clearly, with sustainable homes increasing in value by 10 percent each year. Eventually all the builders joined in with enthusiasm!

Forest City not only provides education in sustainability, it views sustainability as a cornerstone in marketing. Forest City offers education to prospective tenants and buyers in a number of areas, including the selection of green finishing materials. "Nowadays, everyone from builders to developers embraces sustainable principles; they have to in order to stay competitive" (Nicola, 2008).

Another example of education and marketing coalescing includes the former visitor's center at Stapleton. This center showcased new innovations and markets in sustainability for prospective buyers, educating them as to the prices, style, location, and profile of each builder's sustainability practices. Additionally the visitor's center, constructed of 100 percent modular construction, allowed for quick assembly, disassembly, and relocation. Recently, the fully modular visitor's center was disassembled and then moved, creating a new project out of a reused building. This strategy eliminated the energy needed to demolish and rebuild a new building, providing an affordable, practical, and rapidly constructed alternative. Visitors to the site learned about commercial modular construction, its affordability, practicality, and beauty and recognized Forest City for innovative approaches and leadership in the sustainability market.

THE FUTURE FOR STAPLETON

Forest City will finance and build more than $5 billion on Stapleton's development with seven and a half square miles eventually supporting over 12,000 homes and a variety of mixed-use neighborhoods. According to Michael Leccese at Terrain.org, "10 million square feet of office space, 3 million square feet of retail space, six public schools, and more than 1,100 acres of public parks and open space . . . will expand the acreage of Denver City parks by 25 percent" (Leccese, 2005).

According to Tom Gleason, until the most recent economic downturn, the properties of Stapleton have consistently increased in value by

10 percent per year, and held their value during the economic crisis, showing that sustainable development clearly makes good business sense. Forest City's commitment to sustainability extends out in multiple directions, beyond the triple bottom line, to the big picture of measuring the carbon footprint for the entire Stapleton Development, with the goal of one day becoming carbon neutral. To achieve this, Forest City Stapleton continues to research alternatives for onsite renewable energy sources and conservation measures. Working with Denver Water and Xcel Energy, Stapleton's sustainable opportunities continue to evolve into alternate approaches to water and energy concerns in today's and future markets. Evolution, the ability to assess and change, ultimately may be one of the most important tenets of sustainability for Forest City as a developer of sustainable urban redevelopment projects. The evolution of Forest City's process enabled the incorporation of sustainable practices not only on this one project, but also exported to other national and international markets. As technology changed and the company's knowledge increased, Forest City remained flexible throughout the project by adopting alternate approaches and strategies. Forest City at Stapleton will continue to evolve its approach to sustainability and redefining its goals into the future, to midcentury and beyond.

Chapter Outline

History of Forest City Development

- 1905: The Ratner family immigrates to the United States.
- 1920s: The Ratner family's lumberyard businesses grow out of their multiple businesses, and they become their own supplier for their development projects.
- Liberal credit policies for the homeless are established while still making a profit.
- 1950s: Forest City becomes a major player in real estate and development.
- 1995: Stapleton, formerly Denver's airport, was abandoned, and a new airport was relocated northeast of the city.
- November 1998: Forest City is chosen as Master Developer of Stapleton.

Financial Creativity

- Vertical and horizontal financing and variety of financing mechanisms were used for the development of Stapleton.

Strategy

- Forest City, with the help of Melissa Knott, grows into the role of sustainability.
- Forest City adopts sustainability as its core value.
- Some resources fit the needs of Forest City's requirement better than others.

Relationships and Networking

- It is important to attend meetings that educate developers, builders, and architects on new technology and sustainability.
- Networking at work and outside of work is vital to the project's success.
- It is valuable for all involved to maintain an open and helpful attitude.

Changing Challenges and the Roles of LEED Certification

- Knowing how and when to apply LEED standards is important.
- It is necessary to work with standards of the Environmental Protection Agency, the Department of Energy, and Energy Star.

Connection to the Community

- The local paper, *The Front Porch,* is invaluable as an event announcement and information service for tenants and residents.
- Support of events, open space, and charter schools reinforces core values.

Education as Marketing Tool

- It is important to educate prospective buyers on the advantages of green buildings.
- The use of the visitor center is valuable as an education and marketing tool.
- *The Front Porch* is useful for the distribution of sustainable ideas at Stapleton.
- It is helpful to use sustainability to market the Stapleton community as a brand.

Future Plans for Stapleton

- There are plans for becoming carbon neutral.
- It is important to be flexible in regard to goals.

LESSONS LEARNED

(1) "The ambitious scope of the redevelopment of the former Stapleton International Airport produced a range of creative financing mechanisms. The Denver Urban Renewal Authority (DURA) issues bonds for the front-end financing for Stapleton's infrastructure with repayment through tax increment financing (TIF). TIF financing, tied directly to retail sales tax revenue and initially issued through DURA, is retired through the sales taxes generated with the project. As a result of these challenges, a unique partnership evolved."

(2) "If your project managers all understand sustainability and how that applies to your business, then you know you are already light years ahead. It is just like in architecture—you can hire a sustainability consultant, but it is never as successful as when you have an architect or a firm that really understands what to do. Anyway, sustainability became a core value for our company for here and nationally."

(3) Forest City determined that allocating resources toward helping builders and contractors meet the current LEED standards created the most effective approach instead of developing new metrics. The process also featured an inclusive approach that allowed the developer's designers and builders to determine the priorities and timing of various strategies.

(4) "The recent changes to the real estate market require supporting the value of sustainable practices more than ever. A thorough understanding of the balance between the initial cost and the long-term paybacks remains essential to supporting the investment in sustainable practices."

(5) Forest City's approach for implementing sustainable concepts with cost-saving strategies includes the allocation of a cost, a number for sustainability."

REFERENCES

Funding Universe. "Forest City Enterprises, Inc.," http://www.funding universe.com/company-histories/Forest-City-Enterprises-Inc-Company-History.html.

Gleason, Tom. Personal interview. September 2008.

Knott, Melissa. Personal interview. August 2008.

Leccese, Michael. "Denver's Stapleton: Green Urban Infill for the Masses?" Terrain.Org, no. 17, Winter/Fall 2005, http://www.terrain.org/arti cles/17/leccese.htm.

Nicola, Charlie. Personal interview, November 2008.

QuickMBA. "Strategic Management," http://www.quickmba.com/strategy.

Stapleton Development Corporation. http://www.stapletoncorp.com.

RESOURCES FOR FURTHER RESEARCH

Stapleton

http://stapleton.cciconstellation.net/Stapleton-Development-Plan.aspx

Green Book

The City of Denver's Green Council / Green Print Denver: www.denver gov.org

LEED Certification

http://stapleton.cciconstellation.net/Awards-3055_Gold_Leed.aspx

Awards

EPA Recognizes Stapleton Development: http://yosemite.epa.gov/opa/ admpress.nsf/bb1285e857b49ac4852572a00065683f/1413ed6072f4 b580852572f4006b45b4!OpenDocument

Marketing: http://stapleton.cciconstellation.net/Awards-Stapleton_Infin ity_Recognition.aspx

Sustainable Development: http://stapleton.cciconstellation.net/United_ Nations-Sustainable_Development-Model.aspx

U.S. Conference of Mayors Award: http://stapletondenver.com/commu nity/media-pr-resources

Wirth Chair Award: http://www.forestcity.net/company/awards/Pages/ green.aspx

SIX

Boulder Community Hospital

Blair Gifford, Carrie Yasemin Paykoc, and Alan Romero

The concept of sustainable health care is relatively new. It wasn't too long ago when doctors, nurses, and patients were able to smoke cigarettes at the doctor's office. There were even cigarette vending machines in many health care facilities. Secondhand smoke and the message that health care was sending about cigarette smoking were not even minor considerations. We might rationalize that, if our doctor smokes, it must be healthy. The same is true for environmental stewardship. Health care organizations should be willing to take responsibility for their impact on the environment. Health care organizations are in the position to demonstrate correct behavior and act as environmental stewards. The concept of health being unaffected by our environment is as out of fashion as 1970s orange shag carpet. Health care organizations must understand that their role in improving the health of patients does not end when a Medicare claim is submitted or a prescription is filled. Health care providers have a responsibility to ensure the best care for their patients by providing health care in an environmentally and socially sustainable manner. Green health care aims to reduce the amount of waste produced, chemicals used, and energy consumed to positively impact the health and quality of life in the communities served.

Many studies have demonstrated the link between environmental conditions and the quality of health. With the amount of pollutants released into the atmosphere, water supply, and landfills, it is not surprising that our health is suffering. *Environmental Health Perspectives* published a study on the effects of environmental pollutants on children. The study explored the morbidity, mortality, and health care costs associated with environmental pollutants. Treating children with asthmatic exacerbation caused by environmental pollutants equated to $4.6 million in medical expenses in the populations studied and accounted for 30 percent of all asthma patients (Schechter et al., 2002). From economic and logical standpoints, it doesn't make sense to treat patients for asthmatic conditions and then contribute to the problem by creating additional pollutants. Each year, hospitals produce roughly 3.5 million tons of waste (Teleosis Institute, 2008). Instead of creating more ailing patients, health care organizations should be part of the solution by using renewable energy sources, lowering carbon emissions, reducing the use of volatile organic compounds, eliminating waste, and composting. These are some of the solutions that positively impact the environment and can positively impact patient health.

From a business perspective, sustainable health care makes economic sense, and it can save organizations capital. Environmental initiatives at Boulder Community Hospital in Colorado produce $500,000 in cost savings and cost avoidance annually (Abelkis, 2009). To effectively transition hospitals toward a more sustainable model requires innovation, leadership, and risk taking, which are characteristic of the staff and leadership at Boulder Community Hospital.

Numerous hospitals and health care organizations are moving toward providing health care that is in sync with environmentally sustainable practices. Not only do sustainable health care facilities operate in a way that is better for the environment, they are able to reduce their operating costs through renewable energy and energy efficiency. Hospitals' impact on the environmental can be minimized by reducing the amount of energy consumed and reducing the amount of waste produced. In comparison with other facilities of various industries, hospitals are among the largest consumers of energy and producers of waste (Beidler, 2008). According to *JAMA*, the *Journal of the American Medical Association*, the U.S. health care industry sector accounts for 8 percent of total carbon emissions in the United States (Chung and Meltzer, 2009). The majority of hospitals' energy consumption is in lighting, heating, and ventilation.

Completing an energy audit and making the necessary facility changes to become more energy efficient will reduce a facility's environmental impact and reduce operational costs. With limited monetary resources, health care organizations are under pressure to reduce the amount they spend on energy. On average, hospitals spend $1.67 per square foot on electricity and $0.48 per square foot on natural gas (Consortium for Energy Efficiency,

2005). Energy audits are conducted by numerous organizations, including local energy providers. Xcel energy (the utility company for Colorado and several other states) performs energy audits for homes and businesses and offers a free online energy audit for businesses. It compares the energy used with that used in similar facilities and provides recommendations for low- and no-cost improvements and breakdowns on energy consumed. Xcel also provides resources specific to hospitals on how to minimize energy consumption. "In a typical hospital, lighting, heating, and hot water represent about 60 percent of the energy use, making those systems the best target for energy savings" (Xcel Energy, 2009).

Renewable energy also can make a sizable difference in a hospital's monthly energy bill. After the initial investment, the cost of solar energy is minimal. Hospital systems continue to grow to accommodate the aging population, and so do their energy costs. Reducing the amount of energy consumed and used even by a small percentage can have a dramatic impact on an organization's financial statements. (Beidler, 2008). The Consortium for Energy Efficiency notes that reducing energy expenses by 5 percent is equivalent to increasing earnings per share by one cent (Consortium for Energy Efficiency, 2005).

The following diagram displays where energy is consumed in a typical hospital.

Hospitals Total Energy Use

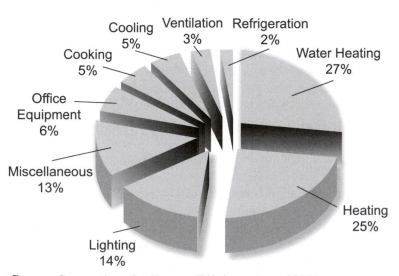

(*Source:* Consortium for Energy Efficiency, Inc., 2005.)

With health care reform and budgetary restrictions due to the current grim economic climate, organizations are looking for ways to reduce costs while not reducing quality. Reducing the energy consumption of health care organizations will ultimately increase their profitability and decrease their impact on the environment. Although many hospitals are now engaged in sustainable practices, Boulder Community Hospital was one of the first green hospitals.

BOULDER COMMUNITY HOSPITAL'S GRASSROOTS BEGINNINGS

In the early 1990s, two nurses at Boulder Community Hospital (BCH) initiated a facilitywide, systematic placement of recycling containers and collection of recycled materials on a daily basis. From this grassroots beginning, other concerned environmental stewards in the organization—doctors, nurses, janitors, and cafeteria workers—began recycling, reusing, and reducing because it was the right thing to do. This effort came naturally for employees who viewed a clean environment as an important element of wellness. It also was natural for the community in which they lived, worked, and played. Boulder's citizens have actively promoted environmental awareness for years. As members of this community, BCH employees valued sustainability efforts long before senior management formalized its importance.

Over the years, these voluntary activities and informal programs evolved and became an integral part of the hospital culture. Hospital administrators and the board of directors took action to formalize and expand sustainability activities, when, in 1995, they adopted a statement of principles to guide the hospital in its environmental efforts. This policy called for specific commitments to limit the use of nonrenewable resources; eliminate emissions of toxic and dangerous substances into the air, water, and earth; and encourage the use of alternative transportation. With official policies in place, the commitment and dedication of the hospital's employees grew rapidly.

The Foothills Campus facility of Boulder Community Hospital subsequently became the first health care project in the nation to achieve LEED Silver certification in 2003. At the time, this was an extraordinary achievement for a hospital. The LEED system is geared toward less-complicated structures such as office buildings. Since then, the U.S. Green Building Council has initiated the development of specialized LEED application guidelines for new construction of health care facilities, focusing in particular on hospitals.

The local community it serves and the global health care industry have recognized Boulder Community Hospital's leadership and commitment to environmental health and wellness. In January 2003, then hospital vice president Joe McDonald received a highly coveted Pacesetter Award for his contributions to the environment and improving the quality of life in the Boulder area. The annual Pacesetter Awards are presented by the *Boulder Daily Camera,* the largest newspaper serving the community, to individuals who have helped transform the county in numerous positive ways. Under McDonald's guidance, the hospital has become a leader in recycling; using wind energy; promoting alternative transportation; and developing green, high-performance, sustainable buildings.

In 2006, Hospitals for a Healthy Environment (H2E) recognized BCH with awards for environmental leadership and for making medicine mercury free. H2E is an organization founded by the American Hospital Association, the U.S. Environmental Protection Agency (EPA), Health Care Without Harm, and the American Nurses Association. The Environmental Leadership Circle is permanent recognition by H2E of facilities and systems that exemplify environmental excellence in health care. This award recognizes health care facilities that are setting the highest standard for environmental practices. The Making Medicine Mercury-Free Award recognizes facilities that have virtually eliminated mercury and have made a commitment to be mercury free. BCH also received Zero Waste certification in 2007 from Eco-Cycle (Boulder Community Hospital, 2010).

BCH is a nonprofit hospital where senior leadership had a strong motivation to promote community benefits. In many ways, the Boulder community expects locally owned businesses to take a leadership role on sustainability issues. With shared values for sustainability from all stakeholders in the community and in the hospital, resistance to change has not been much of a problem.

THE IMPACT OF HOSPITALS ON THE ENVIRONMENT

The reality of widespread environmental degradation and the presence of environmental health hazards in many aspects of our daily lives pose significant and increasing challenges to human health. Poor environmental quality is stated to be directly responsible for about 25 percent of preventable ill health worldwide (World Health Organization, 1997).

We trust and value health care providers and institutions as places to find healing and healthy environments as well as knowledge of environmental risks. Surprisingly, however, conventional medical practices have vastly contributed to the deterioration of the environment. U.S. hospitals produce an average of 6,600 tons of waste each day, according to the American Hospital Association's *Primer on Hospital Environmental Sustainability Topic Position on Waste Management, 2008.* It is thus ironic and unacceptable that the current system of conventional medicine, though at times highly effective, also poses a significant threat to human and environmental health.

Traditional methods of medical waste disposal include incineration and autoclaving, which involves sterilizing the waste at high temperatures before it is taken to a landfill. Infectious waste is regulated by states, because no federal regulations specifically govern disposal of medical waste other than hazardous waste. Furthermore, officials do not anticipate any federal involvement in medical waste regulation in the near future, other than medical waste incineration reform.

The health care industry generally recognizes that, to fulfill the medical ethic to "first, do no harm," it has a responsibility to manage waste in ways that protect the public and the environment. Hospitals and clinics are among those reevaluating their waste disposal methods.

We can and we must do better.

ECOLOGICALLY SUSTAINABLE MEDICINE

Mercury and Vinyl Plastic

A typical large hospital might easily have more than 100 pounds of mercury on site, incorporated into hundreds of different devices in dozens of separate locations, unless it has undertaken a conscious and sustained effort to eliminate mercury (Hospitals for a Healthy Environment, October 2000). The EPA has identified medical waste incineration as the third-largest source of dioxin air emissions and the fourth-largest source of mercury air emissions. While no longer the leading source, medical waste incineration is still a source of dioxin pollution, due in part to the large amount of disposable polyvinyl chloride (PVC) plastic products used by hospitals. Many other hazardous pollutants have been identified in the emissions from medical waste incinerators, including furans, acid gases, heavy metals, and particulates.

Mercury is found in thermometers, blood pressure devices, lab chemicals, cleaners, and other products used in health care. PVC is the most widely used plastic in medical products, accounting for 27 percent of all disposable plastic medical products. Medical devices such as intravenous (IV) bags and tubing, also contain PVC and can leach the phthalate DEHP.

Dioxin is a known human carcinogen. According to the EPA, current general population exposure to dioxin may cause a lifetime cancer risk that is 1,000 times higher than the EPA's "acceptable" risk level. Other health problems that may be associated with dioxin exposure include birth defects, learning disabilities, endometriosis, infertility, suppressed immune function, reduced IQ, and hyperactive behavior in children.

Mercury is a potent neurotoxin that attacks the body's central nervous system. It can also harm the brain, kidneys, and lungs. It can cross the blood-brain barrier as well as the placenta. According to the U.S. Centers for Disease Control and Prevention (2010) up to 1 in 10 women in the United States already carry enough mercury in their blood to pose a threat of neurological damage to the fetus.

Phthalates can damage the liver, kidneys, lungs, and reproductive system—particularly the developing testes—according to animal studies (Food and Drug Administration, 2002). Several government agencies have concluded that some patients are likely to be exposed to potentially unsafe amounts of DEHP while receiving medical care, and researchers (see Green et al., 2005) at Harvard School of Public Health have found that babies in neonatal intensive care units have high exposure levels to this reproductive toxicant.

MEDICAL WASTE

Hospitals generate between 8 and 45 pounds of waste per bed per day in the form of general trash, infectious (red bag) waste, hazardous waste, and low-level radioactive waste (Health Care Without Harm, 2001). Waste minimization and segregation are critical first steps in avoiding medical waste that is otherwise difficult to treat. A medical waste audit is therefore a useful tool for discovering the sources of waste, its composition, and rates of generation in a health care facility. An audit also may provide information on waste minimization and handling practices, segregation efficiency, overclassification, regulatory compliance, and costs. After completing an analysis of its hospital waste, the facility is in a better position to define its needs. A strategic framework for health care organizations entails the implementation of an effective waste collection, transport, and storage system; development of waste management and contingency plans; occupational safety and health considerations; and proper selection of nonincineration technology.

Minimizing waste not only protects people and the environment, but it can save facilities substantial amounts of money. BCH, for example, estimates that it has saved $500,000 annually (Abelkis, 2009). Waste minimization techniques include the following activities:

- **Resource Recovery and Recycling:** BCH emphasized this approach of recovering and reusing materials from the waste stream from the very beginning. Most of the waste from health care facilities is surprisingly similar to that of an office building or hotel—paper, cardboard, and food waste. Hospitals can implement simple programs that divert these materials from the solid waste stream and lower the costs of disposal. Furthermore, many, if not most, on-site medical waste incinerators burn not only infectious waste but also readily recyclable items such as office paper and cardboard, destroying resources and preventing cost savings that could be recouped through recycling.

- **Segregation:** By separating different types of waste at the point of generation and keeping them isolated from each other, appropriate resource recovery and recycling techniques can be applied to each separate waste stream. Amounts of infectious waste, hazardous waste, and low-level radioactive waste that must be treated according to special (and usually costly) requirements are subsequently minimized.

- **Source Reduction:** Toxicity of waste can also be reduced by minimizing or eliminating the generation of waste at the source through techniques such as product substitution, technology change, and good operating practices.

While BCH is currently exploring waste segregation, it already has taken major steps to avoid creation of hazardous waste in the first place. Implementing a program that includes segregation, source reduction, recycling, and other pollution prevention techniques reduces the amount of infectious waste that needs decontamination. Fortunately, safe, cost-effective nonmercury alternatives exist for nearly all uses of mercury in health care. Becoming mercury free, as BCH has done, involves identifying mercury-containing items, investigating mercury-free alternatives, and implementing a mercury-free purchasing policy. Furthermore, PVC-free and DEHP-free alternatives are available for almost every use of PVC in the health care setting, including medical devices, office supplies, building materials, and furnishings.

PVC-free IV and blood bags are available in Europe and the United States for all but one product—packed red blood cells. PVC-free bags are cost-effective and technically competitive with PVC bags. PVC-free or

DEHP-free tubing is on the market for most medical applications. Alternatives for disposable PVC gloves are also readily available. Manufacturers continue to respond to customer demands for PVC-free health care products, with new items coming to market more and more frequently.

In addition to medical devices, PVC-free construction and furnishing products are widely available and are often cost-competitive. PVC-free mattress covers and shower curtains are examples of such products. Infectious waste is estimated to be about 15 percent or less of the overall waste (Emmanuel and Diliman, 2001). The following categories are commonly used in describing the components of infectious waste: cultures and stocks, pathological wastes, blood and blood products, sharps, animal wastes, and isolation wastes.

An infectious waste stream must be treated to prevent the spread of disease, and cost-effective alternative technologies are available. These alternative technologies are safer and cleaner than incineration and are just as effective at rendering medical waste harmless. These technologies can be used on all types of medical waste, including pathological and chemotherapy waste. Four basic, nonincineration processes are used in medical waste treatment: thermal, chemical, irradiative, and biological.

Thermal processes rely on heat to destroy pathogens (disease-causing microorganisms). They can be further classified as low-heat thermal processes (operating below 350° F), medium-heat thermal processes (between 350° F and about 700° F), and high-heat thermal processes (operating from around 1,000° F to over 15,000° F). The low-heat processes utilize moist heat (usually steam) or dry heat. High-heat processes involve major chemical and physical changes that result in the total destruction of the waste.

Chemical processes employ disinfectants to destroy pathogens or chemicals to react with the waste. Irradiation involves ionizing radiation to destroy microorganisms, while biological processes use enzymes to decompose organic matter. Mechanical processes, such as shredders, mixing arms, and compactors, are added as supplementary processes to render the waste unrecognizable, improve heat or mass transfer, or reduce the volume of treated waste.

Given that alternatives to incineration are available, a complete phaseout of medical waste incineration is possible and appropriate. However, no single nonincineration technology offers a panacea to the problem of medical waste disposal. Each technology has its advantages and disadvantages. Facilities must determine which nonincineration technology best meets their needs while minimizing the impact on the environment, enhancing occupational safety, and demonstrating a commitment to public health.

HEALTHY BUILDINGS

Building facilities that are healthy for people and the environment protect the immediate health of building occupants, the health of the surrounding community, and natural resources and the health of the global community.

Patients in green hospitals have greater emotional well-being, require less pain medication and other drugs, and have shorter hospital stays and subsequently lower costs per case. "Green hospitals seek to reduce use of and exposure to toxic chemicals and provide a healthier healing environment" (*Green Guide for Health Care,* 2008). "By employing green practices, whether incrementally or from the ground up, many hospitals are managing to lower energy bills, reduce waste, and achieve healthier indoor air quality" (California Green Solutions, 2007).

Numerous studies have shown dramatic increases in the health, happiness, and productivity of people who live and work in green buildings, and hospitals are no exception. Nurses, doctors, and other staff work long hours in a high-stress environment, and providing them with a safe and comfortable workplace is vital to both their health and the health of their patients. Improvements in the working environment increase staff effectiveness and satisfaction, reduce errors, and contribute to the quality of patient care (*Green Guide for Health Care,* 2008).

The health care industry represents $16 billion and more than 100 million square feet of construction per year (*Green Guide for Health Care,* 2008). While the BCH Foothills Campus was the first health care facility to receive LEED certification, many other health care managers are looking for green guidelines that address specific construction and operational issues unique to the health care market. Relative to other building owners, health care providers have far less flexibility in balancing ecological and operational performance. For example, compromised air quality can be a matter of life and death, not personal discomfort. So typical energy-saving strategies in the mechanical systems are often rejected on operational grounds. "We save lives, not energy," is how the skeptics put it (Walsh, 2005).

The most controversial health issue in LEED certification standards is the perception that they give excessive weight to energy-related issues over issues concerning toxic impacts on human health. Construction materials, furnishings, and furniture products account for approximately 75 percent of all PVC use. For most health organizations, this is a critical point. Health care participants that treat cancer patients want centers built without materials linked to cancer. When treating patients, they also want facilities free of chemicals that trigger asthma.

The *Green Guide for Health Care* (2008), therefore, offers self-certifying guidelines that use LEED standards as a basic framework but also adds guidance tailored to the particular structural and regulatory challenges of health care buildings, introduces health policy reasons for each of its credits, and incorporates design elements that enhance patient healing and staff well-being. Recognizing the full range of construction, operations, and maintenance activities associated with the health care sector, the *Green Guide* applies to new freestanding facilities, additions to existing facilities coupled with renovation, extensive rehabilitation/adaptive reuse projects, and existing facilities Best practices in the *Green Guide for Health Care* include the following:

- incorporating healing design elements such as daylight and views of nature
- using innovative technologies to reduce energy and water use
- reducing hazardous chemicals, such as mercury, lead, dioxin, cadmium, phthalates, and halogenated flame retardants
- implementing green operations, ranging from organic food to housekeeping and landscaping protocols

FOOD

Ecological thinking means looking at things in their whole context while seeking to understand the interconnections between parts. It recognizes that nothing exists in isolation; everything is part of a larger system. This approach is important for health care food decision making, because the production and distribution of food has a multitude of heath-related impacts often removed from the immediate hospital environment.

Food is sustenance. But what we eat and how we eat can also contribute to death, disease, and rising health care costs. Obesity, the leading health concern of the day, is a symptom of poor eating habits and sedentary behavior. Poor nutrition is a risk factor for four of the six leading causes of death in the United States—heart disease, stroke, diabetes, and cancer. Nutrition-related chronic diseases are placing new demands on an already overburdened health care system and taking their toll on human productivity and quality of life.

As places of healing, hospitals have natural incentives to help prevent food-related health concerns by modeling good nutrition in their institutions and by influencing how food is produced and distributed. With its size and purchasing power, the health care industry can provide market leadership by adopting food purchasing policies and practices that steer the entire food system in a more positive direction.

By adopting food procurement policies that are ecologically sound, economically viable, and socially responsible, health care systems demonstrate an understanding of the inextricable links between human, public, and ecosystem health. Hospitals can adopt food procurement policies that provide nutritionally improved food for patients, staff, visitors, and the general public and that support and help create food systems that promote the well-being of the whole community. Institutions can also establish food-purchasing guidelines and set target goals that are realistic for their institution and geographic area. What works effectively for one institution may not be appropriate for another. A hospital should both lead a community with a vision of health and look to the unique attributes of its community for ideas on how to meet patient and staff nutritional needs in an ecologically responsible manner. A few ideas for food-purchasing guidelines for health care organizations include the following actions:

1. **Start a conversation about healthy food.** Providing access to healthier food promotes wellness among patients, visitors, and staff. Healthy food is defined not only by nutritional quality but also by how and where it is raised, grown, processed, and distributed. Consider developing a food team that explores the food issue and identifies ways your institution can get involved.

2. **Implement purchasing policies for meat and poultry that is raised without nontherapeutic antibiotics.** Antibiotic-resistant bacteria are an increasing concern to health care professionals. The scientific consensus is that antibiotic overuse in food animals contributes to antibiotic resistance in humans. Your health care institution can contribute to the solution by buying meat raised without the use of nontherapeutic antibiotics.

3. **Buy milk produced without recombinant bovine growth hormone.** Recombinant bovine growth hormone (rBGH, also known as rBST) is given to dairy cows to increase milk production. The use of this hormone is not allowed in Canada, Australia, New Zealand, Japan, and all 25 nations of the European Union. Health care systems can purchase non-rBGH milk from their suppliers.

4. **Buy organic and other certified food.** By purchasing products that are certified organic, health care systems can help protect the health of their patients while also helping to protect agricultural workers and air and water quality in the communities where food is grown and raised. Because hospitals are bulk buyers of food, they can create markets that support healthy, environmentally friendly growing practices.

5. **Buy from local producers.** Buying locally produced foods avoids the massive fuel consumption and air and water pollution associated with long-distance transport. Buying local also helps to build relationships between the urban and rural communities and supports the local economy. Some health care systems plan menus and preorder produce from local growers before the growing season, providing security for both the grower and buyer.

6. **Become a fast food–free zone.** Ironically, 6 of the 16 Honor Roll hospitals listed in the 2001 *U.S. News & World Report* ranking of America's Best Hospitals currently have one or more fast food chains located in their institutions. Hospitals can review food service operations within their facilities (patient food, cafeteria food, catering, vending machines, and coffee carts) and evaluate whether the food choices offered are consistent with the promotion of healthy dietary patterns for patients, staff, and the larger community (Cram et al., 2002).

7. **Limit use of vending machines and replace unhealthy snacks with healthy choices.** The types of food and snacks offered in vending machines should be consistent with dietary recommendations for healthy snacking. Vending machine options could include whole fruit, low-fat and low-sugar snacks, and water or juice beverages. Hospitals can draft a policy that outlines the types of food that would be acceptable in vending machines (i.e., no trans fat, low in processed sugars and fats, no artificial ingredients, and no preservatives) as well as outlining food packaging standards and energy efficiency of machines.

8. **Host a farmers market on hospital grounds.** On-site farmers' markets and farm stands provide fresh produce to staff, visitors, and patients. Farmers markets support efforts to incorporate healthy foods into diets by increasing the availability of fresh, locally grown foods. Farmers markets also generate goodwill in a community, support local growers, and create new community partnerships.

9. **Create hospital gardens to grow fresh produce and flowers.** Vegetable and herb gardens on hospital grounds provide not only healthy foods but also much-needed, thriving green spaces. Cut flowers can be

sold or used in your facility. Hospital gardens can foster a sense of community and pride in hospital staff, offer a place of respite for patients and staff, and create opportunities for community members (students, seniors, and others) to be involved.

10. **Compost, divert, and reduce food waste.** Food waste comprises approximately 10 percent of a hospital's waste stream. Food and other organic waste can be diverted, composted, or otherwise beneficially reused instead of being landfilled. Hospitals can further improve their environmental performance by purchasing recycled napkins, using paper or compostable dishware for take-out items, and recycling kitchen cans and bottles.

11. **Buy certified coffee.** Coffee is the United States' largest food import and second most valuable commodity after oil. Most coffee is grown in developing countries under conditions that require clear-cutting and heavy use of pesticides and where agricultural workers toil for little pay. Buying certified coffee supports community development, health, and environmental stewardship.

BROMINATED FLAME RETARDANTS

Flame retardants are all around health care. IV pumps, televisions, computers, hospital beds, waiting room chairs, and hospital privacy curtains all share the need to be fire resistant. To meet fire safety standards, manufacturers add chemicals known as flame retardants. Unfortunately, many flame retardants do not remain fixed in the product, but slowly leak into the air, dust, and water and eventually enter our food and bodies. Evidence shows that a subset of these chemicals, called brominated flame retardants (BFRs), is likely to persist in the environment, to bioaccumulate in the food chain and in our bodies, and to cause adverse health effects in children. The breast milk of U.S. women contains the highest levels of BFRs in human breast milk found anywhere in the world BFRs do not remain bound to a product but release and attach to dust particles. Scientists have measured significant BFR levels in common household dust, window film, and clothes dryer lint. The manufacture, use, and disposal of products containing BFRs have resulted in contamination of the outdoor environment, where scientists have found that BFRs rapidly accumulate in wildlife tissue. Similar to polychlorinated biphenyls, concentrations of BFRs increase with each step of the food chain, indicating these chemicals are readily absorbed and not easily broken down by the body. Therefore, human exposure to BFRs is thought to occur through ingestion and inhalation of dust particles containing BFRs and through ingestion of food containing BFRs, including breast milk.

Based on available data, we know that BFRs are associated with several adverse health effects in animal studies, including developmental effects that include permanent changes in memory and learning, interference with normal thyroid function, and reproductive effects. There is evidence that some BFRs can cause immune suppression, endocrine disruption, and cancer. Measurements in humans are troubling, because some levels are rapidly approaching those associated with adverse effects in rodent studies. The available literature on BFR toxicology is incomplete, so more studies are needed. However, based on the available data, switching to safer available alternatives might prove prudent in health care settings.

In health care settings, BFRs are as pervasive as they are in our homes and offices. Patient rooms, mattresses, foam pads, and other bedding materials may contain BFRs. Other furniture and textiles in patient rooms may be treated with BFRs, including furniture cushions, lampshades, cubicle curtains, privacy curtains, draperies, and window blinds. Electronic equipment such as televisions, pulse oximeters, monitors, ventilators, and IV pumps likely have BFRs in the plastic housing. At nursing stations, BFRs may be in computers, printers, fax and copy machines, and assorted office furniture. In the cafeteria and other eating areas, BFRs may be in microwave ovens, refrigerators, and other appliances. In nearly every area of the hospital—from shipping and receiving to the operating rooms—foam packaging is found that can contain BFRs.

Many products that do not contain BFRs are available, effective, and affordable. Health care institutions can make efforts to reduce the use of products and materials containing BFRs. In purchasing practices, institutions can choose products, when available, that meet flame retardant standards without any added flame retardants—products that are inherently flame resistant such as wool or Kevlar®. To learn more about the flame retardants used in products, hospitals can require disclosure of the name and the Chemical Abstracts Service registry number of all added flame retardants used in the products purchased. Moreover, hospitals can express a preference for products that do not contain toxic, persistent, bioaccumulative toxicants and alert vendors that, as more information on flame retardants becomes available, they will choose products with flame retardants that have been comprehensively tested for health and safety (see Health Care Without Harm: Issues Flame Retardants, 2008; Health Care Without Harm, 2010; U.S. News Health, 2010; and HealthCareWithout Harm, Press Release, 2005).

ELECTRONICS

Computers, televisions, lab analyzers, electrocardiogram monitors, and other types of electronic equipment used in hospitals every day contain many hazardous constituents—from lead in cathode ray tube monitors to chlorinated plastics in cable wiring, brominated flame retardants in circuit boards and plastic enclosures, and mercury in liquid crystal displays. The hazardous substances found in electronics have been linked to human health effects such as cancer, birth defects, and hormone disruption.

Improper disposal of electronic equipment poses a significant threat to public health and the environment. When electronic products are incinerated or landfilled, they can release heavy metals and other hazardous substances that contaminate groundwater and pollute the air. There is also concern around the export of hazardous electronic waste to developing countries that are less equipped to handle the hazardous materials; in many cases, this export is in violation of international law as well as domestic laws in the importing countries.

By focusing on the way they purchase and discard electronic equipment, hospitals can improve their environmental and public health impact in many ways:

- When purchasing electronics, applying a total cost of ownership approach that incorporates end-of-life disposal costs in the product and services costs
- Negotiating contracts that require products and practices to meet specific environmental criteria
- Establishing manufacturer take-back requirements for obsolete electronic equipment
- Extending the life of electronic equipment through upgrades and reuse
- Recycling old electronics with a vendor who has signed the Electronic Recycler's Pledge of True Stewardship

PESTICIDES AND FRAGRANCES

Despite their role as places that promote health and healing, hospitals and other health care institutions use a surprising number of highly toxic chemicals on their premises, including pesticides, cleaners and disinfectants, and fragrance chemicals. These volatile organic compounds contribute to poor overall indoor air quality and are associated with a host of health problems.

Pesticides are toxic substances designed to kill or repel pests. But in addition to being harmful to pests, they can cause acute symptoms in humans, including nausea, headaches, rashes, and dizziness. Many are also linked to chronic diseases and conditions such as cancer, birth defects, neurological and reproductive disorders, and to the development of chemical sensitivities.

Most people have no idea that most health care institutions use chemical pesticides on a regular basis, both inside and outside of their facilities. People generally visit health care facilities because their health is already impaired in some way. They may have compromised immune, neurological, digestive, and respiratory systems that put them at increased risk of suffering harmful effects from exposure to pesticides. The elderly, pregnant women, chemically sensitive individuals, and infants and children are especially vulnerable to the toxic effects of pesticides.

Everyone expects a hospital to be clean. However, many traditional cleaning products, floor strippers, and disinfectants present a variety of human health and environmental concerns. They often contribute to poor indoor air quality and may contain chemicals that cause cancer, reproductive disorders, respiratory ailments (including occupational asthma), eye and skin irritation, central nervous system impairment, and other human health effects.

In addition, some of these products contain persistent bioaccumulative toxins, are classified as hazardous waste, and/or otherwise contribute to environmental pollution during their manufacture, use, or disposal. Less-toxic, environmentally friendly maintenance products exist for almost all health care facility needs. More products are being developed all the time.

Hospitals also use a variety of methods to disinfect and sterilize surfaces and equipment. Some of the most commonly used products, however—such as glutaraldehyde and ethylene oxide—have been shown to cause serious health effects. Alternatives to these products offer effective disinfection while protecting health care workers and the environment.

Triclosan, an antibacterial biocide increasingly prevalent in liquid detergents and soaps (janitorial products), could enhance the ability of bacteria to resist antibiotics and poses a long-term threat to wildlife and to human health (traces of triclosan are found in human breast milk).

The EPA estimates that indoor air pollution is one of the top five environmental risks to public health, potentially causing eye, nose, and throat irritation; headaches; loss of coordination; nausea; cancer; and liver, kidney, and central nervous system damage. Patients are particularly vulnerable to indoor air quality threats, as many have compromised respiratory, neurological, or immunological systems and/or have increased chemical sensitivities. In the United States, the Joint Commission on Accreditation of Hospital Organizations has expressed concern over the growing number of respiratory problems among health care workers (Health Care Without Harm, 2009).

To many people, the word *fragrance* means something that smells nice, such as perfume. We rarely stop to think that scents are chemicals. Fragrance chemicals are organic compounds that volatilize or vaporize into the air—that's why we can smell them. They are added to products to give them a scent or to mask the odor of other ingredients. The volatile organic chemicals emitted by fragrance products can contribute to poor indoor air quality and are associated with a variety of adverse health effects.

Exposure to fragrance chemicals can cause headaches; eye, nose, and throat irritation; nausea; forgetfulness; loss of coordination, and other respiratory and/or neurotoxic symptoms. Many fragrance ingredients are respiratory irritants and sensitizers, which can trigger asthma attacks and aggravate sinus conditions.

Fragrance chemicals are the number-one cause of allergic reactions to cosmetics—not only to the primary users but also to those who breathe in the chemicals as secondhand users. Phthalates in fragrances are known to disrupt hormones and are linked in animal studies to malformations of the penis and adverse effects on the developing testes.

In health care facilities, fragrance can come from a number of sources:

- scented cleaning products
- fragrance-emitting devices and sprays
- workers, patients, and visitors who are wearing perfume, cologne, or aftershave; scented cosmetics, skin lotions, or hair products
- clothes that have been laundered with scented detergents, fabric softeners, or dryer sheets.

Indoor air quality can be greatly improved in health care facilities by adopting a hospitalwide fragrance-free policy that prohibits the use of fragrances by employees and in maintenance products. Using unscented green cleaners can reduce maintenance costs, help protect the environment, safeguard the health of building occupants, increase employee productivity, and improve indoor air quality.

The good news is that health care facilities can manage pests and provide a clean and sanitary environment without the use of toxic pesticides, cleaning products, disinfectants, or fragrance chemicals. There are safer, effective methods of controlling pests and disinfecting that will not harm the health of workers, patients, and the public. The use of safer cleaning products and less-toxic disinfection methods and the adoption of integrated pest management and fragrance-free policies improve indoor air quality and promote health.

GREEN PURCHASING

Health care group purchasing organizations (GPOs) work by achieving economies of scale. GPOs work with large numbers of hospital clients to leverage their buying power to get lower prices and better contracts for medical supplies.

The same advantages of scale can be used to improve the environmental performance of products produced for the health care sector. The power that GPOs hold to help hospitals achieve cost management and quality improvement can also enhance a common mission to protect the environment and human health.

GPOs are also taking up the charge to provide mercury-free products to their hospital clients. In addition, Novation, Premiere, Broadlane, and Amerinet have announced commitments to support labeling of PVC and DEHP medical products and offer DEHP-free alternatives; to encourage suppliers to identify products that have BFRs; and to identify environmentally preferable building products in contracts.

HEALING ENVIRONMENT OUTCOMES

What can be gained by "greening" of health care facilities? Some benefits can be seen immediately, such as improved patient health and greater productivity and satisfaction among staff. Other benefits are less readily apparent but perhaps more significant from a longer term perspective. Summarized below are key areas of impact experienced by Boulder Community Hospital and other institutions that have committed themselves to providing an environment that is ecologically and socially sound and sustainable.

Tangible and Intangible Bottom-Line Benefits

- Significantly save over time due to energy and design efficiencies
- Reduce costs with better waste management, smaller building footprints

- Increase philanthropic opportunities
- Receive federal, state, and municipal incentives for green design
- Increase purchasing power and economics of scale to buy green alternatives at equal or lesser price

Improve Patient Satisfaction

- Reduce stress (emotional well-being)
- Increase comfort (less pain and other drug medication)
- Positively influence patient perception and well-being
- Improve performance-related outcomes (shorter hospital stays, lower cost per case)

Protect Health

- Enhance indoor and outdoor air quality
- Reduce exposure to carcinogens, reproductive toxicants, allergens, asthma triggers
- Curtail building-related illness
- Reduce chronic diseases linked to hazardous chemicals

Attract and Retain Staff

- Improve emotional and physical well-being
- Reduce injuries and absenteeism due to illness
- Strengthen recruitment opportunities
- Improve health and retention with views, outdoor walking areas, natural light

Reduce Fossil Fuel Emissions

- Reduce costs with energy-efficient technologies
- Reduce dependence on fossil fuel
- Support renewable energy initiatives
- Mitigate global warming associated with carbon dioxide releases from burning fossil fuels

With such impressive results, it is surprising that Boulder Community Hospital's sustainability program began with a simple grassroots effort. Today Boulder Community Hospital has a full-time sustainability coordinator—Kai Abelkis—who analyzes and minimizes the hospital's footprint to ensure that BCH is environmentally, economically, and socially sustainable. He has worked at BCH for over 15 years, and he is clearly dedicated to making BCH an environmental steward. The ultimate goal for Abelkis and Boulder Community Hospital is to make the hospital completely energy independent and produce zero waste. Today, BCH's parking garage and atrium are lined with solar panels that supply power for a portion of the hospital's energy needs.

Although Boulder Community Hospital has made significant efforts in using renewable energy, it has a long way to go before becoming energy independent. Abelkis is very aware of the direct relationship between the quality of the environment and the health of the community (Abelkis, 2009). Health care organizations must recognize the relationship between health and the environment. We are responsible for providing health care in a manner that allows future generations to enjoy the same, if not better, quality of life.

Many hospitals attempt to emulate Boulder Community Hospital's sustainability efforts. Some organizations are able to make the transition, and others are not so successful. The difference lies in the upper management support and the culture of sustainability that extends to every staff member. Boulder Community Hospital's employees and management team truly believe in the importance of environmental health. Management has repeatedly demonstrated its willingness to act boldly, reward innovative thinking, engage employees, and consider and act upon the environmental implications of all decisions. While many changes are initiated through grassroots methods, management supports the necessary changes and risks associated with the change. An institution whose leadership provides only lukewarm support to their staff's environmental initiatives, or whose employees are not fully engaged on a day-to-day basis, will not be able to make the transition to sustainability.

LESSONS LEARNED

(1) "Health care organizations should be willing to take responsibility for their impact on the environment. Health care organizations are in the position to demonstrate correct behavior and act as environmental stewards."

(2) "From a business perspective, sustainable health care makes economic sense, and it can save organizations capital. Boulder

Community Hospital's environmental initiatives saved the organization $500,000 in cost savings and cost avoidance annually."

(3) "Over the years, voluntary activities and informal programs evolved and became an integral part of the hospital culture. Hospital administrators and the board of directors took action to formalize and expand sustainability activities. With official policies in place, the commitment and dedication of the hospital's employees grew rapidly."

(4) "Boulder Community Hospital's employees and management team truly believe in the importance of environmental health. Although the changes are initiated through grassroots methods, management supports the necessary changes and risks associated with the change."

REFERENCES

Abelkis, Kai. Director of Sustainability at Boulder Community Hospital. Personal interview, August 19, 2009.

American Hospital Association (AHA). *Executive Primer on Hospital Environmental Sustainability Waste Reduction.* December 2008. http://www.hospitalsustainability.org/topic_waste.shtml

Beidler, Aurae. *Energy Efficient Healthcare Center.* February 1, 2008. http://saving-energy.suite101.com/article.cfm/energy_efficient_healthcare_center

Boulder Community Hospital. *First and Awards.* April 18, 2010. http://www.bch.org/green-hospital/firsts-and-awards.aspx

California Green Solutions. *Green Hospital Program Launched: Green Hospitals Program Is Being Developed by USGBC and Green Guide for Health Care.* May 12, 2007. http://www.californiagreensolutions.com/cgi-bin/gt/tpl.h,content=1478

Chung, Jeanette W., and David O. Meltzer. "Estimate of the Carbon Footprint of the US Health Care Sector." *Journal of the American Medical Association* (2009), 302(18), 1970–1972.

Consortium for Energy Efficiency. "Commercial Building Performance Healthcare Facilities." Sector Fact Sheet 2005. http://www.cee1.org/com/bldgs/hc-fs.pdf

Cram, Peter, Brahmjee K. Nallamothu, A. Mark Fendrick, and Sanjay Saint. "Fast Food Franchises in Hospitals." *Journal of the American Medical Association* (2002), 287, 2945–2946.

Emmanuel, Jorge, and D. Diliman. Healthcare Without Harm Organization. "Best Environmental Practices and Alternative Technologies for Medical Waste Management." Excerpt from the United Nations Development Programme GEF Project on Health-Care Waste, the Environmental and Engineering Research Group President and University of the Philippines, 2001. http://www.noharm.org/seasia/issues/waste/alternatives.php

Fischer, Brandy E. "Dissolving Medical Waste." *Environmental Health Perspectives* 104, no. 7 (1996).

Green Guide for Healthcare. 2008. http://www.gghc.org/about.php

Green, Ronald, Russ Hauser, Antonia M. Calafat, Jennifer Weuve, Ted Schettler, Steven Ringer, Kenneth Huttner, and Howard Hu. "Use of di(2-ethylhexyl) phthalate containing Medical products and urinary levels of mono (2-ethylhexyl) phthalate in neonatal Intensive care unit infacts." EHP Environmental Health Perspectives. Published by the National Institute of Environmental Health Sciences, June 8, 2005. http://dx.doi.org

Health Care Without Harm Organization. "Medical Waste Treatment Technologies." *Healthcare Professionals Resource Guide, 2001.* www.noharm.org

Health Care Without Harm Organization. *Cleaners, Pesticides, and Fragrances: Global Overview.* 2009, http://www.noharm.org/all_regions/issues/toxins/cleaners_pesticides/

Health Care Without Harm Organization, Issues Flame Retardants, 2008, http://www.noharm.org/us_canada/issues/toxins/bfrs/alternatives.php

Health Care Without Harm Organization, "Environmental Health Group Applauds Toxic Retardant Phase-Out," HCWH News, January 19, 2010, a http://www.noharm.org/us_canada/news_hcwh/2010/jan/hcwh2010-01-19.php

Health Care Without Harm Organization, Press Release, June 23, 2005, "Evidence Mounts About Problematic Flame Retardants, Press Release Arlington, Virginia, available at: http://www.sustain.org/hcwh/details.cfm?type=document&id=1099

Hospitals for a Healthy Environment (H2E) Fact Sheet, October 2000, published by the Environmental Protection Agency (EPA), http://www.epa.gov/pbt/pbs/h2efactsht2.pdf

Schechter, Clyde B., Jeffrey M. Lipton, Marianne C. Fahs, Joel Schwartz, and Philip J. Landrigan."Environmental Pollutants and Disease in American Children: Estimates of Morbidity, Mortality, and Costs for

Lead Poisoning, Asthma, Cancer, and Developmental Disabilities." *Environmental Health Perspectives* 110, no. 7 (2002): 721–728.

Teleosis Institute: Health Professionals in Service of the Global Environment. "Green Health Care." Year End Report 2008 (available at www.teleosis.org).

U.S. Centers for Disease Control and Prevention. Data Statistics. December 9, 2010. www.cdc.gov/DataStatistics.

U.S. Food and Drug Administration. *FDA Public Health Notification: PVC Devices Containing the Plasticizer DEHP.* July 12, 2002. http://www.fda.gov/MedicalDevices/Safety/AlertsandNotices/PublicHealthNotifications/UCM062182

U.S. News Health, "Scientists Raise Concerns about Flame Retardants." October 28, 2010. http://health.usnews.com/health-news/managing-your-healthcare/environment/articles/2010/10/28/scientists-raise-concerns-about-flame-retardants.html

Walsh, Bill, National Coordinator of the Healthy Building Network. *Imagine, Cancer Treatment Centers Built Without Carcinogens: Green Guide For Health Care Co-Director Robin Guenther, AIA.* April 20, 2005. http://www.healthybuilding.net/news/guenther-042005.html

World Health Organization. *World Health Report 1997.* http://www.noharm.org/all_regions/issues/toxins/cleaners_pesticides/

Xcel Energy. *Online Energy Assesment.* December 10, 2009. http://www.xcelenergy.com/Colorado/Business/SaveEnergy_Money/Pages/Online_Energy_Assessment.aspx

SEVEN

The Digital Frontier

Kenneth Bettenhausen and Natasha Gleichmann
Contributing Research by Jennifer Mich

Interviews with The Digital Frontier President Mark Scott and Sales Manager Rick Moravec were conducted in July 2008 by Jennifer Mich.

INTRODUCTION

One has only to peruse the Web site of The Digital Frontier, an offset printing company located in Wheat Ridge, Colorado, to observe the company's commitment to sustainability. From the initial image of grass growing and "We Are Green" banner, to the use of JavaScript to discourage mindless printing of the site's contents, to the multiple links urging consumers to be mindful in their printing practices, company president Mark Scott portrays The Digital Frontier as enthusiastically devoted to sustainability and seems committed to pursuing this position to its fullest.

With the growing movement toward sustainability in the business world, this position might not seem shocking, but for a business in the printing industry, sustainability is anything but typical. Indeed, The Digital Frontier's path to sustainability was not one clearly planned, but rather a path that Scott stumbled upon accidentally. Eventually, sustainability was embraced as a key part of the business's mission and strategic positioning.

SOME BACKGROUND

The Digital Frontier was founded in 1994 to take advantage of the growth in desktop publishing. Previously, highly skilled graphic artists and special equipment were needed to prepare print jobs such as catalogs, brochures, flyers, business cards, and letterhead stationery. Designers sketched alternative layouts by hand. Text and illustrations were sized; type was ordered and then pasted by hand onto camera-ready poster boards for the printer. If a proofreader found a typo or a client wanted to add a sentence or change the design, the type had to be reordered and the affected copy boards created anew. As personal computers became more powerful and more prevalent, desktop publishing software allowed freelance and in-house graphic artists to create more elaborate projects and to make changes quickly and easily. With PCs, customers and printers can easily proof copy and review multiple designs. When the project is approved and ready to be printed, the entire project can be sent to the printer electronically.

In its early years, The Digital Frontier focused preprint services on helping clients, such as advertising agencies and end-user companies, to prepare their work for printing. From the digital image supplied by the client, the company would prepare the plates needed for printing on a printing press. Printing presses apply only one color of ink at a time. Single-color print jobs can be completed with one pass through the printing press, and two-color jobs require two passes, but projects that include full-color images, such as photographs, must be separated into four fundamental colors, red, yellow, blue and black. A different plate is made for each color of ink, and each sheet of paper makes four perfectly aligned passes through the press to recreate the full-color image. The Digital Frontier created color separations for customers and retouched photos and corrected or altered their color balance. It also helped clients prepare their artwork for publication in magazines and newspapers, resizing the design to correspond with different publication formats.

In 1998, The Digital Frontier bought its first digital press, enabling the company to not only help clients with their prepress production needs but to complete the process from start to finish. Adding the Heidelberg DI offset press allowed them to bid competitively on larger orders, ranging from 200 to 20,000 sheets. Today, The Digital Frontier has annual revenues of $2 million and employs 13–15 people. The company specializes in digital printing, direct-to-press offset printing, and super–wide format printing jobs such as banners, posters, and signs as large as 80 inches wide and as long as a client desires. It continues to provide a full range of digital pre-press services and a variety of finishing solutions and business services, from designing posters and business cards to developing elaborate corporate identities. "Anything that a client can have printed, we can do it," says Scott. "Banners, postcards, and everything in between."

TRADITIONAL PRINTING PRESSES

It must be acknowledged from the start that printing is not a very green industry. While photo-imaging technologies are improving rapidly, economies of scale dictate that all but very small print jobs be completed using offset printing presses. Offset presses work on the principle that oil and water do not mix. Similar to the photographic process, the printer creates a plate, or negative image, of the desired printed image. Water fills spaces that are to remain white, and oil-based ink fills the remaining spaces. The ink is then transferred from the plate to the paper, which must dry before it is sent through the printing press again to apply a second color of ink or to be trimmed to size.

Throughout a print run, water and ink run constantly. Excess ink and chemically tainted water can be caught, but more typically they flow down the drain after being diluted with more water. Plates are typically created using chemical solutions and water baths that are discarded down a drain. Generally, after a press run is completed, the ink-soaked plates are discarded in the trash along with ink-contaminated solvents and rags used for cleaning. In addition to the chemical and water waste, print jobs using more than one color of ink must be perfectly aligned in the presses, a process that takes up to 100 sheets of paper per job. Because the cost of setting up the press constitutes a large fixed cost, companies typically order more copies of a product than they need.

In contrast, The Digital Frontier has adopted a different process. All its printing presses use the greenest available technology. Its Xerox iGen is the greenest press for digital printing, a process that is especially cost-effective for small print jobs. Because clients pay by the sheet, they print exactly the number of pieces they need, and because digital printing does not require aligning multiple plates, the process doesn't waste paper or ink. Large-format jobs are printed using a Vutek press with UV ink sets. And large jobs are printed with the Heidelberg DI offset press. Unlike traditional offset presses, the Heidelberg DI uses titanium plates etched by a laser. When the run is complete, the plates are returned and reconditioned by the manufacturer, to be used again and again. The Heidelberg DI is also more precise than traditional presses, so alignment creates far less paper waste. Still, nothing can eliminate the paper waste created when print images fill the entire page or the print job is designed for less than a full sheet of paper. In these cases, paper must be cut to size, and the scrap discarded. The Digital Frontier greens this aspect of the printing process as much as possible by donating usable scrap paper to elementary schools and recycling what can't be used. Proceeds received from recycling are donated to scholarships administered by the Printing and Imaging Association, a trade association for printers. Finally, whenever possible, The Digital Frontier uses soy-based rather than petroleum-based inks and encourages its customers to use paper stock that incorporates high percentages of post-consumer (recycled) content.

A SUSTAINABLY FORTUNATE DISCOVERY

Although The Digital Frontier now operates as a sustainability-focused business, this was not always the case. "We're the greenest printer in Colorado, but we sort of backed into it about three years ago when a client, running shoe maker Pearl Izumi, approached us to print their marketing materials and asked, 'How green is your process?'" relates Scott. "At the time we didn't know." So Scott did some research.

The company had recently purchased a Heidelberg DI offset printing press because of its state-of-the-art technology, not because it was green. During his research, Scott learned that the Heidelberg DI used a printing process that was greener by far than the offset printing presses used by larger and more established Colorado printers. Scott reported to Izumi what he had learned about the press along with his bid, and he won the job. Scott admits, however, that The Digital Frontier didn't truly recognize the potential value of its green printing press until six months later, when they were at a pet product industry trade show. Scott was discussing trends with other exhibitors when someone said about their product line, "Everything is green except the printing."

"That was the catalyst," Scott recalls. "I decided we should start blowing our horn. I started a marketing campaign to get the word out."

THE PATH TO SUSTAINABILITY

The main difficulty Scott noticed along his company's journey was a lack of guidance and support from industry trade associations. Printing is an industry whose history includes the routine dumping down the drain of toxic chemicals and in which change is not necessarily resisted, but is so expensive that it is not feasible for many companies. Scott found The Digital Frontier often had to create its own path. "No one is going to hold your hand," Scott relates. One area in which he expresses a particular desire for industry assistance is in the measurement of waste. When it comes to evaluating the entire printing process, Scott knows that, because The Digital Frontier uses soy-based inks and the Heidelberg DI offset press, he has the greenest printing process available. However, he has not yet been able to produce metrics to adequately compare his company to other companies in the industry—metrics that would give The Digital Frontier both the opportunity to more clearly explain its sustainability efforts to consumers and the chance to educate consumers and others in the industry about the level of waste created by specific elements of the printing process. Scott believes that measuring the carbon footprint of the company "should be handled by our trade association. They should have a group that you could just say, 'I need to be measured,' and they could come out and do it."

A second, lesser, difficulty has been employee buy-in. The Digital Frontier's sales manager, Rick Moravec, says, "We're all aware we're a small company, and Mark drives the company, and if Mark's on board with it, that's the way it is." Still, Scott has sometimes found it difficult to really drive home the full message. Employees realize that this is the way the business is run, and the process itself is as green as possible, but policies such as recycling are not always adhered to. "I still find myself fishing through trash cans, asking, 'why isn't this being recycled?'" Scott relates. Both Scott and Moravec, however, believe that the level of buy-in is steadily increasing, and they have no concern that employee resistance will pose any problems in the long run.

AHEAD OF THE INDUSTRY

One difficulty encountered early on was that the company was ahead of the industry in adopting and marketing a low-waste, sustainable printing process. The Digital Frontier was able to present itself as a green printer but found that the actual process of obtaining information needed to assess the environmental impact of inks, papers, and other supplies was difficult and cumbersome. Scott notes, however, that "over the past couple of years, the paper industry's been really proactive. Once they started seeing that this is a potential market, they changed with it." The Digital Frontier has gone from receiving paper sample catalogs from suppliers that contained little to no information on the recycled content of paper to receiving books with an organized array of recycled options, detailing percentage of recycled, postconsumer content. This change by paper wholesalers has expedited the company's production process and made presenting options to The Digital Frontier's customers more streamlined. Such advances can, of course, have a negative marketing impact on the company, in that such publicity makes it simpler for other companies to market green printing options and provide competition in this area, but Scott emphasizes that the improvement in streamlining the process of identifying paper stock containing recycled content has been very helpful.

While paper and ink suppliers are working to jump on the sustainability bandwagon, there are still areas in which finding and ordering the greenest materials possible is anything but streamlined. A recent technology, for instance, has made possible the production of a biodegradable banner material, which begins to decompose within three months in landfills, as opposed to the vinyl currently used, which never decomposes. After discovering this product, Scott began to search for a supplier and was surprised to find that his current suppliers could provide this material. "The suppliers don't come to you and let you know what they have," says Scott. The company must discover sustainable, innovative products on its own and subsequently research to discover which of its suppliers can provide them. This can slow down the process of beginning to use new, sustainable products, and it is an area in which The Digital Frontier must constantly be vigilant.

SHARING THE COST—MAKING A SUSTAINABILITY FOCUS POSSIBLE

The Digital Frontier was fortunate to have purchased the Heidelberg DI and continued to make sustainable choices from that point. Moravec reports that the company has yet to make up in sales the extra costs incurred by purchasing more sustainable equipment, operating in a sustainable way, and changing the company's marketing to emphasize its green focus. He estimates that these costs will likely take a long time to recoup. Scott, however, notes that these are now viewed as "the costs of business." For instance, he notes, "It costs us a little more to use soy-based inks than regular inks, but that's a situation and a choice we made a long time ago, so I don't want to look at that as saying, 'Oh boy, that cost me more,' 'cause that's just a cost." The company provides the greenest printing process currently available, absorbing these costs as part of the business.

In order to stay in business, however, the company does have to share some of the cost of printing green with its customers, and it is in the choice of printing stock (paper) that the company does so. The Digital Frontier makes it as simple and as clear as possible for customers to understand and choose among various levels of recycled, postconsumer paper stock. Scott explains, "The commitment on their end really comes down to the paper, because that's where they're going to make a financial investment in sustainability." While printing on paper that has little or no recycled content is not necessarily in line with the values of the company, The Digital Frontier will print on nonrecycled paper if the client is unwilling to bear the expense of using recycled paper. In a highly cost-driven industry, both Scott and Moravec emphasize that the higher price associated with using recycled stock would make them uncompetitive with other printers for all but their most green-focused customers. Therefore, when the company bids on a job, it provides the option of printing on a variety of grades of recycled paper and hopes that, as a result of education provided by the company, customers will, over time, increase both their use of recycled stock and the percentage of recycled content in the paper they choose for their print jobs.

MARKETING GREEN IN A COST-DRIVEN INDUSTRY

In the printing industry, the only green most customers are concerned with is the amount of money they are spending. The Digital Frontier is fully aware of this reality and focuses its marketing on education and awareness. Moravec believes that, in today's society, as more and more companies become increasingly concerned about sustainability, customers may be on their own trajectories of awareness, moving from no interest in reduced waste and using environmentally friendly inks to considerable interest, sometimes rather rapidly. The Digital Frontier wants its customers to realize that it is the greenest printer available. As for whether the customer is concerned with sustainability, Moravec says, "If they are, that's great, but if they're not, that's fine also. But there may be a way down the road that we can direct them." Until that point, Scott and Moravec simply want to keep customers and potential customers informed.

One of the company's biggest expenses when transitioning to sustainability was the change in its marketing campaign. A new logo was developed, using the color green and the slogan "Saving the Planet, One Impression at a Time." On each of the company's products, Scott added a paragraph listing the product's green aspects. Scott also began to tout the company's use of recycled paper, as it prints all its marketing materials only on recycled stock. The Digital Frontier redesigned the company's Web site to both emphasize the company's commitment to green production and educate the consumer on issues related to sustainability in the printing industry, burnishing this new image. Moravec acknowledges that this changeover in marketing was a major one-time expense, but he asserts that it was certainly worthwhile.

Since the printing industry is highly cost-driven, The Digital Frontier cannot force its customers to print on more expensive recycled paper stock. It is in the area of selling the use of recycled stock that Moravec notes the need for sensitivity to individual customer needs. Moravec focuses on maintaining positive customer relationships while educating, where he can, about the recycled options available. "There's places I can talk about recycled stock, and 100 percent post-consumer waste stock, but there's other places I wouldn't even dream of mentioning it." During hard sales, it is important that the sales force work to educate without alienating. Moravec notes that "the industry is price-driven, so when you start talking about the price difference between stocks, they just shake their heads and say, 'Well, why should I do that?' Some of them just don't understand . . . they don't get it. And it's a struggle." In the end, the company can do everything in its power to educate the consumer and provide environmentally sustainable options, but it is the consumer who makes the final choice of whether to use recycled stock and, if so, the percentage of its recycled content.

When it comes to soft sales, or working from education on sustainability to an actual sale, the process is less tricky. Both Scott and Moravec speak at conferences and educate industry members, environmental advocates, and potential customers about the ways in which one can print in a sustainable manner. This approach can also be seen on the company's Web site, which functions to educate consumers on what it takes to be green in hopes that customers will choose to take the reins from that point and use The Digital Frontier to help achieve their sustainability goals.

COMPETITION

When it comes to competition, price is obviously a key factor, but when a potential customer actually cares about whether a company is sustainable, The Digital Frontier runs into more problems than one might imagine. Unfortunately, as Moravec relates, when making a sales pitch, "I go in and tell them I print green, and someone else can come in five minutes behind me and say that they print green, even though they really don't. We're bidding against somebody that has a different press and may be making plates and using chemicals and using press washes and foam solutions, but they're printing on a recycled stock and they're telling their clients they're a green printer. That's what I'm fighting." Because the Printing and Imaging Association has yet to establish firm metrics or any certifications on the process of printing, it is difficult for consumers to distinguish between a company that is truly green and one that simply claims to be green because it offers recycled stock.

As far as maintaining its differentiation from less sustainable companies, The Digital Frontier is fortunate to have purchased the Heidelberg DI. Printing presses are extremely expensive capital investments, and they are not normally replaced unless absolutely necessary. Moravec explains that "there are presses that are 40 years old that still run great. No printer in their right mind is going to trash a press that's running great just to buy one that might be eco-friendly. It just isn't going to happen. They're too expensive. You can't afford to throw that away." Many competing companies may even strive to be green and will change every other element of their company and the way they do business, but until the printing press is replaced with a press as eco-friendly as the Heidelberg DI, the company will not be as sustainable as The Digital Frontier. Moravec adds that, because most printing companies do not have a large market cap, and because the demand for green printing, while rising, is still a small percentage of the total printing demand, he has not seen any Colorado printers adopting the same printing process. He does, however, foresee this happening eventually. The Digital Frontier's green printing process is based on its printing on the eco-friendly Heidelberg DI press. As new printing companies enter the market and as established printers buy new equipment, they can be as green as The Digital Frontier by printing with soy-based inks on a Heidelberg DI press. It's even possible that The Digital Frontier may find itself lagging behind if technology advances and a press is made that is even greener than the Heidelberg DI.

CERTIFICATIONS

Regardless of the lack of direct imitators, Scott notes that *green* is a big buzzword right now. For this reason, even companies that do little to nothing to ensure their printing process minimizes pollution and waste wish to appear as green as possible. It troubles Scott that some companies simply lie or avoid the truth by implying that by offering recycled paper they are a green printer. This problem is only exacerbated by the certifications currently available to printers.

The primary certification used by printers to indicate that they operate in a sustainable way is the Forest Stewardship Council (or FSC) certification. According to the FSC's Web site, its model of certification "allows products that flow from certified forests to enter the marketplace with a credential that is unique." Scott's perspective, however, is that this certification is more a hindrance than a help when it comes to ensuring sustainable practices in the printing industry, especially for smaller companies. "You pay $8,000 to be certified, and basically, all it consists of—and it's all on the honor system—is when the paper comes off the truck, you can say, well, I put the paper over here, and the paper can't be mixed in with non-FSC paper sources. So it has nothing to do with how you print, or what you're printing on. All they care about is the chain [of custody]," Scott remarks. "What it does is allow the big guys, the guys with a lot of printers, to go get this [certification], and for $8,000 a year, they're the green printer. And yet nothing else has been addressed. So their process could be the worst process in the world, but they have that certification." Additionally, Moravec notes that, while the FSC's intentions are good, "they are still cutting down virgin wood" rather than using recycled content. The FSC does offer certification for recycled paper as well, but Scott asserts the certification does not require meeting stringent standards. Certifications from other organizations are problematic in that they are difficult for the consumer to distinguish. Scott describes some of the companies offering certifications, remarking that they are "almost becoming these third-party logo sellers. And that's really what they're offering is the ability to use a logo and hope their logo gets recognized over someone else's." While Scott notes that the Printing and Imaging Association and other industry groups are trying to establish more reputable and thorough certifications, no standard, reliable certification currently exists. For the consumer, this creates a situation in which distinguishing among printers that are green and those that are not is no simple task.

WORKING FROM THE OUTSIDE IN

Scott is certain that The Digital Frontier is the greenest printer in Colorado, and likely in the surrounding region, and he's obviously proud of that. However, Scott wants the sustainability of his company to stretch beyond its processes and product offerings to its inner workings. For Scott, the realization that his process was green, and the journey that followed, created a passion for sustainable practices that he wants to be embodied in the inner workings of the company. Scott is working to reduce energy-related pollution by researching a switch to wind energy and to ensure the company produces as little unnecessary waste as possible.

Employee buy-in to the idea of sustainability has made this process a challenge. While Scott has experienced no major sustainability-related employee problems, he believes that most employees "just look at it as our new marketing plan" and do not necessarily feel a more profound connection with the consequences of their actions on the environment. While the employees accept sustainability as the way of the business, it is in these areas not connected to the printing process where he believes the company still has much room for improvement. Moravec notes that it is difficult to make certain aspects of the business sustainable because the company does not own its own building. "It's really tough to stick a lot of money into a building that you don't own," he says.

In certain areas, however, Scott refuses to accept anything less than the most sustainable avenue possible. For instance, many clients return vinyl banners to The Digital Frontier for disposal. Because vinyl banner material does not biodegrade, Scott is constantly researching ways to reuse the material. He keeps all of this used material in his storage facility, and refuses to dispose of it unless it is being given to an organization that plans to reuse it. "We've been storing them in our back room. We have hundreds and hundreds of signs from customers who've said, 'You can just throw this away,' and I'm not going to throw it away because I know where it's going." Scott similarly saves foam board in an attempt to find a method of reuse, and he donates leftover paper to local schools.

Scott realizes that sustainability encompasses people as well as planet, and he makes an effort to contribute to society. "We take the proceeds from the recycled paper and we donate that to the PIA, which is the Printing and Imaging Association. They have a scholarship fund, and we just donate those proceeds to them. It keeps that whole loop going, of sustainability." The company also donates 5 percent of all profits to charity.

CONCLUSION

The Digital Frontier has taken the sustainability of its printing process and made that sustainability the center of its business. While this focus has helped the company to exploit a specific marketing niche, Mark Scott's emphasis on sustainability goes beyond the scope of a marketing campaign. The Digital Frontier stands head and shoulders above its competition with regard to sustainability, primarily because industry norms are very far from green. Yet Scott refuses to settle for anything less than 100 percent commitment to this focus on sustainability. Scott's enthusiasm drives his company's efforts, and, as Moravec comments, "Everyone is really focused on sustainability. Everybody knows it; it's in the back of their minds all the time—when they're talking to clients, it's there. It's at the back of their mind and at the forefront. People are always aware of it, and it's due to Mark. It's due to Mark doing his research and pushing it . . . Mark drives it home."

The company's commitment to sustainability is certainly driven by the passion and dedication of its founder. For Scott, sustainability was never simply a way of marketing his company; it was his way of running his company and a way of life. As he repeatedly emphasized throughout our interviews, "It's the right thing to do."

LESSONS LEARNED

(1) Staying nimble pays dividends: Customer requests and inquiries can alert you to opportunities and spur innovation.

(2) Optimal sustainability is a joint effort between you and your suppliers and customers. You can adopt the greenest processes, but not every customer is ready to accept the cost of going green. Educating them about greener options is an investment in the future of your green business.

(3) Green certifications are often misleading. Truly green companies would benefit from tougher and more universally applied standards.

(4) As sustainability gains broader acceptance, business practices change in both subtle and dramatic ways. It's easier to find green sources of materials, and industry trade associations are providing needed information and support.

EIGHT

Boulder Valley Credit Union: "Better Banking Naturally"

Elizabeth S. Cooperman
Contributing Research by Clint McCarver

STARTING OUT

On a sparkling, sunny spring day in 2007, Rick Allen, chief executive officer and president of Boulder Valley Credit Union (BVCU) peeked out of his window and realized it was time to begin a project that managers had been discussing: purchasing a solar electric system that would produce clean, emission-free solar electricity for BVCU's main branch. Living in or near Boulder, Colorado—a city of about 280,420 people nestled at the base of the beautiful foothills of the Rocky Mountains—employees were already committed to protecting the environment. Many bicycled to work, composted, used energy-efficient lightbulbs, recycled, and insulated their homes.

BVCU decided to purchase a 10-kilowatt Sun Power solar electric system from Namaste Solar Energy, Inc., that would produce emission-free clean solar electricity. The net effect of the system would be an offset of 14 tons of CO_2 pollution per year for the system's 30- to 40-year life. In environmental terms, the pollution reduction per year would be equivalent to planting 1,078 trees or reducing car travel by 30,500 miles. From an economic perspective, energy costs would be lower and fixed each year over the life of the system. Additional panels could be installed later to further increase solar electricity production. Convincing board members, representing BVCU's depositors (member) owners, was easy given the future energy savings, fixed electricity costs, and environmental benefits. As BVCU's board chairman, Wayne Turnacliff, stated at the time, "Saving our members money and helping our environment makes sense, and is the right business decision" (Namaste, 2007).

The solar panels were fully installed by July 5, 2007, and today generate on a yearly basis 11,170.1 kilowatt-hours (kWh) of power (BVCU, 2010). Based on retail prices for electricity (about 9 cents per kWh in Colorado), this amounts to yearly energy savings of about $1,117 per year or total savings of $33,510 to $44,680 over the 30- to 40-year life of the solar panels. Incentives reduced the cost of the system for BVCU by about 52 percent. Around this time in Colorado, for a 10-kWh solar panel system, the average installed price was about $65,000, less an Xcel Energy rebate of $35,000, less a federal tax credit of about $9,000 (30 percent of the net system cost after state rebates are deducted), resulting in a net system cost of $21,000 or lifetime net savings of $12,510 to $23,680. In addition, with net metering, solar systems often produce more energy than utilized, so the excess electricity is returned to the utility grid, allowing energy to be banked for later use (BVCU, 2010).

To allow BVCU's members to see the savings and environmental benefits of the system, managers installed a monitoring system from Fat Spaniel Technologies (www.fatspaniel.com) on BVCU's Web site to provide real-time monitoring of energy generation for the solar electric system on a weekly, monthly, annual, and lifetime basis. As of February 1, 2010, the Web site monitoring system showed that the solar electric system had avoided producing 39,029 pounds of CO_2 and had generated 31,374 kWh of electricity since installation on July 5, 2007 (www.WeCareColorado.com).

With the installation completed, Rick Allen was content with the decision, noting that "We hope that with our leadership, other companies will follow suit by taking action to preserve our environment and public health" (Namaste, 2007). At that time, he was unaware that the installation would lead to a new business model.

ABOUT BOULDER VALLEY CREDIT UNION

In 1959, BVCU began as a state-chartered credit union for the Boulder Valley School system to serve faculty, students, and staff and their family members with their banking needs. Over the years, its membership group expanded and diversified, and its classification was changed to a state-chartered natural person credit union. Today, BVCU has about $211 million in assets and 17,500 members across the Colorado Front Range, including approximately 500 groups in the communities of Boulder County and Estes Park, Colorado. Any current employee in Boulder County or Estes Park, along with their immediate family members, are eligible to be members. Membership groups include employees in the Boulder Valley and Estes Park School Districts, Boulder Community Hospital, Estes Park Medical Center, and the Estes Park YMCA, among other groups.

BVCU employs 52 full-time and four part-time employees at four branch locations in Boulder, Louisville, and Estes Park, Colorado. Members also receive services through a national credit union network that includes over 4,000 branches, over 28,000 automated teller machines, a call center, and services provided on the BVCU Web site (www.bvcu.org). BVCU makes mortgage, auto, and consumer loans, including loans for new and used cars, recreational vehicles, credit card loans, and other personal loans for home improvements such as home solar panels, and provides checking and savings accounts, financial education, and other investment products and services for members.

Credit unions (CUs) are unique by being nonprofit and exempt from taxes and by requiring some type of common bond, including multiple occupation, industry, government, residential, employee, region, and multiple common bond groups, as well as community credit unions. Upon submitting an application and depositing (purchasing) at least one share (often $5), an individual has full voting rights (National Association of Federal Credit Unions, 2010). Member deposit accounts are called shares; members, in effect, are the owners of the credit union and are represented by elected board members.

CUs benefit from strong trade organizations. The Credit Union National Association (CUNA) and its affiliates serve as a support organization. The National Credit Union Administration (NCUA) supervises the National Credit Union Share Insurance Fund for both federal and state CUs, with individual savings insured for at least $250,000. CUs have a mission to assist the financial well-being of their members and to maintain the financial viability and capital of the organization. BVCU's mission is to "provide helpful, friendly, accurate and prompt financial services to its members" (www.bvcu.org). As a credit union with a community focus, BVCU found it easier to engage in activities that would give back to the community and protect the environment.

BVCU competes for deposits and loans in the Boulder–Louisville–Estes Park region with about 30 other depository institutions, including very large interstate bank holding companies with over $5 billion in assets (i.e., Wells Fargo, JPMorgan Chase, U.S. Bancorp), smaller Colorado-based bank holding companies (i.e., FirstBank Holding Company and COBIZ Financial Inc.), and small community banks and savings banks (i.e., United Western Bank and Liberty Savings Bank, FSB). In Boulder, several other credit unions operate with other member group bases, including Ashoka Credit Union, Boulder Municipal Employees Credit Union, Elevations Credit Union, and Premier Members Federal Credit Union. About 116 CUs operate in Colorado, with over 1 million members and $10.27 billion in assets at the end of 2009 (Credit Unions in Colorado, 2010). In 2007, BVCU was the first financial institution in Boulder to take on an environmental focus for all of its operations.

SUSTAINABILITY EFFORTS AND OBSTACLES IN THE BANKING AND CREDIT UNION INDUSTRY

Large Bank Activities

The financial service industry has been under pressure by its stakeholders (stockholders/owners, regulators, the government, competitors, and customers) to become more sustainable, to avoid lending to companies that damage the environment or cause social problems, and to support industries that offer solutions to environmental and social problems. Jeucken (2002) points out that the banking industry, compared to other industries, is a relatively clean industry, but because the industry is so large, it makes a significant environmental impact. Special sustainability issues and obstacles include utilizing enormous amounts of paper for trillions of financial transactions as well as using large amounts of energy for building operations and information systems and other back-office operations. As Jeucken (2002) notes, several large European and British banks started early environmental endeavors and energy-reduction projects. These include UBS reducing its energy costs by 25 percent from 1990 to 1993 and National Westminster Bank (NatWest) lowering its energy costs by $50 million from 1991 to 1995. Triodos Bank, Netherlands, operating in Europe and the United Kingdom, was established in the 1980s with the special purpose of investing in projects benefiting people and the environment. Triodos uses solar power and other forms of renewable energy for all its bank buildings and was awarded the *Financial Times* Sustainable Bank of the Year Award in 2009 (Triodos Bank, 2010).

An example of a large U.S. bank engaging in sustainable activities is Bank of America (BOA), whose board of directors adopted a set of environmental principles in 1991, including guidelines for materials appropriate for purchase and desirable environmental practices for the bank, its vendors, and its contractors. BOA also increased its use of recycled paper and co-founded the Recycled Paper Coalition to allow greater market access to recycled paper. By 1993, about 95 percent of paper purchases at BOA had at least a 10 percent postconsumer content. By 1996, BOA had reached a 26 percent paper reduction from 1994. All copiers were required to include a duplex option, and a comprehensive intranet system was created to reduce paper used for reports and internal communications. By 1999, BOA included environmental principles as a component for purchasing contracts with paper vendors (Sarantis, 2002).

In 2007, BOA made a 10-year, $20 billion commitment to promote sustainability in not only its operations but also through its lending by financing companies engaged in new alternative energy technologies and new products and services. In 2008, BOA invested in a new energy management system for 3,300 banking centers across the nation to reduce its greenhouse gas emissions and cut energy costs, with expected energy cost savings of 50 percent and an expected greenhouse gas emission reduction of 14,000 tons. BOA did this by utilizing Field Diagnostic Services Inc's efficiency technology that allows more accurate heating, ventilation, and air conditioning equipment that allows lower energy and operational costs (Sustainable Business, 2008). BOA offers its employees cash incentives if they purchase hybrid vehicles and provides loan breaks for customers with energy-efficient homes. BOA also created an environment-friendly credit card and debit card with Brighter Planet, allowing a percentage of purchases to assist firms developing renewable energy projects (Bank Vows, 2008; Credit Cards' Latest Pitch, 2007). Many U.S. banks encourage online banking and online bank statements, reducing paper usage and providing cost savings, and many are building new energy-saving buildings. JPMorgan Chase, for instance, recently made renovations to its New York headquarters to make it more efficient and opened its first energy-saving branch in Denver in 2007, which utilizes Energy Star office equipment, appliances, and lighting and includes a comprehensive recycling program (Chase Opens Its First "Green" Bank Branch, 2007). Other regional banks have also built new LEED-certified branches, including Northwest Georgia Bank (Northwest Georgia Bank, 2009) and Chittenden (New Chittendon Bank, 2009).

On the lending side, JPMorgan, Citigroup, and more than 70 other financial institutions have signed on to the Equator Principles, an agreement with guidelines on social and environmental issues in loans to developing countries, which include that banks make environmental assessments of major loans. The Equator Principles established in 2002 initially included just 10 global banks that underwrote about $14.5 billion of project loans (about 30% of these for developing countries). In 2006, the Equator Principles were revised and now apply to all project loans of $10 million or more crossing different industry sectors (Epstein, 2008, p. 122, and www.equator-principles.com).

Large financial institutions also have invested in companies that provide clean energy. Barclays, a UK bank, for instance, funded a multimillion-dollar project involving wind farms that was expected to provide energy to 13,000 homes. Wells Fargo loaned more than $1.7 billion for approximately 35 LEED projects that included construction loans and some permanent financing, with growing interest on the part of its long-time customers. Large banks, such as U.S. Bank in Colorado, have also launched home equity loan programs to finance environmental improvements for homeowners at lower rates than those of standard home equity loans (see Epstein, 2008, pp. 122–123; Home Equity Loan, 2009). Chittenden, the largest bank in Vermont, offers customers the option of foregoing high interest rates in return for putting their money to use to provide funds for community projects (Scheer, 2004; www.chittenden.com/socially-respon sible.htm).

Problems for project financing for environmental projects remain. As noted by Scott Muldavin, executive director of the Green Building Finance Consortium in San Rafael, California, in a *National Real Estate Investor* article in 2008, green finance provides a challenge to appraisers and underwriters. Because they are unfamiliar with value and risk aspects of sustainability, they have difficulty valuing future energy savings and revenues over the life of a building or project. Yet he points out that an appreciation for energy savings and marketing benefits is growing (Hudgins, 2008).

A 2010 article in the *Financial Times* observes that, despite financial institutions' strong voice for actions to be taken against climate change, they received low scores in a PricewaterhouseCoopers/Climate Group survey for not lending to low-carbon companies. This included even the most climate-friendly financial institutions (Credit Agricole, HSBC, Standard Chartered Bank, Munich Re, and Swiss Re). On a positive note, the article mentions that banks will find it easier to judge companies from an environmental perspective with the recent Securities Exchange Commission mandate that publicly traded firms must disclose information how climate change will affect operations (Harvey, 2010).

SUSTAINABLE ACTIVITIES BY SMALL
AND MEDIUM-SIZED BANKS

Some financial institution managers of small to midsize enterprises (SMEs) argue that it is less feasible for them to develop sustainable management practices. Yet large financial institutions often face obstacles that smaller firms do not have to face, such as less flexibility to make changes quickly, gaining board and stockholders' approval, and greater challenges with changing employee culture within huge organizations. Community banks, savings institutions, and credit unions have an advantage by being more cooperative and willing to help each other in different endeavors and by having community-service missions.

Some SMEs are already finding ways to both educate customers and engage in environmental activities. Citizens Financial Group, Inc., a regional commercial bank holding company headquartered in Providence, Rhode Island, offers a customer environmental education Web site (www.citizens bank.com/greensense). The site includes an offer to pay enrolled customers 10 cents every time they make a paperless transaction such as online bill paying, automatic bill payments, and debit card use. Umpqua Bank in Oregon, has an eco-banking division that provides pro-environment loans to small businesses, educating customers on business energy tax credits and federal tax credits for installing solar panels and other energy-savings efforts.

A community bank in Houston, Redstone Bank, was adapted to become a sustainable bank in 2006 and rebranded as Green Bank. With $275 million in assets, Green Bank has taken incremental steps in sustainability, including moving into a new LEED Gold–certified headquarters building; developing standard loan terms for green projects, including lower interest rates; and offering other environmental services and paperless checking accounts. A new community bank in Austin, Texas, One Earth Bank, also emphasizes sustainability (Hudgins, 2008).

Other new alternative banks include: (1) New Resource Bank that began in San Francisco to provide loans that conventional banks do not finance; (2) First Green Bank of Florida, established to promote environmental and social responsibility; (3) Common Good Bank in western Massachusetts, which is implementing a new community network structure; and (4) e3bank, a community bank in Philadelphia that offers a diverse, grassroots ownership structure for the bank, with most of its business done online, reducing its carbon footprint and operating costs and allowing lower loan rates for more sustainable firms. Some established community banks that focus on energy conservation and facilitating investment in energy efficiency and alternative energy include ShoreBank in Chicago, ShoreBank Pacific in Washington and Oregon, and Wainwright Bank and Trust Company in Boston (Green Banks, 2010).

In 2006, Alpine Bank, an independent community bank operating on the Western Slope in Colorado with $1.46 billion in assets, obtained an ISO 14001 certification for its environmental management, which includes efforts to use clean energy, conserve water, recycle, select and use recycled paper products and green cleaners, and safely store chemical products. Alpine Bank's employees started a grassroots effort called the Green Team in 2005 that led to a more formalized program and an environmental management system to provide a framework that measures the bank's progress and impacts and to continually make improvements (Alpine Bank, 2010). Alpine Bank has a formal environmental policy and projects underway with targets for reduction in energy use, paper use, water consumption, and courier fleet fuel consumption. A green initiative section on Alpine Bank's Web site links customers to organizations that can assist them with questions on renewable energy, energy-efficient products, preventing pollution, and reducing greenhouse gas emissions. The bank serves as a dropoff point for customer recycling.

In February 2009, Alpine Bank (now $2.7 billion in assets) introduced a new automated disk-drive platform made by Nexsan that reduces storage costs by 30 percent and energy use by over 20 percent by reducing the power and cooling used by current disk-drive systems. Alpine replaced all its incandescent lighting in its 10-story office building and purchased Canary tags offered by the city of Aspen Canary Initiative to offset the bank's carbon emissions. Canary tags are sold by the city of Aspen, and the funds are invested in local, state, and regional renewable energy and energy efficiency projects to reduce greenhouse gases on a firm's or individual's behalf. Alpine Bank South Rifle, a new facility, was awarded a LEED certification in 2009 (Alpine Bank, 2010).

In addition to BVCU, credit unions that have engaged in sustainability efforts include: (1) Permaculture Credit Union in New Mexico, whose members follow an ethical code whereby funds are invested in sustainable projects and the local community, with no loans allowed to exploitative types of business (Scheer, 2004; Permaculture Bank, 2010); (2) Arizona State Credit Union, which provides loans to community-focused firms engaged in sustainable practices, including in 2009 the financing for Hope Construction for Flagstaff's first solar-powered multihousing development (Arizona State Credit Union, 2009); (3) Bellco Credit Union in Denver,

Colorado, which developed in 2009 a partnership with PayITGREEN™ (www.payitgreen.org) to plant trees in customers' honor as a reward for using online banking and e-statements. Bellco renovated its office space to reduce energy usage, including installing sensor light switches, and developed a comprehensive recycling program (Bellco Credit Union, 2009). Because credit unions are limited to providing business loans up to 12.25 percent of their assets, some credit unions, such as Mid-Atlantic Federal Credit Union in Maryland, have found ways to partner with banks to allow larger business loans beyond their loan caps, providing a new niche for the credit union (Williams, 2009).

BVCU is a leader in the movement of credit unions that are becoming environmentally oriented in the United States Jason Bauer, vice president of marketing at BVCU, noted in an interview that, although environmental and socially responsible efforts may never be as extensive as those at the largest financial institutions, small and medium-sized firms can be forerunners, with a limited window of opportunity to be a sustainability leader. Small to medium-sized institutions should be willing to go ahead and "go, go, go" to make the commitment now (Bauer, 2008).

GETTING STARED WITH A SUSTAINABLE BUSINESS STRATEGY

With the installation of the new solar electric system for Boulder Valley Credit Union, its marketing managers decided to make this event a celebration. This would set an example for other firms to follow BVCU's lead. The announcement also became a positive marketing event for BVCU and a point of pride for customers and employees. Managers marked this milestone by taking an additional step to allow customers to be more eco-conscious by rewarding customers for engaging in positive ways to reduce their carbon footprint. Members would be offered special low-rate financing for home solar electric systems and lower auto loan rates for fuel-efficient vehicles. New members received an environment-friendly gift during the celebration. BVCU also launched a Web site with energy efficiency tips to reduce costs for customers and help the planet (www.bvcu.org/green).

With its new solar panel initiative, Boulder Valley Credit Union received quite favorable press locally, regionally, and in industry publications. As a result, credit unions in Colorado and across the nation became aware of BVCU's efforts. One day, Jason Bauer answered a phone call in his office from a credit union colleague from a small town in Oregon. The colleague eagerly talked about BVCU being in the forefront as a leader in sustainability for credit unions nationwide. At the time, with just the early efforts, which didn't seem all that momentous, Bauer thought this was comical and laughed out loud. Although the attention was complimentary, he wondered how Boulder Valley Credit Union had developed the reputation as an environmental leader in the industry.

Suddenly, it clicked that perhaps BVCU could be in the forefront. BVCU's managers and employees were engaged in practices to protect the environment. Why couldn't Boulder Valley Credit Union take the environment into consideration for every decision that was made from an organizational perspective? Perhaps BVCU could set an example for other financial institutions in Colorado and nationally. Bauer suddenly realized that this was the "right thing to do," since environmental efforts characterized what BVCU was and how it chose to do business. BVCU should become fully committed and not just go half way as an overall strategic effort. It should go beyond current practices by financial institutions, such as using recycled paper, providing customers with online statements, and online bill paying. As Bauer pointed out in a 2009 interview in *ColoradoBIZ* magazine, "We wanted to set an example. There is no financial institution that has really set the example. So that's what we decided to do, do the right thing" (Ringo, 2008; Bauer, 2008).

Just two weeks after the phone call from Bauer's colleague in Oregon, the business model for BVCU changed, including how decisions were made internally. Greener was more important than cheaper for BVCU's community mission. Plans were made for additional solar panels for the main branch and other branches the following year. BVCU forged partnerships with Eco-Cycle and other environmentally conscious charities and businesses. Environment-friendly office supplies would be used, and all marketing materials would be printed on recycled paper using soy- or corn-based inks. In addition to changing the company's culture, employee attitudes had to be changed. Each employee would be expected to recycle, compost, use recyclable products, and conserve energy and materials and be a mentor for members.

The new strategy included education and assistance to help customers become more environmentally aware and efficient in their use of energy. Every new member signing up at BVCU would receive an energy-efficient lightbulb. A powerful message was sent with each compact fluorescent lightbulb: "If every household in America changed one light bulb to one of these, this would be equivalent to taking 800,000 cars off the road." BVCU's new business model included "education, awareness, and commitment," for employees, managers, customer/members, and other businesses (Bauer, 2007a).

A new brand was launched, with BVCU becoming the first financial institution in Boulder to be fully ecologically conscious. Concern for the environment would be taken into consideration throughout its decision making and operations. As pointed out by Bauer, BVCU's environmental focus would be a way of doing business versus "a novelty promotion." To mentor members, a new, more detailed Web site was launched (www.We CareColorado.com), which included member environmental efforts and environmental promotions and partnerships with other environmentally conscious firms in BVCU's region. The new site would serve as a resource center for environmentally friendly living strategies. Bank managers and employees would mentor and work with members to assist them in their sustainability journeys by providing discounts on loans for purchasing fuel-efficient automobiles, installing solar panels, and making other home improvements that would reduce their energy costs and help the environment.

As Rick Allen stated, "Our eco-friendly efforts are to take a first step to further our culture of environmental responsibility within the communities we serve. We encourage our members to take the step with us in order to reduce the footprint we leave on our environment." Bauer summarized BVCU's new philosophy as: "It all starts with this first step, and in our view committing our entire organization to this philosophy is the right thing to do. It's no longer about doing small things here and there; it's who we are" (BVCU Press Release, November 13, 2007).

PARTNERS AND TOOLS

To take steps toward becoming a zero-waste company where all products are reused, products and packaging are designed for reuse with recycling in mind, minimal trash is sent to landfills, and responsibility is taken for the entire life cycle of products, BVCU partnered with Eco-Cycle, a Boulder, Colorado, firm that provides zero-waste services. These services include recycling, composting, education, and tools and information to help firms generate zero waste (Eco-Cycle, 2010).

Robin Burton, the zero-waste services coordinator with Eco-Cycle, noted in December 2007, "We are excited that Boulder Valley Credit Union made the decision to go beyond recycling by conserving, composting and purchasing eco-friendly products." Eco-Cycle works to make production systems cyclical rather than linear, managing resources from the design of products to their disposal, and provides zero-waste services for discards, including hard-to-recycle materials. Eco-Cycle's zero-waste system includes four key concepts:

1. *Changing the rules* to support resource recovery
2. *Producer responsibility* to hold the industry liable for creating less toxic and more efficient products
3. *Purchasing for zero waste* to use buying power as a voice for zero waste
4. *Resource recovery infrastructure* to build the processing and recovery systems to move to zero waste (BVCU Press Release, December 3, 2007).

BVCU's efforts to move to zero waste included purchasing energy-efficient lighting, office equipment, recycled-content paper, and office supplies; printing all marketing materials on at least 30 percent postconsumer recycled paper; and having employees recycle, compost, and conserve energy.

BVCU also organized recycling events with Eco-Cycle for staff and volunteers to bring in old computers, monitors, television, VCRs, and DVD players to dispose of these items in an environmentally responsible way. Reusable computers were donated to nonprofit groups with the permission of owners, and used equipment was sold to companies with the highest recycling rates. BVCU members benefited from the proceeds (BVCU Press Release, March 28, 2008).

BVCU formed partnership with 54 Colorado companies and nonprofit organizations engaged in sustainability efforts (www.wecarecolorado.com/partners.html). These organizations include the following:

1. Sustainable hotels (St. Julien Hotel and Spa and Boulder Outlook Hotel and Suites)
2. Renewable energy and engineering and construction companies (Renewable Choice Energy and Architectural Energy Company, Brickey Solar, and Brickey Construction)
3. Organic grocery stores (Whole Foods)
4. Nonprofit sustainable business trade associations (Colorado CORE)
5. Green printing companies and business centers (Copy Experts)

BVCU also contributes to and partners with charitable organizations such as the Forest Stewardship Council, the Rainforest Alliance, the National

Arbor Day Foundation, and the Thorne Ecological Institute. BVCU welcomes other environmentally friendly organizations to become preferred financial partners for their financial needs.

For its new mission and branding, BVCU participates in community educational projects in Boulder. In April 2008, BVCU hosted the first Earth Day Eco-Expo featuring more than 30 Boulder-based eco-friendly and sustainable-managed companies showcasing pro-environment products and services. Attendees were educated on proactive approaches to reducing carbon footprints; tasted solar oven–cooked food; test-drove electric cars, trucks, and scooters; and played fun games and activities. BVCU benefited from considerable nonmember traffic and potential new members. The BVCU Earth Day Eco-Expo continues to be an annual event.

OVERCOMING OBSTACLES

BVCU has a simple organizational structure and little bureaucracy or red tape, which allows it great flexibility. BVCU also has leadership that is committed to incorporating sustainability into the credit union's business model. The new business strategy could be implemented quickly; yet managers realized that there could be some resistance. Managers surveyed a sample of customers and found considerable customer/member enthusiasm in favor of the changes. Managers also talked to other sustainably managed businesses for advice. BVCU did not need a cultural change, since concern about the environment was already part of its culture and identity as perceived by its managers and employees. A few members were not entirely committed to the idea because of concerns about higher costs. Some products that did less damage to the environment could cost a little more. There was also the challenge of ensuring that the credit union was fully committed to the new business model across all branches. Management decided to conduct a complete audit to determine opportunities for process improvements pertaining to environmental stewardship.

A composting and recycling commitment needed to be incorporated across branches. Composting and recycling areas needed to be set up at employee desks. Vendors and suppliers needed to be following the best environmental practices. Some vendors already fit this model; others had to be let go and new ones found. Partnerships needed to be made with other eco-companies. For some items, this reduced costs for BVCU; for example, recycled ink cartridges were cheaper. The biggest financial commitment was to print all marketing materials on recycled paper using soy- or corn-based ink and all statements on recycled paper. Old statements on other paper would be used for scratch pads. All paper products needed to be recyclable, from toilet paper to copy paper to any paper used for financial statements. A new marketing initiative was implemented to encourage member/customers to use online statements to eliminate paper altogether. Messages were posted in bathrooms to remind employees to turn out lights to save energy. And signs at teller windows encouraged customers to switch to online banking and financial statements.

When the energy-efficient lightbulbs were given to new members, one or two new customer/members expressed concerns about possible mercury leakage if the lightbulb broke and about recycling the lightbulbs. Members/customers also noted difficulties finding recycling for computers and other difficult-to-recycle products in trying to follow BVCU's lead and practice sustainability. Members were given the address for the nearby Center for Hard to Recycle Material, and managers ensured customers that BVCU would also accept and recycle such materials. Branches in Estes Park and Louisville would accept compact fluorescent lightbulbs that needed to be recycled.

Managers needed to ensure that all branches were complying, look out for any areas of waste, and check that employees correctly composted and recycled at their desks. The janitorial staff and other employees were provided with recycling training to ensure they understood the new aspect of their jobs. One branch was slower to fully commit to the changes and showed some resistance, using nonrecyclable supplies that it had on hand. To surmount this problem, these supplies were taken away and donated to other organizations to have full compliance to BVCU's policy of only using recyclable paper. With this change, every branch came on board, and a new enthusiasm was generated as the remaining branch became fully sustainable. Customers could see that BVCU was fully committed. Employees and members realized that BVCU was doing grand things, that this sustainable culture defined who they were, and it was not going away. BVCU had differentiated itself with a true commitment for being fully environmentally conscious; the credit union was doing something employees and managers truly believed in.

SUSTAINABLE COSTS AND BENEFITS

As pointed out in a 2009 *ColoradoBIZ* magazine article (Ringo, 2009), BVCU invested over $90,000 in its new pro-environment business model. Costs encompassed employee training; building improvements including solar panels for branches, new windows and shades, and energy-efficient lighting; a new Web site, www.wecarecolorado.com; and equipping every employee's work station with a recycling bin. Although in difficult economic times, small firms might be afraid to make a significant initial investment, to fulfill its new mission, BVCU realized that significant savings—such as energy savings from the solar panel system—would occur farther in the future,. Today, smaller amounts of efficiency savings pay off; a few thousand dollars per year are saved by using products that are environmentally friendly such as toner and ink for copy machines. Some costs rose a bit, such as an extra dollar or so for a ream of recycled paper. Any extra costs BVCU could afford to put in its budget, with other savings, such as lower paper use (Ringo, 2009).

Steve Carr, the public relations specialist for BVCU, notes that it took four to six months for BVCU to fully implement its new business model. As advice to other credit unions engaging in new sustainable business models, he notes that it takes patience to implement training and education. Some small changes, such as providing electronic statements instead of paper statements, can make a big difference in cost savings and in saving hundreds of trees. Jason Bauer pointed out that partnerships with other area businesses have forged significant business benefits, with BVCU offering membership as a benefit to partner employees. In the 15 months previous to BVCU's new green strategy, BVCU had signed on three new partners. In the first year after implementation of its green strategy, it signed on 40 new partners. Partner companies, such as Standard Renewable Energy, use the credit union now for personal banking as well as a source of financing for clients that need financing for renewable energy. Other partners recognize that it is the right thing to do to support BVCU and other organizations that are environmentally responsible (Moed, 2007; Ringo, 2009).

From a financial perspective, BVCU performed well during the financial institutions and markets crisis of 2008 to the present, remaining well capitalized and having a positive return on average assets that was higher than the peer average for similar-sized credit unions in the nation and in Colorado and superior to the national average for commercial bank and savings institutions. While many banks suffered large net loan charge-offs during the financial crisis, BVCU's net loan charge-offs remained well below the peer credit union and bank/savings institution averages (NCUA, 2009; Federal Deposit Insurance Corporation, 2009). From July 2007 to September 2009, BVCU's assets grew by 35 percent from $148 million to about $199 million, an annual compound growth rate of 16 percent per year (compared to 7% for credit unions nationally) and higher than peer and national averages for banks and savings institutions as well (CUNA, 2009).

AWARDS AND THE FUTURE

In addition to changes throughout the organization, BVCU applied for and received certification through Partners for Clean Environment (PACE) in Boulder. BVCU became the first PACE-certified bank or credit union in Boulder County and its markets. BVCU continues to grow greener each day, forging new partnerships, introducing new products, and making daily organizational changes. BVCU also partnered with Eco-Cycle in Boulder to become the first financial institution in Boulder County and in the markets it serves to take steps to become a zero-waste company.

BVCU has received a number of awards for its sustainability efforts:

- 2009: Boulder Camera's Boulder County People's Choice Gold Award as the Best Local Employer (Gold Award Winner in 2008)
- 2009: Eco-Cycle Zero Waste Winner for BVCU's Office-Based Activities (http://www.ecocycle.org/events/communityawards)
- 2008: CleanTech Sustainable Business Silver Medal of Honor Award presented by the Colorado CleanTech Initiative at the Colorado CORE Sustainable Opportunities Summit
- 2008: Boulder Camera's Boulder County People's Choice Gold Award winner for the Best Financial Institution (Silver Winner in 2009)
- 2008: First Place in the Credit Union Excellence in Lending national competition for mortgage lending sponsored by the Credit Union National Association Mutual Group and the CUNA Lending Council

BVCU's managers and employees continue to work on its sustainability strategies, develop new ideas, and encourage other firms and individuals to join efforts to protect the environment and reduce energy costs. Ideas for the future include developing more business connections and partners and supporting these businesses in their green efforts, including possibly having classes on anything related to becoming more sustainable. Boulder Valley Credit Union demonstrates that a small financial institution can become a community environmental leader.

LESSONS LEARNED

(1) Boulder Valley Credit Union began its sustainability journey with small steps that led to a new business model for the firm, with BVCU becoming the first fully eco-conscious credit union.

(2) "BVCU forged partnerships with Eco-Cycle and other environmentally conscious charities and businesses."
(3) "In addition to changing the company's culture, employee attitudes had to be changed. Each employee would be expected
to recycle, compost, use recyclable products, conserve energy
and materials, and be a mentor for members."
(4) "As advice to other credit unions engaging in new sustainable
business models, Steve Carr notes that it takes patience to implement training and education. Some small changes, such as
providing electronic statements instead of paper statements,
can make a big difference in cost savings and in saving hundreds
of trees."

REFERENCES

Alpine Bank, 2010, https://www.alpinebank.com/go/about-alpine/green-
initiative
"Arizona State Credit Union: Lending Green Fuels Solar Growth," *Business Wire,* March 3, 2009, p. 1, http://www.businesswire.com
"Bank Vows $20 Billion for Green Projects," MSNBC, February 6, 2008,
http://www.msnbc.msn.com/id/17500301
Bauer, Jason, "Better Banking. Naturally." *Healthy Planet—Colorado Edi-
tion,* December 2007a.
Bauer, Jason, "Better Banking Naturally." *Elephant Magazine,* December
2007b.
Bauer, Jason. Personal interview by Clint McCarver, April 2008.
"BoA to Reduce Energy Costs 50% in Banking Centers," *Sustainable Busi
ness.com,* August 1, 2008, pp. 1–3, http://www.sustainablebusiness.
com/index.cfm/go/newsdisplay/id/16516
"Bellco Credit Union Introduces PayItGreen™, *Business Wire,* April 20,
2009, pp. 1–2.
Boulder Valley Credit Union, http://www.bvcu.org
"Boulder Valley Credit Union Goes Beyond 'Going Green,'" BVCU Press
Release, November 13, 2007.
"Boulder Valley Credit Union Installs SOLAR Electric System and Helps
Make the Decision To Add Solar Panels More Affordable for Their
Members," BVCU Press Release, June 15, 2007, http://www.bvcu.org.

"Boulder Valley Credit Union Leads the Way Towards Being the First Zero Waste Financial Institution in Boulder Via Partnership with Eco-Cycle," BVCU Press Release, December 3, 2007.

"Boulder Valley Credit Union Continues To Sustain Their Reduce, Reuse, and Recycle Commitment," BVCU Press Release, March 28, 2008.

"Chase Opens Its First 'Green' Bank Branch in U.S.," CSR Press Release, *Corporate Social Responsibility Newswire,* August 3, 2007, http://www.csrwire.com/press/press_release/16175-Chase-Opens-its-First-Green-Bank-Branch-in-U-S-

"Credit Cards' Latest Pitch: Green Benefits," *Wall Street Journal,* November 30, 2007, https://online.wsj.com/article/SB120225763311445823.html

Credit Unions in Colorado, 2010, http://www.cardreport.com/dirs/credit-unions-colorado.html

Credit Union National Association, *U.S. Credit Union Profile, 3rd Quarter 2009,* prepared by CUNA Economics and Statistics, December 15, 2009.

Eco-Cycle, 2010, https://www.ecocycle.org

Epstein, Marc J. *Making Sustainability Work: Best Practices in Managing and Measuring Corporate Social, Environmental, and Economic Impacts.* Sheffield, England: Greenleaf Publishing, 2008.

Federal Deposit Insurance Corporation, *Statistics at a Glance, 2009* http://www.fdic.gov/bank/statistical/stats/2009sep/industry.html

"Green Banks Offer Mega-Bank Alternative," *Progressive Investor,* January 15, 2010, pp. 1–3, http://www.sustainablebusiness.com/index.cfm/go/news.feature/id/1759

Harvey, Fiona, "Banks Not So Hot on Green Projects Says Study," *Financial Times,* January 29, 2010, p. 5.

"Home Equity Loan from U.S. Bank for Colorado Green Projects," *Mortgage News,* September 16, 2009, http://www.financingandmortgage.com/blog/home-mortgage/home-equity-loan-from-u-s-bank-for-colorado-green-projects/

Hudgins, Matt. "Banks Cultivate Green Loans." *NREIonline,* June 2, 2008, pp. 1–4, http://nreionline.com/brokenews/greenbuildingnews/banks_cultivate_green-Loans_0602/

Jeucken, Marcel, *Sustainable Finance and Banking: The Financial Sector and the Future of the Planet.* London: Earthscan Publications, 2002.

Moed, Joyce, "How 1 CU Flipped the Switch To Help Turn on Members To Saving the Environment," *American Banker: Credit Union Journal,* November 26, 2007.

NAFCU Services Corporation, 2010, http://www.culookup.com

Namaste Solar Electric Inc. and Boulder Valley Credit Union, Press Release, June 15, 2007, http://www.bvcu.org

NCUA Reports for National and State Peers and for Boulder Valley Credit Union for 2009, http://webapps.ncua.gov/ncuafpr/FPROnLineRatio.aspx

"New Chittendon Bank Building in Middlebury Receives LEED Certification," *VermontBiz,* December 8, 2009, http:www.vermontbiz.com/news/decembernew-Chittenden-bank-building-middlebury

"Northwest Georgia Bank Awarded LEED Certification for North Shore Branch," *The Chattanoogan,* December 11, 2009, http://www.Chattanoogan.com/articles/article-164786.asp

Permaculture Bank, 2010, http://www.pcuonline.org/

Ringo, Kyle, "Sustainability Spotlight: Boulder Valley Credit Union," *ColoradoBIZ,* March 1, 2009, pp. 1–3, http://www.cobizmag.com/articles/sustainability-spotlight-boulder-valley-credit-union

Sarantis, Heather, "Business Guide to Paper Reduction: Case Study of Bank of America," *ForestEthics,* September 2002, pp. 16–24; pdf available at http://sustainability.tufts.edu/downloads/BusinessGuidetoPaperReduction.pdf

Scheer, Roddy, "Credit Where It's Due: Green Credit Unions Do Well by Doing Good," *E: The Environmental Magazine,* May–June, 2004, pp. 1–3.

Triodos Bank, 2010, http://www.triodos.co.uk/uk/Investment-banking/

Williams, Geoff, "Small Banks Really Want Your Business," *AOL Small Business,* December 2009, http://smallbusiness.aol.com/article/_a/small-banks-really-want-your-business/20091209154209990001

NINE

New Belgium Brewery

K. J. McCorry
Contributing Research by Liz Lowry and Maria Elena Price

INTRODUCTION

New Belgium Brewing is the third largest craft brewery nationally and one of Colorado's leaders in sustainable business. This ethically driven and values-driven company has a devoted staff and loyal customers. Based out of Fort Collins, Colorado, its beer is now sold in 26 states. From the early stages, New Belgium believed in corporate social responsibility not only for the environment but for its employees and community as well. New Belgium has won numerous national awards for both its exceptional products and its pioneering sustainability initiatives. New Belgium's dedication to its values is reflected in the company's mission statement: "To operate a profitable brewery which makes our love and talent manifest." In 1998, it became the first brewery in the United States to subscribe to wind energy, thanks to a unanimous vote by the employee owners. It was one of the first microbreweries that had a full-time sustainability officer dedicated to implementing various sustainability initiatives. This Colorado company has shown that cultivating a culture of sustainability can enable a business to become profitable, successful, and even an industry leader.

A BIKE, A MAP, AND A LOVE OF BEER

It all started when Jeff Lebesch embarked on a bicycling trip in Belgium back in 1989. Not only did he love the countryside, but he also loved the beer that had been brewed for centuries in various monasteries around the country. Upon returning home to Colorado, this electrical engineer tinkered with old dairy equipment and set up his own home Belgian brewing operation in his basement. His friends and family loved his concoctions, and he decided to take it to market in 1991.

The company initially remained in Jeff's basement, and he and his wife, Kim Jordan, personally hand-bottled all the beer, filling about 60 cases an hour. Kim, a former social worker, supported her husband's endeavor in other capacities and soon took on the roles of sales representative, distributor, marketing director, and financial planner. Her role eventually expanded into chief executive officer, the position she currently holds.

Jeff and Kim named their first beer Fat Tire Amber Ale, symbolizing Jeff's inspirational trip in Belgium. This brew has become the signature beer of New Belgium. As the company grew, it moved into an old railroad depot located in Fort Collins. In 1995, it moved from the depot to a 50-acre lot near the Fort Collins downtown area, where they custom-built a new brewing facility, which they still occupy today.

New Belgium has found that its customer base wants variety now more than ever. Beyond its signature Fat Tire beer, the company also offers a variety of permanent, seasonal, and special release beers and pilsners. The standard line includes Sunshine Wheat, Blue Paddle Pilsner, 1554 Black Ale, and, of course, the best-selling, Fat Tire Amber Ale. Seasonal beers include 2°Below, Frambozen, Mighty Arrow, Skinny Dip, and Hoptober Ale. Explore series beers, created for more adventurous beer drinkers, include, La Folie, a wood-aged sour brown, Mothership Organic Wit, Abbey Belgian Ale, and Trippel. The company also hosts employee contests to create original brews, which are available only in the brewery's tasting room.

With more than 300 employees, New Belgium Brewing is the third largest craft brewer in the United States. Its products are carried in 26 U.S. states. It bottles more than 700 bottles per minute in its current facility, which produces more than 500,000 barrels per year and has the growth capacity of 850,000 barrels. The company generates more than $100 million in revenue annually. It has had a growth rate of about 10 percent for the last five years, whereas the craft beer industry, according to Morgan Stanley, has dropped to 8 percent growth, down from 10–12 percent just a few years ago. In 2009, New Belgium enjoyed 17 percent growth.

THE AVERAGE NEW BELGIUM CONSUMER

New Belgium Brewery tends to attract customers who like the outdoors, are community oriented, and care for the environment. Although New

Belgium Brewing targets all customers who would drink a craft beer, the average New Belgium craft brew consumer definitely has distinguishing traits. They tend to be male, in their late 30s, and earn an annual salary of $95,000. Although these consumers most of the time drink local craft beer, they also one-third of the time will drink domestic and imported beers. They live in urban areas where there is a sense of culture and community. They tend to purchase products from values-based environmental and socially minded companies. They are risk takers and tend to travel to other countries and dabble in the stock market. New Belgium has found that usually one out of five beers drunk will be a New Belgium brew for the average New Belgium consumer.

NEW BELGIUM'S SUSTAINABILITY JOURNEY

Both Jeff and Kim knew from the start that they wanted their company to be environmentally responsible. In 1991, they went on a hike in Rocky Mountain National Park to discuss the overall company purpose and vision. During this expedition, they decided that New Belgium would be an environmental and social steward. What they wrote that day is still true to the company's aspirations today:

- Lovingly care for the planet that sustains us.
- Steward natural resources by closing the loops between waste and input.
- Minimize the environmental impact of shipping our beer.
- Reduce our dependence on coal-fired electricity.
- Protect our precious Rocky Mountain water resources.
- Focus our efforts on conservation and efficiency.
- Support innovative technology.
- Model joyful environmentalism through our commitment to relationships, continuous improvement, and the camaraderie and cheer of beer.

The initial response from employees was enthusiastic, and Kim and Jeff were pleased that striving to become an idealistic company had real meaning to their employees. As with many of New Belgium's key decisions, the founders engaged their employees in developing ideas about how the company could effectively live out this vision. Many New Belgium employees can recite most of these values offhand to visitors, and this sustainability outlook has been embedded in the corporate culture.

In a concerted effort to live by the aspirational goals set forth in 1991, New Belgium has implemented a variety of initiatives over the years, with the intention of reducing the company's environmental impact and improving the local and global community.

As with all craft breweries, a key to profitability is maximizing raw materials. The raw materials used in beer manufacturing cost so much that even a small change will make a big difference in the bottom line. New Belgium is continually looking at ways to maximize its raw materials, decrease energy use, and reduce waste.

ENERGY

In 1998, New Belgium conducted its first energy audit, which showed that the single biggest emitter of CO_2 was the electricity used by the coal-burning plants in Fort Collins that supplied energy to all company facilities. In an effort to reduce its CO_2 impact, the company entertained the idea of subscribing to wind energy at an increased energy cost of 2.5 cents more per kilowatt-hour. Management felt they had to have employee support, because this decision would greatly affect the bonus pool at year end. During a staff meeting, they explained the audit findings and the recommendation to subscribe to wind energy for the company's electrical needs. At a historic moment in the industry and for the company, the employees demonstrated unanimous support for the wind energy program, and, in 1999, New Belgium became the country's first brewery to purchase the equivalent of 100 percent of its electricity from a wind power program. This decision enticed the city of Fort Collins to erect an additional turbine just to service electricity for New Belgium over the next 10 years.

Beyond participation in the wind power program, New Belgium constantly strives to reduce energy needs across the company. Jeff, as an electrical engineer, was able to design more energy efficiency into the operations and equipment. Natural gas is used for thermal energy to heat water and create steam in the brewing process. The company also has designed heat recovery systems that conserve natural gas by closing the heat loops in the production process. In 2002, New Belgium commissioned an on-site process water treatment plant that produces energy in addition to cleaning all of the production wastewater. Methane gas, created as a by-product of the water treatment process, is piped back into the brewery to run equipment.

This process meets up to 15 percent of the company's total demand for electricity. Over the years, the company has worked diligently to automate the brewing process to save energy as well as time.

New Belgium began its partnership with the U.S. Green Building Council in 2002 to take part in a pilot program with the Leadership in Energy and Environmental Design (LEED). This opportunity allowed the company to begin incorporating new green building technologies in its existing facility. In June 2007, it opened a new bottling and packaging facility that incorporated many green building and energy conservation measures, while doubling bottling capabilities. This facility cost $26 million and was constructed $2 million under the original budget.

Unique features in the building include skylights and sun tubes that provide natural light and reduce the need for electricity during the day. Light sensors and computer-controlled lighting minimized the additional lighting needed during the evening and on cloudy days. The heating, ventilating, and air-conditioning system is fluorocarbon-free and uses innovative displacement-ventilation technology. Around the facility, xeriscape landscaping has been implemented to minimize the need for water. A porous concrete surrounding the building also enables water drainage. The building was constructed with insulated panels and mostly green building materials. The facility is furnished with sustainable office furniture made of compressed newspaper and woodchips. The carpet was purchased from Interface, a leading manufacturer of recycled carpet products. Even the art hanging in the foyer is made with recycled bottles! Despite all its green building accomplishments, New Belgium was not able to apply for LEED certification. LEED certification focuses more on building performance, and over 50 percent of the building improvements were focused on improving New Belgium's packaging process. In 2009, New Belgium implemented a 200-kilowatt solar array that can produce up to 16 percent of its peak electrical load. The 870-panel system is the largest privately owned solar array in Colorado.

In its Top 10 Business Risks for 2008, Ernst and Young includes energy shocks as number 9. With expected sharp increases in energy costs, it is important for companies to look at options to reduce energy. New Belgium sees energy conservation as an ongoing issue and one it takes very seriously. The company makes continuous strides to purchase equipment that is energy efficient, educate employees to reduce consumption, and design with energy conservation in mind. This initially does involve more upfront expenses, but the management feels certain the costs will be gained back in reduced energy needs and lower future costs.

WATER

One of the key ingredients used in the brewing process is water, and lots of it. Breweries can commonly use up to 5 gallons of water to produce 1 gallon of beer. New Belgium has worked diligently to reduce water consumption over the years and now is down to an average of 3.9 gallons of water for every 1 gallon of beer. That is a savings of 34 gallons of water per barrel of beer, or more than 15 million gallons of water saved annually, compared to the national industry average. The company has realized the most significant water savings by reusing the water used to rinse the insides of bottles on the final exterior rinse during the bottling process.

RECYCLING

New Belgium strives to reduce waste through recycling, inventive reuse strategies, and responsible purchasing. All of the spent grain, created as a by-product of the brewing process, is sold to local cattle and pig farmers as feed. Keg caps are reused as table surfaces, and an extensive recycling program is in place at the company headquarters. On site, a wide range of materials are collected for recycling and safe disposal, including cardboard, bottles, cans, polystyrene, plastic, chipboard, stretch wrap, wood, wire, office paper, ink cartridges, computers, plastic bags, oil, steel, mercury, and other hazardous waste. Employees who are unable to recycle some of these items through curbside programs are encouraged to bring them to the plant for recycling. From office and promotional products to packaging materials and even beer coasters, purchases are mainly made from manufacturers who use sustainable and recycled materials, and preference is given to local manufacturers.

PACKAGING

Another common sustainability challenge for the beverage industry is packaging. Glass is the largest single contributor to the carbon footprint of most breweries. The manufacturing of glass requires a considerable amount of energy and resources. In addition, the weight of glass bottles demands that more fuel be used for transportation. Using recycled glass reduces the carbon footprint considerably. New Belgium purchases its glass bottles from a Colorado local supplier to reduce transportation cost and greenhouse gas emissions. The amber glass manufactured has only 10 percent recycled content. To increase recycling in the Fort Collins community, New Belgium established the Brown Bottle Recycling Program, which is free for its retail accounts and completely financed by the brewery.

ALTERNATIVE TRANSPORTATION

To discourage driving, after one year of employment, all employees are given a customized cruiser bike, just like the one pictured on the signature Fat Tire beer label. This was one of the company's earliest initiatives to promote alternative transportation and good health. Multiple bike racks donning these coveted bikes sit outside the brewery's front entrance.

PHILANTHROPY AND COMMUNITY INVOLVEMENT

With Kim's social work background, she was motivated to incorporate more philanthropy and community-based initiatives into the company's work. This has happened through New Belgium's generous support of community partnerships, charitable giving, and event sponsorships. To date, the company has donated more than $4 million to various organizations and communities. This number is calculated on a percentage of national sales. Funding decisions are made by an internal philanthropy committee comprised of employees who select nonprofit organizations that are actively involved in the community and demonstrate an innovative approach to their mission. To engage the New Belgium staff locally, there is a community bulletin board in the facility where various community activities and volunteer opportunities are posted. The company also invites nonprofit groups to use its facility for meetings and special events. New Belgium sponsors between 150 and 200 events per year. One of the most popular events is the Fort Collins Tour de Fat, which supports bicycle and environmental advocacy groups. Through these events, New Belgium has successfully engaged key stakeholders like city programs and nonprofit organizations, which in turn have become advocates and champions of New Belgium Brewing.

AN ONGOING PROCESS

Although New Belgium has supported many remarkable and progressive sustainability initiatives, it continues to work toward reducing its environmental impact. In March 2008, the company contracted an outside firm,

Climate Conservancy, to conduct a life-cycle analysis for a six-pack of Fat Tire. A life-cycle analysis, or assessment, investigates the raw material production, manufacturing, distribution, and disposal related to a product's existence. The sum of all those steps and resources used to create a product is the life cycle, or footprint, of the product. New Belgium found in this assessment that 55 percent of the footprint came from retailing the product because of refrigeration, 5 percent from distribution, and 14 percent from glass manufacturing. What it found surprising was that transportation of the product was on the lower end of the life-cycle percentage. Because of this, the company is focusing on ways to reduce refrigeration and packaging before addressing transportation.

To assist in managing all these sustainability initiatives, New Belgium created a full-time sustainability position in early 2000. This was a proposal by one of the tasting room employees, Hillary Mizia, who had a degree in resource management and recognized the opportunity for the company. She titled this new position "sustainability goddess." The position has become so valued in the company that it was promoted to executive level in May 2007. Jenn Orgolini has been the director of sustainability since 2007. Beyond researching and implementing a wide variety of sustainability projects, Jenn also works to cultivate a culture of sustainability within the company and provides a forum for employees to suggest ideas and offer feedback.

CORPORATE CULTURE

New Belgium may have become a role model for sustainability through high-profile initiatives, but what truly speaks to the company's success is the extent to which environmental and social responsibility has been ingrained in the corporate culture. New employees are hired based on their values, not just their skill set and background. After one year of employment, not only do they get the red cruiser bike, but they also become part of the stock ownership plan. This stock ownership plan is set up as a retirement plan and is part of each employee's benefit package. More importantly, it signifies employee ownership.

New Belgium focuses on the fact that each employee is an owner and provides opportunities for employee owners to give input and feedback. Every year, the company hosts an all-staff retreat to review the strategic plan, gain employee insight, and ask for volunteers to become stewards of new projects and initiatives. It also reviews financial statements so that each employee understands how his or her work impacts the bottom line. Not only does this all-staff retreat provide employees with the opportunity to contribute above and beyond their job description, it attests to the fact that all employees are accountable for the success of the business.

As the company and staff count grow, management has noticed that it is becoming harder to keep all employees active and engaged. They continue to strive to keep employment at New Belgium a meaningful experience. Early on, company leaders decided they didn't want the formal hierarchy of an organization chart. They wanted to create interdisciplinary teams and break down usual barriers between departments and divisions, although each employee does have a manager who conducts annual reviews and provides feedback. This staff structure presents more challenges as it grows, but employees seem to like it and remain proud affiliates of New Belgium Brewing.

PROMOTING SUSTAINABILITY

It wasn't until a few years ago that New Belgium began to market its sustainability achievements. This was because of the company's humility, fear of being labeled as greenwashing, and uncertainty about consumer attitudes. Through its own consumer surveys, it found just the opposite. When typical New Belgium consumers knew about the brewery's environmental and social accomplishments, it created a brand preference. In addition, the surveys revealed that consumers wanted to learn more about these sustainability initiatives.

New Belgium has begun to market its sustainability initiatives gradually. It has a Web page dedicated to its sustainability initiatives. It produced its first sustainability report in 2008, which is available for download from the Web site. The company prefers to speak with actions rather than focus on direct marketing, and it does this through support of other organizations and community-sponsored events. Since 2007, it has asked one member from every Tour de Fat city to trade its car for a bike. Thirty-three individuals have met the challenge. The Tour de Fat has been a huge success for New Belgium; in 2009, the event drew more than 50,000 participants.

New Belgium has been recognized in the media for its sustainability efforts through numerous environmental awards. It was recognized in *Business Ethics* magazine for dedication to environmental excellence. In 2006, the Gold Level Medal of Honor for innovations in clean technology and sustainable business was given by CORE (Connected Organizations for a Responsible Economy), and that same year New Belgium also received the Colorado Environmental Leadership Award by the Colorado Department of Public Health and Environment. Other awards in environmental stewardship have been given to New Belgium by Colorado Renewable Energy Society, Colorado Environmental Partnership, Colorado Association for Recycling, and the Environmental Protection Agency. It also won honorable mention in the Better Business Bureau's 2002 Torch Award for Outstanding Marketplace Ethics competition.

New Belgium sees these sustainability marketing efforts as an important differentiator between it and other craft breweries. The company has found that a key component to keeping its customer base loyal is its environmental and social values and ideology, along with making great beer. This has distinguished New Belgium Brewing from its craft beer competitors. New Belgium hopes to become more in the forefront of sustainability marketing but recognizes that this process must happen organically and slowly.

With the hit of greenwashing in the media, companies can be singled out for hypocritical actions. Now more than ever, company actions and what the brand promotes must be synchronized. New Belgium cautions other companies who are engaging in green initiatives to be truthful and honest and, more importantly, authentic. It has realized that there are no perfect companies and, through its marketing, provides consumer awareness that it is always striving to do better.

THE SUSTAINABILITY CHALLENGES

All companies experience challenges and obstacles to growth, and New Belgium is no exception. With the investment in the new bottling facility and the capacity to double its growth, continuing to make the right environmental decisions becomes more complicated. Through the recent life-cycle analysis, New Belgium realized the importance of collecting all the data and understanding the facts and options before making decisions. In the past, the company headed straight for action without examining relevant metrics, assessments, or return on investment (ROI) calculations. Given this, New Belgium did make some good intuitive decisions with great outcomes. Although it has come to realize doing proper ROI has value, it also shouldn't be the only decision tool for making sustainable choices.

FUTURE SUSTAINABILITY INITIATIVES

The next steps for New Belgium are taking actions based on the finding of the life-cycle assessment. It has started packaging beer in cans in addition to bottles because cans ship lighter and therefore reduce carbon emissions involved in transport. It wants to improve current bottling recycling programs within the 26 state distribution areas. It intends to develop ways to reduce the need for refrigeration and hopefully store beer at room temperature in retail outlets. This nonrefrigeration goal is complex and will require adjustments in the brewing process. In addition, it is developing procurement policies and guidelines to improve its supplier and raw materials sources. Each vendor will be asked to participate in a sustainability valuation program as part of the contract process.

In early 2010, New Belgium implemented a 200-kilowatt solar photovoltaic system, thanks to recently allocated grant funding. The company was awarded $4 million in the form of a Fort ZED Grant in the spring of 2008. This is a Fort Collins city initiative to produce enough power from renewable resources and conservation to exceed the energy used by its residents and businesses. This grant will also allow New Belgium to spend two years on research and development to create another cogenerator 500-kilowatt system, which will produce enough electricity on site to meet refrigeration needs during off-peak hours. Cogeneration is the production of electricity using waste heat (as in steam) from the brewing process.

Table 9.1   New Belgium Brewery's Sustainability Journey Timeline

Year	Sustainability Initiative
1991	New Belgium Beer enters Colorado market
1991	Developed sustainability vision
1995	Employee stock ownership plan was introduced
1998	Conducted first energy audit
1999	Unanimous employee vote to purchase 100 percent wind energy
2000	First full-time "sustainability goddess" was hired as the company's sustainability officer
2002	Participated in the U.S. Green Building Council's Leadership in Energy and Environmental Design for Existing Buildings (LEED-EB) pilot program
2002	Commissioned water process treatment plant
2004	Began filling Brewery Direct Service (distribution within Fort Collins) trucks with B20, a mixture of biodiesel and diesel fuel
2005	Became a member of the Chicago Climate Exchange

(*Continued*)

Table 9.1   (*Continued*)

Year	Sustainability Initiative
2005	Started local brown bottle recycling program
2006	Developed a sustainability management program
2006	The first brewery to use recycled material for beer coasters
2007	Opened new bottling and packing plant on 50-acre site
2007	Sustainability officer promoted to executive-level position
2008	Donated, to date, over $1.6 million to community philanthropic organizations
2008	Conducted first life-cycle analysis for six-pack of Fat Tire beer and produced first sustainability report
2010	Implementation of an 870-panel 200-kilowatt solar array system at the facility

LESSONS LEARNED

(1) "From the early stages, New Belgium believed in corporate social responsibility not only for the environment but for its employees and community as well." To support this, they incorporated environmental and social values in the company mission and vision.

(2) "In 1998, [New Belgium] became the first brewery in the United States to subscribe to wind energy, thanks to a unanimous vote by the employee owners. It was one of the first microbreweries that had a full-time sustainability officer dedicated to implementing various sustainability initiatives." It is important to instill sustainability in the company culture by engaging employees in the process through ideas, discussion and engagement.

(3) "New Belgium strives to reduce waste through recycling, inventive reuse strategies, and responsible purchasing. All of the spent grain, created as a by-product of the brewing process, is sold to local cattle and pig farmers as feed. Keg caps are reused as table surfaces, and an extensive recycling program is in place at the company headquarters."

(4) "Using recycled glass reduces the carbon footprint considerably. New Belgium purchases its glass bottles from a Colorado local supplier to reduce transportation cost and greenhouse gas emis-

sions. To increase recycling in the Fort Collins community, New Belgium established the Brown Bottle Recycling Program (BBRP), which is free for its retail accounts and completely financed by the brewery."

(5) "Conduct a life-cycle analysis on products. It is important to gather the necessary metrics, benchmarks, and environmental footprint data before making decisions regarding sustainability measures."

REFERENCES

Beers, Brendan, New Belgium Brewery Packaging Materials Purchaser, personal interview, May 2, 2008.

Dwoinen, Alex, New Belgium Brewery House Manager, personal interview, May 2, 2008.

Ferrell, O. C., "New Belgium Brewing: Ethical and Environmental Responsibility," Working Paper 2007, Colorado State University.

Giske, Meredith, New Belgium Brewery Marketing Manager, personal interview, May 2, 2008.

"New Belgium Brewing Bottling and Packaging Facility," Packaging Gateway, downloaded July 24, 2008, http://www.packaging-gateway.com/projects/newbrewery/.

New Belgium Brewery, "Brand Tracking Survey," presentation, February 2008.

New Belgium Brewery, "New Belgium Brewery Case Study," presentation, September 2009.

New Belgium Brewery, "New Belgium Brewing Company: Sustainability Management System," March 2008, http://www.newbelgium.com/Files/SMS%203rd%20edition,%202009%20for%20external%20release.pdf.

New Belgium Brewery Project Profile, 2007, U.S. Department of Energy Intermountain Clean Application Center, http://www.intermountaincleanenergy.org/profiles/New_Belgium-Project_Profile.pdf.

New Belgium Brewery, "The Sustainable Purchasing Guidelines Project," presentation, 2008.

New Belgium Brewery, "Sustainability at NBB," October 19, 2007.

New Belgium Brewery, 2007 New Belgium Sustainability Report.

New Belgium Brewery, "Waste Not, Want Not," Blog Post, May 8, 2009.
New Belgium Brewery, "Who Is the New Belgium Consumer," May 2008.
Orgolini, Jenn, New Belgium Brewery Director of Sustainability, personal interviews, March 20, 2008, and May 2, 2008.
Owsley, Greg, "Sustainable Branding Strategy," March 27, 2007, New Belgium Brewery.

TEN

Guaranteed Recycling Xperts: A Cleantech Business That Wasn't

Graham Russell

On November 6, 2008, CBS's *60 Minutes* aired a story titled "Following the Trail of Toxic e-Waste" ("Following the Trail," 2008). On August 27, 2009, CBS rebroadcast the item on *60 Minutes,* now updated and titled "The Electronic Wasteland." It featured a carefully orchestrated investigation by the network in partnership with an environmental watchdog group, the Basel Action Network (BAN), based in Seattle, Washington. The reporters traced the journey of a 40-foot shipping container from the yard of an electronics recycler in Denver to the village of Guiyu in southern China. Guiyu and the surrounding area is one of the most toxic sites in the world, its water and air polluted beyond belief by the primitive processes used to extract minute amounts of gold and other metals from the carcasses of old computers, printers, and other electronic equipment, almost entirely imported into the region from developed countries, including the United States.

Back in 2002 the Guiyu region had been the subject of a documentary by BAN called "Exporting Harm: The High Tech Trashing of Asia" (Puckett, 2002), which had exposed the horrendous environmental and social degradation caused by the dumping of U.S. and other developed countries' electronic waste (e-waste) in the region. Since that date, nearly everyone in the emerging U.S. electronics recycling industry was aware of the terrible consequences of shipping old U.S. electronics to the world's poor countries. Yet numerous U.S. electronics recyclers like the one in Denver that was the subject of the

60 Minutes story continued to illegally export e-waste to places like Guiyu, Nigeria, Pakistan, Bangladesh, and other poor countries, where it provided the basis of a meager livelihood.

The costs to the local environment, not to mention the health of the local inhabitants, of this economic model were staggering. Investigations have shown that 7 out of 10 children living in Guiyu have blood lead levels that vastly exceed those that are considered safe in the United States. Water and sediment samples taken from rivers and irrigation ditches by BAN and others around Guiyu have been found to contain levels of various heavy metals ranging from 100 to 2,000 times the maximum acceptable standards in the United States and Europe. At the time of the BAN documentary, the local water was so polluted that fresh water had to be trucked in by tanker truck from 30 kilometers away. Local medical studies have shown that many children suffer from serious respiratory problems (Huo, 2007).

A STRATEGY BASED ON SUSTAINABLE BUSINESS PRINCIPLES—WHY?

Mike Wright had sold his successful systems integration business in 2002 and spent the next year or more looking for his next entrepreneurial venture. In 2004, he settled on a tiny Denver-based electronic waste recycler called Guaranteed Recycling Xperts (GRX). GRX had been founded in 1999 and had carved out a small but established niche in what was beginning to become a growth industry: the disposal of old computers, printers, keyboards, and other obsolete electronic equipment. Twenty years after the first mass use of computers and related electronic devices, the volume of obsolete equipment looking for a final (end-of-life) resting place was growing exponentially. GRX's former owner operated the company out of a house full of dogs and surrounded by a junkyard.

For some years prior to Wright's purchase of GRX, scientists and others were beginning to warn of the dire consequences of simply dumping all this stuff into the nation's landfills because of the large amounts of lead, cadmium, and other toxic metals in the equipment, which it was feared would contaminate the underlying aquifers. The European Union had put in place laws requiring a gradual reduction in the volume of toxic materials permitted in the production of electronic equipment and had also begun to impose obligations on electronic equipment manufacturers to take back obsolete equipment at the end of its useful life for responsible recycling and reuse. Even in the United States, states were increasingly restricting the disposal of e-waste in landfills, although the Environmental Protection Agency (EPA) had not then begun to concern itself with this issue at the national level. It was clear to Wright that there would be increasing pressure to find ways of keeping e-waste out of the landfills and to recycle the constituent materials from which electronic equipment was made (see RoHS, 2002).

Wright readily admits that he wasn't particularly looking for a clean technology (or cleantech) business for his next venture. Neither did he purchase GRX with the specific objective of creating a sustainable business model. Like any good entrepreneur, he could see that the market for e-waste disposal would grow quickly in the next few years, and his objective was to build the business rapidly and make money out of it. Very early on, however, he saw the BAN documentary on the appalling environmental and social problems being created in Guiyu and other Third World dumping grounds for U.S. e-waste and resolved that he would not be a contributor to those disastrous conditions. It was at this point that he realized he had to create a responsible—and sustainable—business model for GRX.

WHEN CLEANTECH ISN'T SUSTAINABLE

There is a great deal of buzz about cleantech as the potential driving force for a new, green U.S. economy. Cleantech may be defined as technology that increases the level of efficiency with which we use resources (energy, water, and other natural resources), and/or reduces or eliminates waste. These technologies are sometimes described as eco-friendly, which means they reduce the impact of economic activity on the environment and/or eliminate waste.

However, it's important to realize that, just because a company advertises a product or service that is intrinsically eco-friendly and calls itself a cleantech company, that doesn't mean it has a sustainable business model. This is currently the case with quite a few renewable energy technologies (notably in the biofuels arena, where the impact on local water supplies and agriculture can be extremely negative). These types of negative consequences may or may not be recognized by the cleantech business owner, but they represent a set of consequences that will eventually destroy his or her competitive advantage and render the business model unsustainable in the long run.

The opening paragraphs of this chapter described one electronics recycler that quite clearly did not have a sustainable business model despite touting his business as a responsible disposer of e-waste and promising the public that any old electronics they brought to his facility would be disposed of in such a manner that they would do no harm to the environment. As the story of Guiyu shows, there were hundreds more like him, both in the United

States and Europe. It's difficult to believe that these operators didn't know what was happening to the waste they sent out of their yards in those 40-foot shipping containers.

Unsustainable cleantech business models occur frequently in the early stages of a new industry that is brought into existence by regulations designed to reduce the environmental impact of improper disposal of toxic material. What happens is that the regulations come into existence before anyone has properly thought out the technical or operating standards that need to be in place for the regulations to have the desired effect. These types of regulations often foster the entry of all sorts of unscrupulous entrepreneurs, slick operators out to make a quick buck in a hot new industry and get out before the backup rules and certifications are in place requiring that the new industry adheres to high standards of environmental and social responsibility.

This was the case with the environmental laboratory industry in the early 1980s, where new regulations requiring the testing of water and hazardous waste encouraged the establishment of STET thousands of small laboratory companies. The owners of many of them were not only technically unqualified to conduct chemical testing, but maintained ethical standards that allowed them to disregard the question of whether the data they were producing was valid by taking shortcuts with the published analytical methods. In the worst cases, lab owners would accept bribes in exchange for delivering an analytical result that would keep the owners of the material they were testing off the regulatory hook. Eventually, rules establishing relevant operating standards and certification systems were put in place, and most of the fly-by-night operators fell by the wayside—but not before a lot of damage had been done and many unsuspecting customers had been bilked out of a great deal of money or found themselves in regulatory trouble for not having paid attention to operating standards of their testing laboratory.

When Mike Wright bought GRX in 2004, despite the emerging regulations and the well-publicized environmental and health disasters shaping up in places like Guiyu, the young U.S. electronics recycling industry was characterized mainly by irresponsible operators who largely ignored the adverse environmental and social consequences of their business models. The industry, while portraying itself as an emerging, sophisticated, technology-driven cleantech industry, was, for the most part, operating in an entirely unsustainable fashion.

E-WASTE RECYCLING: HOW IT WORKS

In principle, e-waste recycling is quite simple. Old equipment is broken down into its constituent materials, which are then recycled into the manufacture of other products. One of the major challenges in 2005, as Wright began to develop his corporate strategy for GRX, was (and in fact still is) that certain of these materials were extremely difficult to recycle. The most valuable materials were the gold and other precious metals used in the circuit boards of computers, and there was a good market for these with companies such as Noranda (Canada) and Umicor (based in Belgium) that had sophisticated processes for extracting these metals and either incinerating the balance of the material or otherwise disposing of it in an environmentally responsible fashion. Wright found that he could also easily find a market for the steel, aluminum, and other basic metals that formed the casing and other structural components of computer towers, printers, and other devices. Scrap metal recycling has been around for decades, and there were plenty of competing local processors with a good environmental track record in this business.

Other constituent materials were (and still are) much harder to recycle. Computer monitors, like TVs, contain cathode ray tubes (CRTs) made of thick glass, part of which contains large amounts of lead to protect viewers from the hazardous effects of the radiation inside them. Apart from the difficulty of accurately separating the plain glass walls from the leaded glass screens, the market for recycling leaded glass in 2005 was rapidly shrinking as flat panel displays replaced the bulky CRTs that had been used for decades in TVs and computers. Despite numerous efforts to find alternative uses for leaded glass from CRTs, the only practical recycling option for leaded glass consisted of reusing it in the manufacture of new CRTs. The last CRT manufacturing plant in the United States had been closed by Sony at the end of 2005.

Even though CRTs continued to be manufactured in developing countries, the volume of leaded glass pouring onto the market as people replaced CRTs with flat panel displays began to exceed demand, and prices collapsed. A U.S. recycler could establish an operation to separate leaded from unleaded glass, sell the unleaded glass in the United States, and still obtain a modest price—depending on the quality of the leaded glass stream—from an overseas manufacturer of CRTs such as Videocon in India and Samsung. However, to protect themselves against unscrupulous operators that cut corners in the process of separating leaded from unleaded glass, the latter have continued to ratchet up quality control standards, imposing stiff penalties on subspec batches or even rejecting them outright. There has been the additional difficulty of establishing whether an overseas CRT manufacturer really is using all of the leaded glass in a remanufacturing process or whether the manufacturer is dumping a large portion of it locally, thereby opening the responsible U.S.-based recycler to potential liability.

The only viable alternative for disposing of leaded glass responsibly was to send it to a lead smelter like Doe Run or Noranda that would smelt out the lead for reuse, leaving behind an essentially inert silica-based slag that could be landfilled safely. Here again, however, the demand was such that the smelters were requiring increasing prices from the e-waste companies. At the time of writing in 2009, the option of separating leaded from unleaded glass and selling these recycled material streams respectively to overseas CRT manufacturers and domestic glass product manufacturers (e.g., brewers) is the better option. However, as the global demand for old-style CRTs diminishes, it's questionable how long that market will represent a viable option for leaded glass recycling. The electronics recyclers, therefore, have found the responsible disposal of glass to be an increasing challenge, potentially compromising the amount they can earn from the back-end sale of constituent materials from e-waste processing.

The situation with plastics has been even worse. Although many plastics can be viably recycled into new products, there are well over a dozen different types of plastic used in electronic equipment manufacture, and the process of separating them out from one another is extremely difficult. In 2005, as Wright was building GRX, there were just a few organizations in the United States with semiestablished technologies for separating plastic types using various density-based techniques. None of these technologies has proved to be viable for large-scale recycling of plastics used in the manufacture of electronics equipment. There are operations in China that remanufacture e-waste plastics into low-grade plastic products, such as switch box housings and cheap plastic furniture. They will pay 10 to 14 cents per pound for plastics that have been sorted by broad type. However, from a sustainability standpoint, uncertainty always exists about whether they are genuinely reusing the material or dumping a large portion of it locally in an irresponsible fashion. For U.S. recyclers trying to do a responsible job, whether any revenue can be generated from the plastics or whether they incur a cost to send them to a hazardous waste incinerator as a fuel—the only other environmentally responsible option—has continued to be an issue.

IGNORANT CUSTOMERS + IRRESPONSIBLE VENDORS = MAJOR STRATEGIC CHALLENGE!

As already implied, in the electronics recycling industry of 2005, precious little material recycling was taking place at all. Most owners of old electronics who wanted to get rid of it didn't care where it went and how it was disposed of. Those few who knew enough to be concerned about where it ended up for the most part trusted the statements of the recyclers to the effect that it was being disposed of responsibly.

The business model of many recyclers, including the company that eventually became the subject of the *60 Minutes* investigation and many others in Denver and in cities all over the country, was fairly simple:

- Fix up any equipment of fairly recent origin that could be sold for a small profit to schools, churches, nonprofits, and other organizations that couldn't afford to buy new gear.

- In the case of equipment that couldn't be fixed up and resold, strip out the circuit boards and a few other items containing high-value precious metals on which they could collect a decent price from smelters such as Noranda, Umicor, and Boliden.

- Load the balance into 40-foot shipping containers and sell it for a minimal amount to a broker in the United States or elsewhere who would arrange for its transport to one of the toxic hell holes in China or Bangladesh, where primitive open-fire plastic burning and open bath-acid leaching techniques would be used to scavenge the remaining minute amounts of valuable metal, the balance being dumped into former rice paddies or irrigation ditches and left to pollute the local water supply, kill the local flora and fauna, and compromise the health of the local population.

In this model, the revenue from the resold items and the circuit boards sent to the smelters plus the bulk fees collected from the brokers who shipped the balance overseas was sufficient to pay for the cost of collection in the United States plus the salaries of the technical staff who fixed up the reusable items and yield a decent profit. Most of these operators didn't charge an up-front collection fee in 2005—the model worked quite nicely without it. And, of course, the idea of not having to pay to get rid of your old electronic junk had great appeal for customers.

One of the tenets of recycling industry dogma is that reuse is better than recycling. In the case of old electronic equipment, this is a dubious proposition. The incremental life of a three- or four-year-old computer or cell phone is inevitably quite short. In the hands of its second user, who probably has little money (otherwise he or she would have bought new equipment to begin with), the likelihood that it will get recycled responsibly when it does reach the end of its useful life is extremely slim. Many e-waste recyclers seeking to do the most responsible job of recycling take the view that it's actually more responsible to recycle everything and not get into the business of fix-up and resell—more on this later in the chapter.

For responsible recyclers, collection costs, the cost of breaking down the equipment into its constituent material streams, and the questionable economics of disposing responsibly of the leaded glass and some of the plastics exceeded the revenue that could be earned from the circuit boards and basic metals (steel and aluminum), so it has been necessary to charge owners of e-waste a small, up-front collection fee to make the financial model work. The approximate makeup of a viable revenue model for a responsible e-waste recycler in 2005 was 70 percent in up-front fees and 30 percent in back-end materials revenues.

Why would anyone pay additional fees to recycle their old electronics with a genuinely responsible operator when they could get it done for free, especially since those recyclers that did not charge an up-front fee still promised that their operations were entirely eco-friendly? Mike Wright had earned his success in earlier entrepreneurial ventures with a strategy emphasizing doing the right thing and delivering outstanding customer service. He wasn't about to conduct his new business with a different set of values guiding him, especially after seeing the horrific environmental and social consequences of the typical industry model as portrayed in the "Exporting Harm" documentary. It was obvious to him and other responsible operators who the scamsters in the industry were (tell-tale signs included no up-front collection fees, the presence of 40-foot ocean containers on their lots, and a complete lack of transparency concerning how their operation worked and who handled the downstream materials). However, the fact that most customers either didn't care where their old e-waste went or didn't know the right questions to ask to identify a responsible recycler, placed GRX at a severe competitive disadvantage.

Wright knew that, eventually, regulations concerning the proper disposal of e-waste would catch up to the demand in the marketplace (just as they had in earlier segments of the environmental services industry, such as landfill operations and laboratory testing services). However, the strategic challenge in 2005 was how to create a value proposition that would encourage customers to pay an up-front collection fee when there were plenty of operators that would collect their old electronic equipment for free.

THE STRATEGY, THE VALUE PROPOSITION

With the help of an industry consultant, GRX began to see that there were, in fact, certain major liabilities of a nonregulatory nature that might influence an owner of e-waste to think seriously about paying an up-front fee in exchange for a guarantee that all of its electronic items would be completely physically destroyed. Not all recycled e-waste ended up in containers en route to Guiyu and similar places. Stories had emerged in the industry of old equipment turning up in the most unlikely places with the former owners' asset tags still attached. For example, old monitors were found on Bureau of Land Management land in Colorado being used for target practice by a rifle club. The asset tags showed that they had formerly belonged to various school districts and other local government entities. Not great publicity for those involved! In another well-documented case, a property owner in Minnesota who had rented a warehouse to an e-waste recycler suddenly found he was no longer getting paid his monthly rental fees. After all efforts to track down the lessee failed, the owner investigated his property to find several floors stacked top to bottom with old computers and other e-waste. Because the lessee was nowhere to be found, the warehouse owner successfully went after the former owners of the e-waste, many of whose asset tags were still on the equipment. This was a bit awkward for the owners since, in this case, they had already paid the recycler an up-front collection fee and been told their equipment would be disposed of properly.

Another form of liability to owners of e-waste involved equipment ending up in the hands of identity theft shops that made a good living salvaging things like social security and drivers' license numbers from the hard drives and printer buffers of old electronics. One group of students at the Massachusetts Institute of Technology purchased a batch of discarded computers from a recycler and were able to successfully withdraw money from a private bank account using a personal identification number recovered from an old computer hard drive.

It eventually became clear that a strategy based on a solid guarantee that a customer's equipment would be completely destroyed, including any data remaining in it, would persuade owners to pay a fee up front. Wright had been wrestling for some time with the issue of whether GRX should get into the business of fixing up and reselling newer devices, the conventional wisdom in the industry being that a pure end-of-life recycling model couldn't be viable. With hindsight, he credits a portion of GRX's success to the fact that he maintained strategic focus, sacrificing that revenue stream in the interests of maintaining a clear and easily understandable value proposition to his customers—guaranteed total destruction. This decision also necessitated some modest capital investment in the form of a crusher to destroy hard drives, which in a short time became a strong selling point for potential customers.

GRX developed a comprehensive statement of its operating processes that included verifiable information about how the equipment was destroyed and where the constituent materials were disposed of, inviting potential customers to audit the GRX facility and talk to the downstream materials processors about how they handled the materials they received. Coupled with some fairly soft-sell statements about the adverse publicity received by some e-waste owners who had paid insufficient attention to the claims made by their chosen recyclers and liabilities arising from the theft of data from old computers, this began to grab the attention of larger companies seeking to do the right thing with their e-waste.

One of the breakthroughs GRX made at this time was to secure the business of Eco-Cycle, a large, not-for-profit recycler based in Boulder, Colorado. Eco-Cycle has been a force in the Denver metro area recycling industry for many years and has crusaded on the topic of zero waste generation since the late 1990s. Eco-Cycle had been sending two truckloads of e-waste from Boulder to a recycler in Los Angeles that had demonstrated a highly automated process for completely destroying all equipment and mechanically separating out the constituent materials streams for reuse in new manufacturing processes. Once GRX was able to demonstrate its verifiable process for breaking down the equipment and sending the materials to verifiably responsible recyclers downstream, it became a no-brainer for Eco-Cycle to switch its business to the local service provider, because it avoided the carbon emissions and diesel consumption involved in sending two trucks a month halfway across the United States.

Another breakthrough came when GRX recognized that landlords and building managers were becoming concerned about e-waste. In Colorado, the laws illogically allow an individual homeowner to dispose of an old computer, TV, or printer in a landfill, but a business is *not* allowed to do so. Some smaller companies got around the landfill ban by giving each of their employees items of old electronic equipment to take home to dispose of as their own by leaving it out with the trash—yet another of the scams prevalent in the industry in 2005 in the early days of Wright's ownership of GRX.

Another way to deal with the problem was to sneak down after normal business hours and quietly dump old computers in the dumpsters provided by trash haulers under contract to the landlords or building managers, most of whom typically didn't know this was going on. In the event the e-waste was discovered by the trash hauler when it was tipped into the landfill, and assuming the former owners had been smart enough to remove the asset tags, it would be the landlord or building manager who would be subject to regulatory action. Yet another subterfuge used by smaller companies was to disappear at the end of a lease leaving closets full of old equipment that would then become the disposal liability of the landlord or building manager.

GRX began to find a solid marketing opportunity by encouraging landlords and building managers to hold e-waste recycling days, which they would advertise heavily to their tenants. These proved an extremely useful way to concentrate collection activities and, at the same time, promote the company and its responsible recycling activities to a large range of smaller organizations. Similar collection days were organized with local governments anxious to promote responsible e-waste recycling and keep e-waste out of their local landfills.

If we boil down the game plan constructed by GRX to stake out the high ground in an industry in which many of the participants were more than happy to take the low road regardless of the adverse environmental and social consequences, the essential elements are as follows:

- Guaranteed total destruction of all old electronic equipment collected from customers, including hard drives and other data-containing devices.
- Maximum commitment to genuine recycling of constituent materials and landfill diversion.
- Total transparency on all aspects of the company's operations, including an invitation to talk to downstream material processors to verify the ultimate destination of constituent materials.
- An open invitation to potential customers to simply drop in at any time unannounced to conduct an operations audit of GRX's activities.

As this strategy began to take hold in the marketplace during 2005, GRX's volume and revenues started to grow rapidly. The following table shows the growth in volume measured as pounds of e-waste collected by the company's main facility in Denver from January 2005 to December 2007. The compound annual volume growth rate from 2005 to 2007 was nearly 72 percent.

A LEADING PLAYER IN THE INDUSTRY

Many business owners struggling to build a responsible operation in an industry that lacks adequate regulation work hard through the industry association to raise operating standards. Mike Wright has been no exception. Starting in 2005, he has played an increasingly important role in the International Association of Electronic Recyclers (IAER), working particularly on educational issues and helping to raise the visibility of the association as a driver of responsible practices. He also established a very close relationship with the Basel Action Network and encouraged the IAER (later absorbed

Table 10.1   Volume Growth at GRX Denver Facility, 2005–2007 (pounds of electronic waste processed)

	2005	2006	2007
January	97,998	191,474	341,670
February	115,664	247,667	268,993
March	108,923	260,850	390,443
April	157,554	286,706	383,183
May	168,098	480,594	659,761
June	114,305	451,133	539,429
July	118,080	353,271	502,796
August	146,270	595,620	448,956
September	130,492	361,087	399,249
October	129,656	383,046	528,901
November	257,164	414,202	411,910
December	230,985	297,905	361,332
Annual Total	1,775,189	4,323,555	5,236,623

into the Institute of Scrap Recycling Industries) to work with BAN to establish a certification system for electronics recyclers. He was likewise instrumental in forming the e-waste section of the Colorado Association for Recycling and working with the EPA's Region 8 office in Denver with the objective of driving higher operating standards at a local level.

Carrying a torch for higher operating standards and lobbying for tightened regulatory standards is a powerful weapon in many industries where irresponsible activity by unethical operators creates a disadvantage for those trying to do the right thing. That is something every sustainable business owner should pay attention to. Aside from the process of moving the industry to higher ground, being involved and proactive in industry issues builds credibility for a company, and being seen to be a leader in the industry always generates interesting—and often unexpected—business opportunities.

GRX has recently secured ISO 9000 and 14000 accreditation, one of a very few electronics recyclers in the country to achieve these distinctions. Wright believes that his deep commitment to the highest possible operating standards has been the key factor in securing the competitive advantage GRX now enjoys.

WHAT ABOUT THE SOCIAL DIMENSION?

During the early days of his ownership of GRX, Wright believed it would be possible to switch from manual operations in which teams of people used hammers, screwdrivers, and other basic tools to break apart old computers and other electronics to an automated process that would significantly reduce costs. At that time, a number of well-funded, venture-backed companies were investing in sophisticated shredding and sorting equipment (mostly built in Europe), which they hoped would enable them to handle vast quantities of e-waste at very low unit costs, thereby securing a huge competitive advantage over smaller, manual operators.

In fact, while it's easy to shred electronic equipment and reduce it to small pieces of fairly homogeneous material, separating out all of the different constituents into reasonably clean material streams has proved extremely challenging, and most e-waste recyclers' operations—even the larger ones—remain largely manual. After recognizing that GRX had nowhere near enough volume to justify the purchase of automated equipment, Wright nevertheless understood the need to keep operating costs as low as possible in a business where unit margins were very thin and high-volume processing was essential. In pursuit of what he intended to be a socially and environmentally responsible business model, he established relationships with several halfway houses in Denver in the hope that he could build a motivated, low-cost labor force with people recovering from drug and alcohol problems.

This proved challenging at times, mainly due to the tendency of recovering drug and alcohol abusers to slip back into their former habits, leading them to high levels of absenteeism, stealing, and other troublesome activities. As GRX refined its strategy of guaranteeing complete destruction of all electronic equipment received, it found that persistent problems with theft by staff became a serious obstacle to the point where it had to abandon the policy of hiring from halfway houses.

Starting in 2006, the company has sought to build a productive, motivated workforce by offering its relatively unskilled line workers good wages and a full array of health benefits for them and their families. At the same time, Wright has encouraged them to take responsibility for their earnings by introducing a bonus system based on the volume of equipment they disassemble, while making it clear that the company gets paid for delivering clean material streams so that they need to be diligent in their activities. Staff who do not meet minimum production targets or are careless in separating the different materials do not remain with the company long. This combination of high performance expectations and excellent employment conditions has been extremely successful for the company in terms of retaining competent, motivated staff. Wright also helps his staff understand that the job they do makes a contribution to a better global environment, a strong motivator for the company's managerial staff and even for some—although by no means all—of the line workers.

Late in 2005, Wright determined that he should take his responsible employment strategy one step further by deliberately ensuring that he was not employing any illegal immigrants. This resulted in the loss of almost 50 percent of his workforce overnight! One who failed the legal citizenship test found a job with one of the largest hotel chains in the United States with a strong reputation as a socially responsible corporation; another left to join a local school district.

MEASURES OF SUCCESS

Because of its very rapid growth over the past several years, GRX has been unable to develop many meaningful measures of operational sustainability improvement. One important one, however, concerns the percentage of material diverted from landfills.

When Wright bought GRX in 2004, the Denver facility was processing about 30,000 pounds of e-waste per month and a 40-foot container was leaving the yard about once a week with material to be landfilled. By 2008, the same facility was handling about 600,000 pounds per month with only a single container leaving for the local landfill. Wright estimates that the recycling rate is now about 94 percent. Most of the landfilled material comprises wood from old TV cabinets.

The sustainable business model developed during 2005–2006 allowed the company to establish successful start-up operations in Salt Lake City and Omaha, and the company also bought and turned around the struggling operation of a competitor in Colorado Springs. By the summer of 2008, the entire company was handling close to 1 million pounds of electronic waste per month, making it by far the largest operation of its kind in the Rocky Mountain region.

Admittedly aided by soaring global commodity prices in 2007 and 2008, GRX achieved extremely strong levels of profitability during this period (by 2008, the original model of 70 percent up-front collection fees and 30 percent in back-end material sales had more or less exactly reversed itself as the typical revenue breakdown for a responsible e-waste recycler). Although Wright will not divulge specific income figures, the company's financial success and high profile in the industry attracted the attention of a number of potential buyers. After an internal debate about whether GRX should become a major industry consolidator or itself become part of a larger corporation, in the summer of 2008, Wright finally elected to sell the company to Singapore-based Centrillion Environmental and Recycling. At the time of the sale, and including earn-out elements, the purchase price was estimated to be about $7 million. Wright thinks that the final purchase consideration could even be higher depending on the performance of Centrillion's stock price on the Singapore stock exchange.

Part of the sale arrangement was that Wright would remain with the organization for a period following the purchase. Centrillion has been pursuing a consolidation strategy in the U.S. electronics recycling industry and, since the acquisition of GRX, has also purchased Metech, another industry leader with operations in Massachusetts, California, and North Carolina. Wright assumed the role president of the entire U.S. operation, reporting to Centrillion's chief operating officer.

The joint GRX/Metech operation will process about 22 million pounds of electronic scrap in 2009, and Wright has initiated a variety of operational improvements that he estimates will enable the company to accommodate up to 35 million pounds in 2010, making it one of the largest electronics recyclers in the country. Quite a ride for a former systems integration company entrepreneur who bought a broken down little company operating out of a dog-infested junkyard in Denver!

One final footnote: GRX has, not surprisingly, completely overwhelmed all of its local competitors in Denver and across the state of Colorado. However, the company whose story opened this chapter, after a period of several months of inactivity, has apparently recently resurfaced as an active player in the local e-waste industry. Wright knows that the responsible business model he has created for GRX is in no danger of losing out to competitors that continue to engage in unscrupulous business practices, turning a blind eye to the adverse environmental and social consequences of their activities.

On the other hand, Wright wonders why the owner of a business that has been savaged by the media for many months and raided by the EPA would want to raise his head again in the same industry. Perhaps he's learned from his mistakes and deserves a chance to demonstrate his ability to make a positive contribution to the ongoing efforts of Mike Wright and like-minded competitors to turn the e-waste business into a genuinely sophisticated, cleantech industry that provides good domestic employment opportunities and recycles millions of tons of discarded material back into the global manufacturing economy. Perhaps he just doesn't know when he's beaten.

LESSONS LEARNED

(1) "Negative consequences may or may not be recognized by the cleantech business owner, but they represent a set of consequences that will eventually destroy his or her competitive advantage and render the business model unsustainable in the long run."

(2) "GRX developed a comprehensive statement of its operating processes that included verifiable information about how the equipment was destroyed and where the constituent materials were disposed of."

(3) "GRX began to find a solid marketing opportunity by encouraging landlords and building managers to hold e-waste recycling days, which they would advertise heavily to their tenants. These proved an extremely useful way to concentrate collection activities and, at the same time, promote the company and its responsible recycling activities to a large range of smaller organizations."

(4) Essential elements of GRX's game plan include: Guaranteed total destruction of old electronic equipment collected from customers, maximum commitment to genuine recycling of constituent materials and landfill diversion, total transparency on all aspects of the company's operations, and an open invitation to potential customers to drop in at any time unannounced to conduct an operations audit of GRX's activities.

REFERENCES

"Following the Trail of Toxic E-waste," *60 Minutes,* November 6, 2008 (produced by Solly Granatstein, CBS Interactive, Inc.), http://www.cbsnews.com/stories/2008/11/06/60minutes/main4579229.shtml

Huo, Xia, Lin Peng, Xijin Xu, Liangkai Zheng, Bo Qui, Zongli Qi, Bao Zhang, Dai Han, and Zhongxian Piao, "Elevated Blood Lead Levels of Children in Guiyu: An Electronic Waste Recycling Town in China, *Environmental Health Perspectives* 115, no. 7, July 2007. http://www.ncbi.nlm.nih.gov/pmc/articles/PMC1913570/

Puckett, Jim, Leslie Byster, Sarah Westervelt, Richard Gutierrez, Sheila Davis, Asma Hussain, Madhumitta Dutta (edited by Jim Puckett and Ted Smith), Basel Action Network and Silicon Valley Toxics Coalition, *Exporting*

Harm—The High-Tech Trashing of Asia, February 25, 2002, http://www. ban.org/E-waste/technotrashfinalcomp.pdf

RoHS, "Read about the EEC Efforts To Make the Electronic Equipment Manufacturers More Responsible for End-of-Life Issues," *RoHS (Restriction of Hazardous Substances) Guide: Info Guide to the RoHS Directive and WEE Compliance, 2002,* http://www.rohsguide.com/

ELEVEN

Denver Machine Shop: Sustainability through Four Generations

Stephen R. Bernard

Founded in 1916, Denver Machine Shop, Inc., uses sustainable business practices that have been passed down through four generations in this family-owned business. Ethical business practices, community service, and the daily work of repairing equipment to extend its useful life are at the core of this business. Few businesses can claim sustainable business practices for this length of time. The White family emphasized passing forward high ethical standards with each new generation, and this was acknowledged when the family and employees were selected as finalists for the 2008 Business Ethics Award presented by the Colorado Ethics in Business Alliance. What are the business practices that have propelled this company forward with a vibrant business model? Leaders in the emerging sustainability economy can learn from the experiences offered by the owners and employees of Denver Machine Shop.

This chapter explores the hurdles and successes experienced by the company along its sustainability journey. Denver Machine's employees take pride in working together as a team and valuing the experience of each employee. The company has extensive experience in helping other companies with alternatives to the wasteful dispose-and-replace mode of equipment use that is too common today. We can learn from Denver Machine Shop's expertise in extending equipment life through equipment repair, rebuild, and reuse. This important business practice reduces demand on resources while sustaining a vital network of small and larger businesses.

HISTORY

Denver Machine Shop was founded in 1916 by Fred A. White, great grand-father to the current owners, Scott and Eric White. The business was origi-nally located at 1417 18th Street in Denver, moved first to 1409 Blake Street in 1938, and then to its present location at 3280 Denargo Street in 1996 (White and White, 2008; Denver Machine Shop, n.d.; Scott White, 2008).

In 1956, Fred's son, Edwin F. White, assumed management of the com-pany. In 1976, Edwin F. retired, and his son E. James (Jim) White became president. Jim and his wife, Lee, ran the company until 2003, when Scott E. White purchased the company. In 2005, Scott's brother, Eric J. White, joined as a 50 percent partner. Scott and Eric are, therefore, fourth-generation own-ers of Denver Machine Shop. Edwin, Jim, Scott and Eric are all graduate engineers from the Colorado School of Mines. The White family provided the following historical description.

The first picture was taken in the original building on 18th Street in down-town Denver around 1925. The shop was on two floors and had single motors

Denver Machine Shop around 1925. (Courtesy of Denver Machine Shop, Inc.)

turning multiple lathes using shafts, sheaves, and leather belts to drive and change the speed of the machines.

The tooling used to cut the metal was hardened tool steel that was ground to shape by hand. Industry at that time required shafts, pulleys, and gears, much like today. Many parts required casting to get to approximate shapes so that machining was minimized. The castings required carved wooden patterns made by pattern makers, which were then used to form sand castings into which melted steel was poured. Denver Machine Shop operated one of the first sand-casting foundry operations in the Denver area.

The shop flourished with industrialism in the early 20th century. The company's main customers were from the local gold and silver mining industry; the steel industry in Pueblo, Colorado; the sugar industry; and the transportation industry, which needed shafts and wheels for wagons and buggies; and the railroads. Since there were few telephones at the time, much of the business was discussed daily at the business tables in the old Oxford Hotel where industry folks joined for lunch. "Back when my great grandfather ran this company," says Scott White, "time moved at a different speed" (Scott White, 2008). His great grandfather walked regularly to what is now McCormick's Restaurant in the old Oxford Hotel. Over lunch, Fred White would work with a pattern maker for a pattern, a steel supplier for the steel required, an engineer for planning, and other business owners for supplies and tooling to fulfill an order. After lunch or the next day, the supply items were delivered by wagon, the castings were made, engineering completed, and machining undertaken. The bill was settled after job completion, many times at the table in the Oxford. The old ledger books show pricing at that time was sometimes as low as $0.50 for material and $1.50 for labor. The shop had five furnace kilns, many kinds of patterns, and did sand casting. It didn't have ready-made materials like blocks of steel to make items like wheels.

In support of World War II equipment demands, the U.S. government contracted with companies like Denver Machine Shop to manufacture items required for the war effort. The shop moved to a larger facility at 14th and Blake Street in downtown Denver in 1938 and, during the war, was assigned to make howitzer shells and Jeep parts on a priority basis. The crew that was assembled for the war effort can be seen in the second shop photo, taken in 1944.

Edwin F. White went to work with his father at Denver Machine Shop in 1946 after being honorably discharged from army active duty. Ed was familiar with air compressors and related air equipment because he already worked as an engineer. Ed was an army ordnance officer during World War II, and, through these contacts, he negotiated for Denver Machine Shop to be

Denver Machine Shop at its new, larger facility in 1938. (Courtesy of Denver Machine Shop, Inc.)

Denver Machine Shop crew, assembled for the war effort in 1944. (Courtesy of Denver Machine Shop, Inc.)

the Colorado distributor for the LeRoi Air Compressor Company, which became the LeRoi division of Dresser Industries. The distribution business grew to the point where a separate company was created in 1956, Denver Air Machinery Company. While running this business, Ed also oversaw operations at Denver Machine Shop. In 1969, E. James (Jim) White joined his father, Ed, at both companies. Prior to that time, Jim worked for Shell Oil Company as a petroleum engineer and served two years as an officer in the Army Corps of Engineers during the Vietnam War. Jim took over as president of Denver Air Machinery and Denver Machine Shop in 1976, when his father Ed retired. With the downturn of the mining and construction industries in the 1980s, the distribution business was closed and Jim and his wife, Lee, concentrated solely on Denver Machine Shop. At this time, the company was servicing not only the local area but also the mining industry in southern Wyoming. As that mining business dwindled, the company started rebuilding with emphasis on the local companies served. The company continued to grow, and, in 2002, Scott White joined his father and purchased the company. Jim remained for two years in a training capacity before retiring. In 2004, Eric White joined his twin brother as 50 percent owner of Denver Machine Shop. Following college, Scott spent several years as a metallurgical engineer for Caterpillar and served as a reserve officer in the army Ordnance Corps. Eric completed his master's degree in mining engineering then served four years as an officer in the Army Corps of Engineers prior to joining Caterpillar. Both Scott and Eric spent three years with Autoliv in Aurora, Colorado, prior to joining the company.

A MISSION OF SERVICE

Denver Machine Shop has provided general machine work services under the same family ownership since 1916. Scott White, one of the current owners, says, "We rebuild things, so we keep the machines going and keep them tight. That's part of what we do. Rebuilding the machines is a core competency." Competitors typically make a brand new replacement part. "If we can rebuild a part for 60 percent of its value," he says, "most customers will go for the rebuild process. In a lot of cases, parts are unavailable or overseas, or have a six month lead time, and then we get involved with our customers."

REBUILDING AND REPAIRING—A SUSTAINABLE ALTERNATIVE TO BUYING NEW

Often, Denver Machine can change the alloy or material of component parts to make an overall repair more cost-effective. For example, the articulation pivot on an underground bore miner takes 4 hours to change the pin and 20 hours to change the bushing. By making the pin to bear the brunt of wear and tear, instead of the bushing, the machine shop can save the mine 16 hours of down time when the pivot needs repair. Purchasing a new pin and a new bushing from the factory, even if less expensive than the remanufactured parts, is not always the most economical decision.

"A lot of equipment in modern industry is either foreign or it's old," says Eric White (2009). "For example, there's a lot of printing press and food manufacturing parts that are from Italy. So, not only would it be an expensive part if you could find it in Italy, but you would also have the shipping involved in getting it here. It is more economical to rebuild from a cash standpoint if you're going to save the shipping price, and, if the part is old enough, they probably don't even have the part on the shelf." Therefore, a customer often chooses getting the part made since it will arrive sooner and they avoid the shipping costs. Also, with a one- or two-day turnaround, a machine that is sitting idle on a production line with a broken part can get back up and running. "So, economically, that could be worth hundreds, thousands, maybe even millions of dollars to a production line," says Eric. "Shipping impacts the environment because more fossil fuels are used to bring these parts over on the barges and boats," Eric continues. "And, if we can keep things close to our vicinity, not only are we helping our own economy, but it just makes sense as a social responsibility."

To give an example in the mining industry, consider a part on a mining shovel made in Germany, a linkage pin. "That part has to either come from Germany, or it has to get made or supplied here," says Eric. "In that case, let's say that that mining shovel makes a thousand dollars an hour while it's running. Then consider that there are 8 or 10 mining trucks that are sitting behind that mining shovel that are waiting to get filled. So, if the shovel doesn't work, then eight or nine trucks can't work. So, if we can get a part fixed very fast and put back into the overall operation, it can be worth a lot more than what the part is worth."

Quick repair of a fan shaft in a school, another example, can be crucial. If the school must wait to get that fan shaft replaced, then the kids can't go to school and the teachers can't go to work due to the lack of air circulation. The shop would either have to fix the fan shaft quickly or order a new shaft to keep the school running. If the shop can get the repair job done faster, that may be the best overall economical solution.

"Our industry protects the environment by either rebuilding or reusing worn parts versus the purchase of a new part and the worn part is perhaps discarded," Eric says.

TYPES OF PRODUCTS AND SERVICES

Denver Machine Shop serves Colorado businesses such as mining, newspaper printers, and restaurants. It operates on a job-shop basis performing maintenance, repair, and special manufacturing needs, including the following:

- General machine work
- Steel fabrication
- Bearing surface weld repair
- Spray metal surface repair
- Mining and industrial equipment rebuild
- Manufacture of special machinery
- In-field welding and boring service
- Prototypes and samples made
- Custom-made drill steel dies
- Short-run production jobs
- Custom steel fabrication
- Emergency services

A SUSTAINABILITY ETHIC FROM THE BEGINNING

"Back in 1916 when my great grandfather started Denver Machine Shop," says Eric, "sustainability was a way of life because raw materials and other things that we take for granted today—parts that can be flown in on a day's notice—weren't available."

Society was actually quite sustainable in the early 1900s, because equipment had to be repaired or rebuilt out of necessity rather than replaced. Materials used to make new parts tended to be those that were on hand, local, and recycled. For example, steel was, and continues to be, the most recycled material used. Steel "had to be re-melted and poured into dies or recast and then remachined back into a shape that was useful for the product that it needed," says Eric. "With that concept—to repair something rather than throw it away when it's broken and buy something new—is not just a strategy for us, it's our entire business. It's what we do." Denver Machine continues to this day with keeping old machines running for Colorado businesses by making and repairing parts in the machines.

Denver Machine Shop, therefore, didn't initiate a comprehensive sustainability program but used a sustainable management approach that has kept the company in business for almost a century. The family intentionally kept the company small into the current fourth generation and chose to not become one of the giant manufacturing and fabrication companies. The Whites learned and passed down business practices of managing with multiple "hats" in engineering design, marketing, accounting, and other small business essentials.

CUSTOMERS ARE KEY STAKEHOLDERS

Denver Machine starts with customers and helping to keep their businesses running. "If someone's elevator breaks down," says Scott, "the service people come to us and we're the ones that make a new shaft or repair a pulley so that an elevator can be running the next day." Jim White recalled, "When I took over the business, many of our longtime customers would approach me at a Denver Rotary Meeting. 'Jim, never let Denver Machine Shop close because my business can't continue without you.' "Now that's an honor, but more of a responsibility, to the rest of the business community," Jim said (Jim White and Lee White, 2008).

RECYCLING AND EFFICIENCY AT DENVER MACHINE

What has Denver Machine done to make its business more sustainable? "For one thing," says Scott, "we take a beginning-to-end approach." All metal scrap and shavings including steel, brass, and aluminum are recycled. "We reuse materials wherever they can be used, so nothing goes to waste. Our tooling is made of carbide, and even the carbide is collected and recycled."

In this way, Denver Machine contributes to the metals recycling business, which, in turn, is a strong contributor to sustainability. In 2008, the scrap recycling industry processed about 150 million tons of materials, a capacity that supports billions of dollars of investments by the industry in infrastructure and equipment. This is sustainability in practice by actively converting used materials into raw materials that are used to produce new products. These raw materials were an export commodity valued at about $28 billion, supporting trade with over 150 countries in 2008. Recycled scrap materials account for about 40 percent of the world's raw materials. Reduction in energy consumption is another major factor. Recycled steel results in energy savings of about 50 percent of the energy needed to make new steel from ore. Recycled copper and aluminum each save over 90 percent on energy use. By using less energy, the use of recycled metals in manufacturing also reduces greenhouse gas emissions (Institute of Scrap Recycling Industries, 2009).

Denver Machine has several large pieces of equipment. Use of these machines is balanced to minimize wasted energy. All compressors and machines are turned off at night. "It's probably easier to leave them on all the time," says Scott, "but it's less friendly to the environment. So, there is some warm-up period in the morning for our machines because of our practices, but it probably saves us some money as well in the long run."

A LEGACY OF CONTRIBUTION TO SOCIETY

Sustainable business practices also require a social contribution. Denver Machine uses a family-style approach with employment practices. "Every time a person is hired, we review our code of ethics with that person to make sure that they buy into our philosophy," says Scott, "and to make sure that they are a fit." This includes active participation in local community organizations. The owners and employees contribute time on a regular basis to support community service activities. The owners of Denver Machine have supported the Rotary Club of Denver and Rotary International through four generations of membership with annual financial and volunteering contributions. Donations reach the local community as well as all over the world. Ed and Jim served on the board of directors of the Rotary Club of Denver, and Eric is serving on the board in 2010. Eric, Scott, and Jim are also strong supporters with their time and financial contributions to the Colorado School of Mines.

"Though our participation in Rotary," says Eric, "we directly affect the social well-being of our community." Through Rotary, they work with the Denver Kids Club, helping students who are at risk of not graduating from high school. "If they don't graduate from high school," Eric continues, "they go on and lead lives which are not as productive. Eventually this costs society quite a bit more than if we just help them get through the first step and get them on to a responsible job." Lee White personally mentored one Denver at-risk student for a few years. "We have a 90 percent graduation rate," says Eric. "By changing the lives of those individuals, it's really going to better our society in the future. I probably spend at least 10 to 15 percent of my time during the work day working for the Rotary Club." In 2009, they donated to the 9 Health for Kids program, working with schools to help children who would not ordinarily have a chance to get medical help. In 2008, they donated to Totes for Hope, a program of the Food Bank for the Rockies, volunteering to fill backpacks for children with food from the food bank. These at-risk kids are fed normally two meals a day and a snack through the public system, but on Saturdays and Sundays, there's no food in the cupboard for them. "So, they come back on Monday and they haven't eaten for two days," says Eric. "How are they going to learn?"

PASSING SUSTAINABILITY DOWN THROUGH GENERATIONS

Most guidance today pertains to how a business can sustain itself for one generation or less. For a legacy of sustainability that passes through generations, the business has to do things right, including providing a needed service, being ethical, working hard, and wisely investing time and money. "Sustainability is great for one generation," says Jim, "but in order to be able to make a company last for more than 20 or 30 years, like ours, you've got to have some means or some plan to be able to pass the ship to the next generation of managers." What are the sustainability principles used by this family business successfully for the past 92 years?

First, a well-thought-out business plan is essential to get from one generation to the next. "You have to, first of all, identify who that leader, or leaders as in the case of our sons, will be," says Jim White. Once you've identified that person who can continue the business and shares the same ethical standards, then you must train him or her. Then once the new leader is trained, you must transfer the responsibility over to him or her. "The most important thing that most business owners often forget," says Jim White, "is that they have to move aside and let that next generation do their thing. If they continue to try to control everything, they really haven't passed the torch and that's where most businesses that try to change fail: because the older generation tries to hang on too long."

Second, successful transitions require that each new leader be qualified and have the desire to make the transition succeed. A small business cannot afford to pay for a nonproducer, and the family did not take prequalifications for granted. The White family, through four generations, took steps to ensure that each leadership position was filled by a fully qualified person. They even emphasize that if no family member is qualified, then it is critical to find someone else from outside who is qualified if the owner wants the business to continue successfully.

Third, education was always stressed in this family business to prepare passing the operation to each generation. Scott's father, Jim, encouraged Scott and his brother Eric to work in an industry of their choice and hold jobs for several years prior to joining the company as part of the management team, just as his father did for him. They also worked for the company during high school and college and were exposed to the company's operations and high ethical standards. Upon their return to the business, they had the background and experience they needed to begin their training to manage the business. His grandfather ran a different machine shop, educated his son, and his son worked for the company through high school and college. He maintained the books for the company while he was in college.

Fourth, after passing responsibilities to the new person and moving aside so that the new leader has room to grow, then the previous leader should be available during the transition to advise the new management when they ask for help. This provides a valuable advantage with keeping the small business associated with its past successes and in touch with its reputation as it grows and moves forward.

Finally, each qualified successor, along with running the business at a profit, must use high ethical standards, keep the welfare of all employees foremost in mind, and keep the customer's changing needs satisfied. Maintaining these principles should sustain the business from one generation to the next with a thriving business that supports a thriving community and the environment.

SUSTAINABILITY THROUGH ECONOMIC UPTURNS AND DOWNTURNS

"Over a period of time," says Jim, "the economy plays tricks on you, and so businesses cannot thrive on an ongoing, unchanging basis. There's going to be downturns; there's going to be times when the country's at war, times when the country's in a depression." The White family recalls that Denver Machine Shop has been at the top and at the bottom with respect to the economy probably four times for almost a century now. Jim emphasizes, "During the times when you're not thriving, you have to tighten the belt and you've got to continue to serve your customers, and you have to keep the main corners of your business moving forward. But during those times it's real easy to say, well, 'I think I'll just give up,' and a lot of companies do, but you can hang on if you tighten the belt far enough. You have to adjust the business." Unfortunately, twice in Jim's lifetime, Denver Machine had to squeeze the business down to less than four employees. However, because the family maintained their principles, the business has sustained and it now is a healthy business with 24 employees.

WEARING MANY HATS FOR BUSINESS SUSTAINABILITY

Lee White, Jim's wife, says, "I think also that you have to have the ability to wear many hats. If you are very profitable and you have a large workforce, then maybe you don't have to be so aggressive to go out and sell. Maybe you can hire people to sell for you. But, if the economy really goes down, unless you find a different niche, you're going to have to go out yourselves and sell." Other hats a small business needs to wear include everything from watering the plants to handling customers; taking care of the receivables, payables, and collections; ordering materials; and completing computer records. As times improve, you can hire people to take over for you so that you can focus on a priority area. Lee says, "When Jim and I were in the recession of the '80s, we were down to so few employees that I was doing most of the computer input, accounting, and hiring. And so we did everything." Then, as the business grew, they could afford to hire someone to focus on the detail work. Family members needed "to be willing to roll with the times, and be willing to take nothing (in salary) at times. "I was willing to take everything I knew and owned in the world and go with Jim," says Lee, "instead of going off in my own career. And I'm sure that's what Jim's mother did."

Scott says, "I've been very fortunate, because when I bought the business from my folks, they agreed to stay on for a while to help. I still work with my dad quite a bit on the accounting and looking at the books and understanding what's going on and make critical decisions. It's been six years now and we still utilize them as consultants. I appreciate their help and I don't think that anybody, especially an engineer, would go out and have enough confidence to buy a business or start a business, but they were there to say 'yes we can.' This business has been around over 90 years and we can show you how it works. It would have been very difficult to make that transition without having that support network. Our business is built on ethics and how we treat each other." Denver Machine Shop has demonstrated this as finalists for the Ethics in Business Alliance awards in 2007 and 2008.

OVERCOMING HURDLES

"I think that we've always been sustainable," says Scott. "We have a culture of sustainability for our community and for ourselves." One of the hurdles that Denver Machine Shop had recently relates to the building of new high-rise buildings around the shop. The Whites, recognizing that they want to continue being a friend to the community, made a commitment to the city and to the developers that they'll work with them being a good neighbor. They moved their weld facilities so that they don't create smoke and noise pollution. They keep their yards clean and work to coexist as an industry near the newer residential dwellings.

"One thing that I think helps sustain our business," says Jim, "is that we always tried to stay in a certain niche. It's one of the things I worked with Scott on as he wanted to grow the business. I try to pull the reins in. You can't go too fast. You need to keep your capital up with your spending needs. One of the things that kills businesses more than anything else is the fact that they are doing well. More businesses go out of business in good times than in bad times because when they're doing well they grow, business is easy to come by, and the next thing you know, they can't pay all their bills. So, you have to really keep the reins in on the growth. You have to grow steadily, but you have to keep the reins on. Over my lifetime, I've gone from many employees down to two or three employees, two or three times, because you have to keep your expenses in line with what business is there. When the market goes down, you can cut back."

"Our whole concept," says Scott, "is that we're doing it like we always have. We've never moved into the type of business practices where we suddenly needed to turn around and 'become' green. Rather than choosing a path of manufacturing many copies of the same parts, the family made a conscious decision to stay within their repair business niche and to not become a contract manufacturer. This is how they started, how they are now, and how they plan to be in the future.

"One of the biggest mistakes that we've made as a business," says Scott, "occurred a couple of times in past generations. We chose to take care of only one or two major customers and fell into the trap of not taking a community approach to our business." The company lost customers and had to rebuild the business. The owners learned from these experiences, and today they are very concerned about the community and care for their walk-in customer base. Now, Denver Machine Shop works to a model that aims to prevent giving any one customer more than 20 percent of their business. Walk-in customers cost more, but "we see it as service where we're here and available to help a neighbor who breaks her lamp, or a guy who comes in with a snow blower to be fixed. No job is too little, and very few are too large."

SUSTAINABILITY AT THE CORE
OF DENVER MACHINE SHOP

"I think that we're constantly looking for new products and services that we can provide," says Scott, "but, at the same time, we still maintain the core of our business. Old brochures show that the company got its start rebuilding equipment. Sustainability "goes back to the heart of craftsmanship," says Scott. "And craftsmanship is one of our core values. And, as a craftsman, every piece of work that we do is delivered in a spirit of the craftsman. And, so each job is like a piece of art or like something that somebody would be proud of to give to the customer. And it's part of our culture, it's our core values of integrity and craftsmanship, are right there. That's how we achieve the sustainability focus in our company. It's who we are." This remains the core of the business. "So, as we re-direct our marketing efforts, we're very much in the rebuild and the remanufacturing business."

"I would say that we are the leaders in our industry, says Scott. "And that our message of rebuilding and remanufacturing is taken very well by our customer base. I think that, in most cases, if a customer can benefit and if we can benefit from taking the old-fashioned value approach, as opposed to the throw-it-out-and-buy-something-new approach, then that would be our brand. People call us because there is a lot of goodwill built up over a hundred years. People call Denver Machine Shop because they know that we're going to get them out of a jam, and that we're also going help them get going again with the equipment that they've got."

COMPETITION

Most competitors focus on contract manufacturing rather than the repair business, so there is not a lot of competition. Denver Machine fills a niche repairing equipment rather than replacing it. They participate in the Rocky Mountain Tool and Machine Association, where they can collaborate with many of the other shops in town. Scott is currently president of this association.

When asked whether the company's sustainability strategy delivers a real competitive advantage, Scott says, "I would say yes, our competitive advantage is that we are able to work on things that nobody else can. We've got the size, capacity, and ability to take care of major remanufacture projects that very few people in the country can take care of. And so it is a real competitive advantage to be able to offer the rebuild procedure or part."

MACHINE SHOP METRICS

Denver Machine has been profitable for 93 years, with some years more than others. "When you have about 100 years of good will behind you," says Scott, "the customers trust you. They know that you are going to do the right thing, and they believe in your service and your product. I would say that those metrics speak for themselves." As a small business, the company focuses on four shop metrics of on-time delivery, quality, safety, and value. It makes a conscious effort to conserve energy and recently purchased a new shop system that allows the company to computerize most manual functions. "It's allowed us to reduce our preprinted forms," says Scott, "and we've saved over $3,000 a year."

When a customer's critical machine is down, or he has a crew of men who can't work because of a breakdown, getting the customer back in business quickly is the highest priority. It is estimated that Denver Machine Shop has saved hundreds of thousands of dollars for its customers during emergency breakdown situations. For example, the cost of refurbishing a coal-pulverizing roller hub, which retails for over $40,000, is usually less than $6,000. The cost of a new underground loader boom is over $100,000, while the cost of remanufacture from Denver Machine Shop is usually less than $10,000. These types of refurbishments are typical for Denver Machine Shop and represent much of what it does. Sustainability works because, in addition to being less of a burden on the environment and society, it is often the most economical choice.

SUSTAINABILITY AND THE 2009 RECESSION

How is the current economy affecting the business and sustainability? The company's doors are open, but profit is flat in this economy. Much can be learned about how the company is doing by again looking back at the history of the company beginning about 100 years ago. It always served the local manufacturing industry but also retained business diversity. The company's challenges go back to projects like remaking a wagon wheel so that a farmer could take his apples to market. Then, during the Great Depression, their great-grandfather made it through that economy using his basic machinist skills to survive with a limited number of local jobs. Prior to World War II, the company serviced the mining and local industries. During the war effort, the mining and local industries slowed and the company supported the war effort by making howitzer shells and other hardware. Business grew, as shown in the photograph, with over 30 employees. After the war, the company serviced the mining community, including the community in Wyoming that mined trona ore, which is used to make glass for porcelain materials. Denver Machine Shop also continued servicing local industry, including bakeries and food companies. The mining industry dropped in 1984, new equipment was not being bought, and its sister air machinery company had to close its doors. "At that point," says Eric, "my folks concentrated heavily on the industry which was available to them." The industry available was in the city, including elevator repair and food companies like the Safeway canary, and some bakeries. It also serviced sand and gravel operations until the economy picked up again. Then, as Scott and Eric became owners, the company concentrated on servicing equipment for the expanding construction industry, including the Denver International Airport, T-REX highway, and light rail projects by servicing construction equipment.

Now, vertical and horizontal construction has slowed, so the company is servicing machinery in the touring industry, including refurbishing parts of a 1950s vintage transcontinental 21-car train for a touring company. Another example in the new economy is servicing the medical industry with a project to outfit more than 20 vans for a business that takes X-rays of people in their homes. The vans are being equipped with mechanical ramps engineered to move special processing equipment for access into homes. Denver Machine Shop is also servicing the machines for a company that builds orthotics for shoes, including army military boots.

"The point is that," Eric says, "as the economy changes, part of the longevity and the sustainability of this company is definitely its ability to jump from industry to industry to industry" while holding to its core business and ethical standards. "Diversification is the key to sustainability," he continues. "Every generation would have lost everything if we weren't able to adjust into the markets that are available at the time when the economic downturns happened. I'm not saying we've had it easy." This, by the way, includes staying involved with the community. As an active member of the community in up and down economic times, this family-owned business provides support through smaller contributions in nonprofitable years and larger contributions in more profitable years, thereby making a positive difference to society, the economy, and the environment.

LESSONS LEARNED

(1) Know your core business, which, for Denver Machine, is rebuilding and remanufacturing.
(2) Challenge the throw-it-out-and-buy-new approach.
(3) Fill a niche that fulfills a need in society, and service a diversity of clients.
(4) Be a positive community leader.
(5) Apply high levels of ethics in decisions.
(6) Include materials reduction, reuse, recycling, energy efficiency, and associated cost avoidance in business planning.
(7) Apply the three primary principles of sustainability and reduce your costs, improve your environment, and contribute to your community.

REFERENCES

Colorado Ethics in Business Alliance, *Awards: 2008 Finalists,* March 20, 2008, http://www.ceba.org/awards-2008finalists.html

Denver Machine Shop, Inc., n.d., http://www.denvermachineshop.com

Institute of Scrap Recycling Industries, Inc., *Scrap Recycling Industry Facts,* June 2009, http://www.isri.org/Content/NavigationMenu/Industry Information/IndustryFacts/scrap_recycling_industry_facts_6_25_2009.pdf

U.S. Environmental Protection Agency, *Municipal Solid Waste Generation, Recycling, and Disposal in the United States: Facts and Figures for 2008,* http://www.epa.gov, accessed Jan 2010 http://www.epa.gov/osw/nonhaz/municipal/pubs/msw2008rpt.pdf

White, Eric, Personal interview, December 20, 2009.

White, Jim, and Lee White, Personal interviews, September–November 2008.

White, Scott, Personal interviews, March 12, 2008, and October 2008.

White, Scott, and Eric White, Personal notes, 2008.

ADDITIONAL READING

Clasgens, J. Colorado Business Ethics and Sustainability Award Nominee—Denver Machine Shop, unpublished research paper, supporting the Ethics in Business Alliance award in 2008.

TWELVE

First Affirmative Financial Network: Responding to Socially Conscious Market Demand

Graham Russell

In 2007, some $2.71 trillion was invested in socially responsible assets, according to the *2007 Report on Socially Responsible Investing Trends in the United States* (Social Investment Forum, 2007). Some other statistics from the same report include:

1. Nearly one out of every nine dollars under professional management in the United States is involved in SRI.
2. This investment level represents an increase of about 18 percent between 2005 and 2007, compared with an increase of just 3 percent for all assets under professional investment management.

First Affirmative Financial Network, LLC, is a professional investment management firm that has established a successful and leading position in the socially responsible investing (SRI) industry in response to the growing demand from individuals and organizations wishing to direct their investments toward companies that manage their operations in an environmentally and socially responsible manner with a view to creating a more sustainable global economy. The firm's history illustrates the development of a successful business that addresses the investing public's increasing concern about doing a better job of managing and conserving the planet's natural and human resources in order to leave future generations the opportunity to enjoy the same quality of life we enjoy now—or better.

COMPANY HISTORY

First Affirmative was formed in 1987 by a financial planning practitioner, Ed Winslow, in Colorado Springs, which remains its headquarters today, although it also has a satellite office in Boulder, Colorado, under the direction of its president, Steve Schueth. In 1989, George Gay, a former army officer who managed the financial affairs of most business operations at the U.S. Army base at Fort Carson, Colorado, joined the firm as chief executive officer. The company formed a strategic marketing alliance in 1989 with Co-op America, which was the beginning of its focus on socially responsible investing.

From the beginning, the goal of First Affirmative was to create a community of investment management professionals with a focus on the growing demand from socially conscious investors to direct their investments into channels that would address social and environmental needs, as well as generate a competitive financial return. Between 1992 and 1999, the firm was a wholly owned subsidiary of Walnut Street Securities, a registered broker-dealer based in St. Louis, Missouri, owned by MetLife.

Meanwhile, in 1989, Steve Schueth had joined the Calvert Group, then—as now—the largest mutual fund company in the country offering socially screened funds. In 1993, he became president of Calvert Distributors, responsible for handling relationships with broker-dealers around the country. During these years, he established a strong business relationship with George Gay as First Affirmative became a major source of new business for Calvert. In 1999, they joined forces to raise $1 million to buy back First Affirmative and its advisory business (not the commission business) from Walnut Street Securities, because they believed that First Affirmative could better serve the growing market demand from socially conscious investors as an independent organization. At the time of the purchase, First Affirmative had about $100 million of assets under management in fee accounts.

Today, Gay and Schueth own about 55 percent of the equity of First Affirmative, which—as a limited-liability company (LLC)—has about 40 members and is governed by an advisory board comprised of representatives from its six largest institutional members and its six largest network members. The firm has a permanent staff of 15 located in Colorado Springs, Boulder, and Denver and is managed by an executive team of four people, including Gay and Schueth. Its nationwide network of formally affiliated investment advisors has grown to over 100. Another 30 to 40 advisors benefit from the community of like-minded investment professionals that First Affirmative has developed and from various resources the company makes available to advisors dedicated to serving socially conscious investors. Toward the end of 2010, client assets under management had increased to nearly $700 million, down just 3 percent from the peak level prior to the onset of the 2008–2009 financial crisis.

SOCIALLY RESPONSIBLE INVESTING

Wikipedia defines socially responsible investing as "an investment strategy that seeks to maximize financial return and social good." (Wikipedia, 2010). SRI is not a new phenomenon. During the early decades of the 20th century, socially conscious investors sought to direct their investments in such a way as to enhance women's rights and, later—in the 1960s and 1970s—the rights of minority communities. Socially responsible investors' targets during the 1960s and 1970s included labor and management issues, the elimination of chemicals such as napalm (which was used with devastating environmental and human impact during the Vietnam War), the improvement of automobile fuel standards, and improved safety practices in the nuclear power industry (Wikipedia, 2010).

The apartheid regime in South Africa provided a fresh target for socially responsible investors during the 1980s, while major industrial disasters including Chernobyl, Bhopal, and the *Exxon Valdez* oil spill further stimulated the interest of many investors to push for more responsible business practices, as did the terrible working conditions found in overseas factories that manufactured goods for U.S. consumers.

In the 1990s and subsequently, SRI has increasingly focused on the concept of creating a more sustainable global economic model in the very widest sense. Many investors consider climate change, the devastation of the planet's natural environment (such as the destruction of the world's forests and overfishing of the oceans), and the rising prices of energy and many other commodities to be serious risks to companies that are—or are perceived to be—contributing to these problems. In the early years of the 21st century, the rights of indigenous peoples, the destruction of traditional lifestyles in many parts of the world by corporations or governments intent on exploiting natural resources such as oil and minerals, not to mention massive accounting fraud and governance failures in major U.S. corporations, have rounded out a very comprehensive list of sustainability issues that are now the object of the efforts of socially conscious investors.

**Table 12.1   Dollar Volume of Investments Directed to a Socially
or Environmentally Responsible Objective, 1995–2007
(in billions of dollars)**

1995	1997	1999	2001	2003	2005	2007
$639	$1,185	$2,159	$2,323	$2,164	$2,290	$2,711

The *2007 Report on Socially Responsible Investing Trends in the United States* (Social Investment Forum, 2007) showed that the dollar volume of investment directed to some form of socially or environmentally responsible objective has increased sharply over the past several years, as shown in Table 12.1.

It's worth noting that an increasing volume of research suggests that companies with a well-defined and proactive approach to environmental and social responsibility perform better than those that don't (A.T. Kearney, 2009; Aberdeen Group, 2009). The most recent ING Socially Responsible Investments Index (Mutual Funds, 2010), which tracks 50 stocks, returned 48.7 percent in 2009, compared with 39.3 percent for its global benchmark, the MSCI World benchmark, and just 26 percent for the S&P 500 Index, a list of the 500 largest publicly traded stocks in the United States. The same report showed that 65 percent of the 145 U.S.-based socially responsible mutual and exchange-traded funds tracked by Morningstar outperformed the S&P 500 in 2009. And the Social Investment Forum (2009) announced that two-thirds of SRI mutual funds in its universe outperformed their benchmarks in 2009. The increasingly evident correlation between *doing good* and *doing well* in the corporate world has been a major factor in increasing the volume of total SRI assets and seems likely to continue to do so.

TODAY'S SOCIALLY RESPONSIBLE INVESTOR

Philanthropy has, of course, existed for as long as humans have walked on the earth. However, over the past several decades, information concerning the degradation of the world's natural and human resources has become much more available. The public has begun to see both the actual consequences of resource depletion (such as the inexorably increasing price of oil and oil-derived products) as well as the potential risks of allowing our current exploitative economic model to continue unchecked (such as the dangers of human-induced climate change). This awareness has gradually led to the emergence of a large group of individuals in the populations of the world's developed countries with a desire to address some of these sustainability issues. This group is sometimes known as the Cultural Creatives (Ray & Anderson, 2000), who try to integrate their values into all aspects of the way they conduct their lives with the goal—in part, at least—of leaving behind a legacy consisting of an economic system that will allow future generations to have a quality of life at least as good as the one they enjoy.

These socially conscious investors understand that the business community has to play a major role in finding solutions to the world's sustainability challenges, because the massive resources of the world's corporations must be harnessed to get the job done. They also understand that corporations are ultimately dependent on the health of the human societies and eco-systems that provide the natural and human resources on which they depend for their existence. Today's socially responsible investor, therefore, is one who seeks to secure his or her own financial future while directing investment capital toward those business enterprises that he or she believes will consciously endeavor to create a more just and sustainable global economic model. Both individual and institutional investors are increasingly using their capital to force changes in the way public and private companies conduct their operations to address the world economy's sustainability issues.

SOCIALLY RESPONSIBLE INVESTMENT OPTIONS—A BEWILDERING CHOICE

During the 1970s, two mutual funds were created that screened companies for various types of environmental and social activity. A dozen more were launched in the early to mid-1980s. Screens could be either positive or negative (i.e., screening companies in or out of a portfolio). For example, some funds excluded companies in the alcohol, tobacco, gaming, and nuclear industries, as well as those with operations in South Africa during the apartheid era. Other funds embraced firms with strategies specifically aimed at doing some kind of environmental or social good in the way they operated, such as those producing organic foods and other products (such as Whole Foods Market). Some of the earliest socially responsible mutual fund groups included Calvert Group, Domini Social Investments, and Pax World Funds.

Since the mid-1990s, there has been an explosion in the number of vehicles through which socially conscious investors can satisfy their desire to put their money to work to address a specific set of environmental or social objectives. The 2007 SRI trends report (Social Investment Forum, 2007) reported a total of 260 socially screened funds (including mutual funds, exchange-traded funds, alternative investment funds, and other kinds of pooled products) aimed at addressing every conceivable type of value set held by socially conscious investors. In addition, more and more public companies, especially those operating on a global basis, have begun to address in a very deliberate and proactive fashion the demands being placed upon them by consumers, regulators, governments—and investors—to make their operations more sustainable. Examples of major corporations that have embraced sustainability as a fundamental driver of their strategic thinking include DuPont (2010), Walmart (2010), and General Electric (Ecomagination, 2010).

Socially conscious investors, therefore, have been faced with an increasingly bewildering array of SRI choices and have accordingly turned to professionals for investment advice in this area. First Affirmative has built its business model around this growing demand for knowledgeable and objective advice on sustainable and responsible investing, enabling it to successfully carve out a unique, industry-leading position in this steadily growing market.

BUSINESS MODEL

In the earliest days of its operations, the leadership of First Affirmative realized that a small number of traditional investment advisors were recognizing the growing demand from socially conscious investors to align their personal values with their investment portfolios. Many also wanted to put their money to work in helping to create a more sustainable global economic model. Following the rebirth of First Affirmative Financial Network as an independent firm in 1999, its objective was to create a community of such registered professional investment advisors and to act as a focal point for research into, knowledge of, and advice concerning the increasing number of SRI choices available to socially conscious investors. The firm originally tried to establish itself as a cooperative but found that Securities and Exchange Commission regulatory requirements rendered that option cumbersome and risky, eventually substituting an LLC format combined with a system for formally affiliating investment management professionals into its network through a membership system.

From the beginning, the company found that it became a sort of magnet for professionals focused on serving socially conscious investors, partly because almost no one else was operating in the space and partly because it was able to establish an early reputation for knowledge and objectivity in its dealings with them.

First Affirmative manages investment portfolios for both individual and institutional investors. Business is referred to the firm by its network of affiliated investment professionals. First Affirmative assumes full discretion and fiduciary responsibility for client accounts, which means, among other things, that it has full management control over the funds on a day-to-day basis and does not have to seek permission to trade in and out of investment vehicles. The firm's revenue comes from annual fees based on the amount of each account under its management. A portion of this fee is shared with the referring network advisor, who may be a broker or independent registered investment advisor.

Minimum account size is $50,000, and the firm manages accounts in the tens of millions of dollars. Smaller accounts are placed in one of a series of broadly diversified model mutual fund portfolios, depending on the amount of market risk the client can tolerate. Larger accounts can be managed on a more highly customized basis through the use of about 54 separate account managers. Each money manager provides a specific type or style of money management. First Affirmative diversifies client accounts among several managers of domestic and international stocks, fixed income, real estate, and other asset classes (such as Trillium Asset Management Corporation in Boston).

Most managers of traditional separate accounts require a minimum of at least $1 million to open an account. But the managers who work with First Affirmative manage model portfolios to which many First Affirmative clients may be subscribed in smaller amounts. This allows individual clients to access top-notch separate account managers with a fraction of their normal minimum account size requirement. First Affirmative monitors model manager performance, subscribes clients to model portfolios, rebalances across model portfolios, and fires underperforming managers with a few keystrokes.

As part of its client services, First Affirmative invests a portion of clients' money in community service investment vehicles, which direct capital to low-income communities that have difficulty in attracting capital from commercial sources. These community development financial institutions work to alleviate poverty, create jobs, provide affordable housing, and finance small business development in disadvantaged communities. About 3 percent of total money under management with First Affirmative is invested this way.

First Affirmative also votes the proxies of most of its clients. Proxy voting is conducted according to a comprehensive set of guidelines that are reviewed and updated annually and generally reflect the values and priorities of the broadest cross-section of First Affirmative clients. Clients can opt to vote their own proxies. Selectively, First Affirmative will also co-file shareholder advocacy resolutions in support of other, large investment management groups seeking to use their investing clout to encourage more responsible corporate behavior.

An important component of First Affirmative's attraction for professional investment managers with an interest in SRI has been its disciplined approach to understanding the values of socially conscious investors, which are extremely diverse. Like any other investment management firm, First Affirmative has a confidential client questionnaire it uses to understand the investment goals of individual and institutional investors, including their time horizons, return expectations, and risk tolerance levels. In addition, the firm asks a series of questions designed to establish the particular set of environmental and social objectives the investor wishes to support. Most investment management firms—even the larger ones such as Merrill Lynch and A. G. Edwards—do not readily understand the full range and subtleties of such values, so First Affirmative has taken on a mentoring role for brokers from both large and small investment management firms interested in providing SRI advisory services to their clients.

First Affirmative does not have a large research staff. Rather, it relies heavily on research conducted by the staff of socially responsible mutual fund companies like Calvert and Pax World, as well as independent SRI research organizations, to develop a deep understanding of what is really going on inside a company that professes to be committed to environmentally and socially responsible business practices. This has become progressively more important, because, as public pressure has increased on companies to do the right thing, many large companies have resorted to what is known as greenwashing—the practice of portraying their operations as sustainable, when, in reality, there is little substance to the claims. Schueth recalls one early example of this behavior when General Motors (GM) publicly lent its support to Ceres, a nonprofit organization founded in 1989 with the objective of challenging companies to direct their efforts to the well-being of the global environment and the communities in which they operate. At the same time, GM was vigorously lobbying to prevent vehicle fuel efficiency standards from being increased. It is this type of misleading, nontransparent corporate behavior that First Affirmative seeks to bring to the attention of its socially conscious investor clients.

SRI IN THE ROCKIES

One of the most important elements in the success of First Affirmative's development strategy has been an annual conference called SRI in the Rockies (2010). In 1990, First Affirmative was faced with the challenge of how to cost-effectively address its obligations as a supervisor of some 45 investment professionals scattered across the country. The solution was to bring the representatives to a central event in the form of a due diligence meeting, which grew into a conference.

What began in 1990 as a compliance-driven event has become the premier conference in North America focused on sustainable and responsible investing, routinely attracting hundreds of attendees from around the world to hear thought leaders talk about the latest trends and issues in SRI. First Affirmative remains the annual organizer of SRI in the Rockies, and its identification with the conference has been a critical component of the firm's marketing efforts to attract independent SRI management professionals from around the country and to encourage them to join its network.

WALKING THE TALK

Like some of the other case studies in this book, First Affirmative is a company with a business model that is intrinsically socially and environmentally responsible. However, unlike an aluminum smelter or any other company that uses large volumes of physical material in its operations, the firm's potential for reducing its environmental impact or a negative social footprint is somewhat limited. Nonetheless, Gay and Schueth recognize that it is important for the firm to do what it can internally to walk its talk, so the company has taken a number of steps over the years to improve the sustainability of its operations.

The firm has had a comprehensive recycling program since long before it was fashionable, and likewise has used recycled paper and soy-based ink for all of its printed materials. Travel is minimized by utilizing Internet (e-mail and an invitation-only social networking site), telephone, and webinar services to address the needs of its nationwide network of advisors. Senior company officials views the firm's highly visible involvement in the annual SRI in the Rockies Conference as a travel-avoiding event that enables its staff to meet extensively with its network members and potential members without requiring salespeople to chase around the country on airplanes.

When First Affirmative moved its Colorado Springs headquarters in 2008, it paid for the offices to be certified according to Leadership in Energy and Environmental Design commercial interiors (LEED CI) standards, using natural lighting wherever possible, low volatile organic compounds, and recycled furniture. During this effort, the firm was proud to educate the building landlord in some of the principles of green building management. One result is that the entire multistory building is now cleaned using nontoxic cleaning materials.

SRI in the Rockies represents a major opportunity to limit waste and carbon emissions. The firm inserted a green section into its annual request for proposals for the conference venue long before it became the norm in the events and hospitality industry. Schueth notes that hotels and other conference venues are now touting their green practices as a leading competitive advantage, but even seven or eight years ago, most of them didn't understand the concept of a green event. In addition to doing everything possible to minimize waste at the event, First Affirmative purchases carbon offsets for all electricity used at the conference as well as for the travel-related emissions of all attendees.

Like most companies with business models offering products or services that are intrinsically beneficial from an environmental or social standpoint, First Affirmative receives a large number of employment inquiries from people wanting to contribute through their work to making the world a better place. Because of this, the company is able to choose the very brightest and committed professionals, most of whom remain with the firm a long time, thereby reducing recruitment costs and enhancing productivity.

FIRST AFFIRMATIVE'S NETWORK OF ADVISORS— THE STRENGTH OF THE COMPANY

The central plank in the firm's growth strategy has been the creation of a community of professional investment managers dedicated to serving the needs of socially responsible investors around the country. This network— currently comprised of some 110 professionals with client assets under management with First Affirmative and another 50 affiliated or interested investment professionals—is one of the firm's greatest sources of strength. At the same time, growing this network also represents the greatest strategic challenge the firm faces today.

First Affirmative has become a magnet for investment professionals seeking advice and support in their efforts to serve the needs of the rising socially responsible investor market. The firm has fostered relationships with these brokers, financial planners, and investment advisors through a knowledgeable, responsive brand of service such that these relationships have become highly symbiotic. First Affirmative acts as a resource and trainer for its network advisors, supplying them with research information, methods for assisting their SRI clients, an annual world-class SRI education forum, and a range of SRI investment products that caters to every conceivable combination of socially conscious investment objectives. It also feeds them business by directing inquiries and leads to local advisors around the country. Likewise, the network of affiliated representatives feeds business to the firm by arranging for First Affirmative to manage their clients' funds.

MEASURES OF SUCCESS

The fact that First Affirmative's assets under management have grown from about $100 million at the time of the repurchase from Walnut Street Securities to just over $600 million 10 years later is a strong testament to the success of the firm's business model. That is a compound growth rate of approximately 20 percent. Despite the economic downturn and accompanying across-the-board decline in stock prices, the firm remained profitable in 2008 and 2009.

Perhaps the strongest vindication of the firm's approach to identifying the best SRI options for its clients can be found in the performance of its

Table 12.2   Performance of First Affirmative Managed Portfolios versus S&P 500, 2000–2009

FA Portfolio	2009	3 Years	5 Years	Since Inception (December 31, 1998)	Volatility Standard Deviation (3-year–%)
Diversified Equity	26.77	−6.82	−0.44	0.92	19.6
Capital Growth	23.62	−4.68	0.56	2.07	16.8
Balanced Growth	21.60	−3.12	1.08	2.15	14.9
Balanced	19.49	−1.74	1.64	2.82	12.8
Conservative Income/ Growth	16.82	−0.39	2.19	3.50	10.7
Indexes					
S&P 500	26.50	−5.64	0.40	0.85	19.2
Russell 1,000	25.47	−7.37	−1.23	0.92	19.2
Russell 2,000	27.17	−6.07	0.51	5.01	24.5

five core managed mutual fund portfolios. This performance is set out in Table 12.2, which shows the annualized return after expenses for the five managed portfolios, compared with three benchmark indexes for various periods ending December 31, 2009, as well as the volatility index (a measure of risk: the higher the standard deviation, the greater the risk level) for each portfolio and index. Over the 11-year period ending December 31, 2009, all five of them outperformed the S&P 500 stock index, with the best performer returning 46 percent over the decade versus just about 10 percent for the S&P and about 11 percent for the Russell 1,000 at significantly lower levels of risk in both cases. No small accomplishment in what is characterized as "the dismal decade."

Another strong indicator of the extent to which First Affirmative has not only delivered good returns to its clients but has also protected their investments against the devastating effects of some of the most irresponsible business practices of recent years, the firm had virtually zero exposure to the likes of Enron, WorldCom, Adelphia, AIG, and Lehman Brothers. This is a strong testament to the ability of First Affirmative to dig into what is really going on inside an apparently well-performing company and avoid those that have been operating what turned out to be fundamentally irresponsible and unsustainable business models.

CHALLENGES FOR THE FUTURE

Despite its success, First Affirmative faces some challenges in extending its business model. The fact is that the number of investment management professionals who actively target the needs of socially conscious investors on an exclusive, or even a predominant, basis remains very small. Out of some 500,000 licensed investment professionals in the United States, Schueth reckons that no more than about 500 understand the principles and the subtleties of SRI and are willing and able to make a conscious effort to secure the best possible advice in this area for their clients. How can this be, when it's quite clear that a much larger proportion of the general population has awakened to the idea that something needs to be done to create a more responsible and sustainable global economy? And when an increasing body of evidence suggests that socially responsible investments—both individual equities and mutual funds—tend to generate superior financial returns?

The simple answer is that, with the possible exception of the natural resources industry, the financial services industry is probably less concerned with socially and environmentally responsible business issues than any other industry. This has been savagely illustrated in the past several years by the subprime mortgage mess, which has not only destroyed hundreds of billions of dollars of wealth but also has caused untold social damage as families were enticed into buying homes they really could not afford, only to find themselves sliding into financial problems, even to the point of millions of personal bankruptcies. The subprime mess—largely a product of greedy, irresponsible behavior in the financial community—has even caused significant environmental damage in cities like Cleveland and Buffalo, where huge numbers of new homes—thrown up quickly a few years ago in response to the demand bubble created by unsustainable mortgage products—lie vacant, stripped bare of everything that can be removed, sitting in subdivisions that have become environmental wastelands, dumping grounds for garbage, and homes to drug dealers.

The unfortunate reality is that most of those entering the financial services industry in general have not been educated in the principles of sustainability, don't understand them well, and, in essence, believe that nothing matters to investors beyond securing the maximum possible return, typically over a short time horizon. The notion that an investor would balk at investing money in an organization or business model that might do damage to our social or environmental infrastructure is largely outside their frame of reference. As a consequence, any individual or institutional investor with a genuine desire to make his or her money work to promote some set of environmental or social objectives (or avoid investments in companies that do social or environmental harm) and at the same time ensure that he or she gets a competitive return at an acceptable level of risk, is viewed as something of an oddity. Such individuals, in turn, find the services of most financial advisors and investment managers entirely inadequate.

So, while the tight-knit community of First Affirmative professionals dedicated to serving the needs of socially conscious investors lies at the heart of the firm's success, the number of investment management professionals operating solely or largely in the SRI space has not grown as rapidly in recent years as Schueth and Gay anticipated when they took First Affirmative private in 1999. Schueth is puzzled and frustrated by this fact. He calls it the "hourglass problem." In the top of the hourglass sit increasing numbers of Cultural Creatives, which now represent as much as 15 percent of the adult population of the United States and all of whom are at least potentially socially conscious investors. In the bottom are ever-increasing numbers of good socially responsible mutual funds, exchange-traded funds, and other SRI investment products. In the waist of the hourglass sit the 500 or so investment professionals who represent First Affirmative's network targets. This group has not grown commensurately with the upsurge of interest in socially conscious investing or sustainable business.

Given that First Affirmative has achieved a high penetration of this existing small group of investment management professionals in the center of the hourglass, Schueth has concluded that the firm's future growth rate will be limited by what he feels will continue to be a sluggish expansion of this small target market group. He attributes this phenomenon to the fact that most financial professionals are, as described above, simply not attuned to the idea of investing that is driven by any motivation other than maximization of financial return, regardless of the nature of the investment. In any event, he regards this limited growth scenario as First Affirmative's biggest strategic challenge and is busy examining changes in the firm's traditional business model that he hopes will enable it to open up additional markets.

He has identified a group of investment management firms that, while not specifically targeted toward the needs of socially conscious investing, are at least aware of the fact that SRI investing exists and are smart enough to see that there is a growing SRI market that they are not well equipped to address. Most of these professionals, who generally manage their clients' money directly, work for smaller brokerage firms that do not have a wide range of socially responsible investment vehicles for satisfying the SRI requirements of these clients.

Schueth believes there may be as many as several thousand brokers/planners/advisors across the country that fall into this category. The firm is currently developing a program that will provide incremental value to those investment professionals who recognize the market needs but are not specifically intending to build their business focused on this market segment. Since First Affirmative would not be managing the money for these clients, First Affirmative's revenue would consist of a small portion of the total fee charged to the client by the brokerage firm or registered investment advisor. Margins would, therefore, be much slimmer than on assets directly under First Affirmative's own management, but Schueth believes that, as the ranks of socially conscious investors steadily increase, the total volume of business the firm can build through this program could be significant. In any case, it is likely to be the only way to break the hourglass problem.

CONCLUSION

What can we learn from First Affirmative's successful business model? Most importantly, this is a fine example of a company that identified and exploited a market niche that owes its origin and continuing growth to increasing public awareness. People realize that something has to be done about the fact that the world is running out of many of the natural resources on which we all depend and that large segments of the world's population continue to subsist in miserable and socially unacceptable conditions. Moreover, society in general—and on a global basis—is demanding that business must play a critical role in resolving these problems.

These concerns are widespread, but the proportion of the population that is prepared to take personal action to influence business behavior, while growing, remains quite small—perhaps 15 percent of the total in the United States, probably more in Europe. Still, it is these Cultural Creatives who have used their purchasing power to drive the growth and success of corporations like Whole Foods, Patagonia, Lands' End, White Wave Foods, Seventh Generation, and many others that have found a way to deliver products and services to satisfy their needs. Like these corporate giants (most of which only came into existence in the 1970s), First Affirmative has provided services that enable these same socially conscious consumers and investors to find investment vehicles that satisfy their goal of putting their money to work in ways that do good for society while providing a solid financial return.

Unlike some of the companies just mentioned, First Affirmative does not have the size and market power to influence the behavior of suppliers through its purchasing power, and, because its operations don't involve much in the form of tangible products—real estate, vehicles, and the like—it has a minimal opportunity to reduce its environmental footprint. Given these limitations, however, it has demonstrated a solid commitment to walking its talk and, just like the larger firms mentioned, has built an internal culture that allows it to recruit and retain highly competent, committed, professional staff whose objective—beyond earning a paycheck—is to make a difference in the way the business world works.

As business increasingly understands that it must improve its stewardship of the natural and human resources on which it depends, First Affirmative's leaders believe their firm will continue to grow successfully.

LESSONS LEARNED

(1) "An important component of First Affirmative's attraction for professional investment managers with an interest in SRI has been its disciplined approach to understanding the values of socially conscious investors, which are extremely diverse."

(2) Growing public awareness of global environmental and social challenges creates demand for new products and services that smart, innovative companies can take advantage of.

(3) Even companies that have a product or service that is intrinsically eco-friendly or socially responsible can boost their performance and image by walking their talk.

(4) Companies with a sustainability-based business model generally can recruit and retain the very best and brightest young people.

REFERENCES

Aberdeen Group, *Sustainability Matters: The Corporate Executive's Strategic Agenda,* April 2009, http://www.cintellate.com/news/ComplimentaryAberdeenReportonSustainabilityMattersTheCorporateExecutivesStrategicAgenda

A.T. Kearney, *Green Winners: The Performance of Sustainability-Focused Companies During the Financial Crisis,* March 2009, http://www.atkearney.com/index.php/Publications/green-winners.html

DuPont, *DuPont Sustainability,* 2010, http://liveneutraldupont.org/dp_sustainability

Ecomagination, 2010, http://ge.ecomagination.com/

"Mutual Funds: It Pays To Be Good = T.K.," *Business Week,* February 1 and 8, 2010, p. 69.

Ray, Paul H., and Sherry Ruth Anderson, *The Cultural Creatives: How 50 Million People Are Changing the World.* New York: Harmony Books, 2000

Social Investment Forum, *2007 Report on Socially Responsible Investing Trends in the United States,* 2007, http://socialinvest.org/pdf/SRL_Trends_ExecSummary_2007.pdf

Social Investment Forum, *Social Investment Forum: Two Thirds of Socially Responsible Mutual Funds Outperformed Benchmarks during 2009 Economic Downturn,* 2010, http://www.socialinvest.org/news/releases/pressrelease.cfm?id=151

SRI in the Rockies, 2010, http://www.sriintherockies.com/

Walmart, *Sustainability,* 2010, http://walmartstores.com/Sustainability/

Wikipedia: The Free Encyclopedia, *Socially Responsible Investing,* 2010, http://en.wikipedia.org/wiki/Socially_responsible_investing

THIRTEEN

Boulder Outlook Hotel

Natasha Gleichmann and Kenneth Bettenhausen
Contributing Research by Jamie M. Dandar

Boulder, Colorado, nestled against the foothills of the Rocky Mountains, just 35 miles northwest of Denver, is home to the University of Colorado's Boulder campus and the National Center for Atmospheric Research (whose team of climate scientists shared the 2007 Nobel Peace Prize with Al Gore). Boulder is a city known for its natural beauty, outdoor recreation, natural product retailers, and restaurants. Surrounded by a greenbelt of city parks and open spaces, Boulder is consistently included in various "Top 10" or "Top 25" lists. In the past two years, Boulder ranked: #19 Best Destinations in the United States, #9 Best Places to Live, #4 Earth Friendly Cities; #1 Recreational Cities, #2 Healthiest Towns in the United States, #1 Best Cities to Raise an Outdoor Kid; #8 Arts Destinations, #1 Top Town to Live Well, #2 Best Midsize Metropolitan Areas, #4 Most Bicycle Friendly Cities in the World, and #1 Most Educated City in America (City of Boulder, Colorado, 2010).

Boulder is also home to the Boulder Outlook Hotel and Suites. Dan King, the managing owner and self-proclaimed "ambassador of cool," opened the hotel in August 2003 with the goal of creating a place that would "reflect and celebrate the Boulder lifestyle: active, educated, progressive and different" (King, 2007, 2008). The Boulder Outlook is a mid-priced hotel with 162 guest rooms, 60 employees, and annual revenues of approximately $4 million. It offers a high level of services and amenities that, for the price, King says, "No one else in this market offers" (King, 2008).

From the outset, King wanted to run the hotel in as waste-free and environmentally friendly a manner as possible, starting with the building itself. The property first opened nearly 50 years ago as a Holiday Inn and expanded in phases to its present size. King relates, "The plan was to breathe life back into what was a struggling property and essentially recycle the building rather than tear it down and build a new property." Before opening as the Boulder Outlook in 2003, the property was refurbished to meet Leadership in Energy and Environmental Design (LEED) and Green Seal certification standards. High-performance heating, ventilating, and air conditioning systems were installed. From conception onward, the Boulder Outlook has integrated sustainability into every part of its operations and now serves as a proud model to any hotel wishing to follow in its footsteps.

SUSTAINABLE FROM THE BEGINNING

Because sustainability was a central value of the Boulder Outlook from the beginning, King did not face the difficulties that someone running an established enterprise would encounter in changing suppliers and operational procedures to go green. But locating suppliers and creating procedures that supported and were aligned with his values and vision were still critical challenges. King notes that, "as a trailblazer in the industry, it was difficult to locate available supply chain members willing to be a part of the sustainable process." Thankfully, King discovered a number of suppliers that had adopted sustainability as an operating strategy and so was able to extend the hotel's sustainability-oriented value chain beyond the operations directly under his control inside the walls of the hotel.

In addition to identifying compatible suppliers, re-visioning operating procedures was a critical step in creating sustainable practices. For instance, King shared that the hospitality staff had to have four trash receptacles, instead of just one, attached to their carts. It was not a huge adjustment, but it did involve extra work, so successful implementation was dependent upon a willing and motivated housekeeping staff. Through the conceptualization and implementation of adjustments such as this, King has created a hotel environment in which lofty sustainability goals have become realistic targets.

INITIATIVES AND METRICS

Buy the Right Things

Going green does not require dramatic investments. Many of the energy-efficiency strategies adopted at the Boulder Outlook are things any consumer wishing to go green could do. Among the decisions King made to reduce the hotel's environmental footprint were to purchase energy-efficient compact florescent lights, use paper made from 100 percent recycled content, purchase 10 percent of the hotel's electrical needs from wind power, and use green cleaning products.

Energy-efficient lightbulbs are simple to procure, even for individual consumers, and the spiral-shaped bulbs are easily recognizable. These compact fluorescent lightbulbs, known as CFLs, save the user approximately $30 over the life of the bulb, paying for themselves in around six months. The bulbs use 75 percent less energy than a standard incandescent bulb and last around 10 times as long (Energy Star, n.d.).

It is surprising that, in the United States, 90 percent of paper is still made from virgin wood considering paper made from 100 percent recycled content costs only modestly more and does not sacrifice quality. In fact, a study reported by RecycleWorks (of San Mateo County, California) found that recycled paper actually exceeds the standards for quality met by paper made from virgin wood and works without complications in office equipment. "For every 20 cases of recycled paper substituted for non-recycled paper, you save 17 trees, 390 gallons of oil, 7,000 gallons of water, and 4,100 kWh of energy. You eliminate 60 pounds of air-polluting emissions and save 8 cubic feet of landfill space" (RecycleWorks, n.d.). Since most paper suppliers and printing companies now offer a wide selection of papers with recycled content, this is a simple switch that can pay big dividends for a business in its quest to reduce its environmental impact.

The use of wind power is an increasingly popular option in businesses' attempts to go green. In the 2009 issue of *Wind Power Today,* the U.S. Department of Energy reports that, "according to initial estimates, the new wind projects completed in 2008 account for about 40% of all new U.S. power-producing capacity added last year. The wind energy industry's rapid expansion in 2008 demonstrates the potential for wind energy to play a major role in supplying our nation with clean, inexhaustible, domestically produced energy while bolstering our nation's economy" (U.S. Department of Energy, 2009). The wind and the sun are the two primary sources of renewable energy. Along with reducing overall energy usage through efficiency initiatives, greater utilization of clean energy is essential to reducing a business's total carbon footprint.

In an effort to protect both the environment and the health of staff and guests, in 2006, the Boulder Outlook switched from standard cleaning products to Green Solution cleaning products, manufactured by Spartan Chemical Company. These products are made without harmful chemicals and ozone-depleting compounds and do not have hazardous waste characteristics. In addition, because the products contain no carcinogens, mutagens, or teratogens, using these products enhances hotel workers' health and safety.

Water Conservation

Particularly for hotels offering amenities such as pools and hot tubs, water conservation is critical to reducing environmental impact. The Boulder Outlook employs a liquid solar cover and Panatol, a waxy substance added to the water, to reduce evaporation by 80 percent. Additionally, both the hotel's pool and hot tub are chlorine free, instead using ozone and bromine. Ozone decreases the amount of chlorine or bromine necessary to disinfect the pool water but works better with bromine, thus reducing the amount of chemicals needed (OzoneLab™ Instruments, 2010).

While it is difficult to control customers' use of water in their private rooms, water-conserving showerheads and low-flush toilets are used throughout the hotel, and King has installed a waterless urinal in the men's public restroom. Waterless Co. Inc. (2009) states that one waterless urinal can save between 20,000 and 45,000 gallons of water each year.

A major contributor to a hotel's environmental footprint is laundry. The Boulder Outlook reduces its impact by outsourcing its laundry to a local company, NexGen, that is "developing a patent pending laundry system which can reduce water usage by 80%. In addition their system will use less chemicals and a dehumidifying dryer which will recover a large portion of the energy used for drying" (Boulder Outlook Hotel, 2007). Although outsourced laundry operations use less water, soap, and energy than an in-house laundry operation, the fuel required to haul laundry to and from the hotel has an unfriendly impact on the environment. King reports, "Recently we increased our par levels of linen inventory by 33%. While this was a significant capital cost for us, it allows us to reduce delivery from NexGen to once a day, thereby cutting in half the environmental impact of delivery" (Boulder Outlook Hotel, 2007).

Waste Reduction

One of the most noticeable initiatives at the Boulder Outlook is the hotel's deliberate and dramatic journey toward zero waste. In all public spaces, wherever you would normally have found a trash can, you will find four containers—compost, trash, bottle and can recycling, and clean paper recycling—clearly labeled with examples of what should be discarded in each. Guests are educated with signs designed by Eco-Cycle that show where materials in each container will go, including photos of a landfill for trash items to discourage trash. All guestrooms have both a traditional wastebasket and a hand-painted box for recycling. Guests are encouraged to place compostable items in biodegradable bags so the hotel staff does not waste plastic bags transferring this material to the hotel's compost bins. Additionally, King notes in the hotel's corporate sustainability report that all of the hotel restaurant's to-go containers, disposable glasses, and straws are either made from paper or compostable materials manufactured from plant cellulose or cornstarch (Boulder Outlook Hotel, 2007; King, 2007).

"Composting is a natural biological process, carried out under controlled aerobic conditions (requiring oxygen). In this process, various microorganisms, including bacteria and fungi, break down organic matter into simpler substances" (Ecochem, n.d.). Because the Boulder Outlook composts not only soiled paper but also foods from its restaurant, including meat and dairy products, composted materials are taken to a commercial compost facility under a partnership with Eco-Cycle in Boulder, Colorado. Eco-Cycle hauls the compost to the commercial compost facility that uses a high-temperature process that kills undesirable bacteria so these items can safely decompose. King notes that, within 90 days, all of the waste composted by the Boulder Outlook is "back to dirt." Currently, 85 percent of the hotel's waste is disposed of through composting or recycling, but King notes that reducing the hotel's waste stream is an ongoing process that will not cease until the hotel becomes truly zero waste.

Just Say No to Plastic Water Bottles

Consumers are becoming increasingly aware that drinking water from disposable plastic bottles is not good for the environment. However, when traveling, the better practices guests might use at home are often pushed aside in exchange for convenience. It is especially important to drink lots of water at Boulder's high elevation (5,430 feet above sea level). As a result, water bottles and activity-specific hydration packs are a ubiquitous sight in and around the city. Prior to October 2007, when the "Just Say No to Plastic Water Bottles" measure was initiated, hotel guests were greeted with a single-serving plastic water bottle at the front desk, and water in plastic bottles was provided in executive guest rooms and in meeting rooms. Although the hotel offered recycling bins for empty bottles, King was concerned that this was not a very environmentally friendly practice. So the decision was made to stop providing water in plastic bottles. Instead, guests are offered 0.6-liter stainless steel water bottles for $6 when they arrive and can return them for a full refund at the end of their stay. Water purification systems throughout the hotel make this an attractive alternative to bottled water.

While these measures may seem mundane, taken together they have a significant impact. In the first 12 months of the Zero Waste initiative, the Boulder Outlook saved

- 361 30-foot trees
- 306 cubic yards of landfill space
- 150,000 gallons of water
- 120,000 kilowatt-hours of energy (enough to power 13 average U.S. homes)
- 1,300 pounds of air pollutants
- 3,371 cubic feet of methane gas (King, 2008)

In addition, the cost of gas and electricity fell from $129,000 to $100,000, a drop from $4.33 to $3.66 per occupied room, delivering significant savings to the hotel's bottom line.

Continued Innovation

Not content with these impressive accomplishments, King is constantly searching for new ways to increase the hotel's environmental sustainability. As presented in a video on the hotel's Web site, the Boulder Outlook is currently studying the purchase of carbon offsets in an effort to become completely carbon neutral (King, 2007). Another current initiative is using guestroom key cards made from recycled paper rather than plastic. The hotel currently uses 11,000 plastic key cards per year, many of which end up lost or discarded as a result of malfunctions. Replacing plastic cards with recycled paper would reduce the hotel's nonrecyclable waste, moving it closer to accomplishing its goal of becoming Boulder's first aero-waste hotel.

THE GREEN TEAM: EMPLOYEE INVOLVEMENT AT ALL LEVELS

Perhaps because environmental awareness is such a pervasive part of Boulder culture, employee buy-in has not been a problem at the Boulder Outlook. King constantly involves employees in every part of the sustainability process, ensuring that they feel a strong sense of ownership. As described in the company's sustainability report, "From day one the staff was involved. Dan had each staff member bring old paint that had been sitting in cans in their garages and basements to the hotel. On a Saturday afternoon, they and their families painted the cardboard boxes that would ultimately be placed in each hotel room for sorting and recycling purposes. The employees took ownership of the project."

It is in this spirit that King involves employees in all of the hotel's sustainability efforts, relying on their contributions to drive continuous efforts to reduce resource usage and adopt practices that increase sustainability. The hotel's Green Team is led by Diane Schevené, who began working with the Boulder Outlook in December 2005 and whose formal title is Green Goddess. The Green Team is comprised of representatives from each of the hotel's operating units: the kitchen, the restaurant, housekeeping, marketing, banquet services, special projects, and the front desk. The Green Team exists to track the hotel's current position relative to its environmental goals and ensure progress is being made toward improving its overall sustainability. "They meet once a month in order to identify the most effective steps in making the hotel ever more sustainable, to instigate new projects and, subsequently, to communicate with hotel staff, guests and the public about these happenings" (King, 2008).

King admits that his journey toward zero waste has not been without challenges. "Collecting and hauling four different streams of materials (mixed paper, co-mingled containers, compost and trash) from each of our 162 guestrooms and from the public areas of the hotel has required operational changes and ingenuity on the part of our staff" (King, 2008). King credits his line-level staff members with demonstrating leadership in these initiatives and taking ownership of the hotel's efforts.

It is no accident that King's staff buys in so readily to the hotel's sustainability focus. King notes that he often does not have a particular position in mind when hiring. He so strongly believes that the employee's fit with the business's culture will influence his or her contributions to the hotel that he often looks for "the proper attitude and motivation" before considering the technical qualifications of the job.

HOW DO THEY AFFORD IT?

Of course, many business owners would love to make their businesses more sustainable, but, in rough economic times, committing financially to such a process can be daunting. Surprisingly, when asked about the expenses associated with his hotel's environmentally friendly initiatives, King remarked that the financial benefits greatly outweighed the costs. King termed "negligible," the cost differentials associated with the green products and cleaning supplies used by the hotel. He reported it costs the Boulder Outlook approximately $600 a month to maintain the zero-waste initiatives, $150 of that specifically attributable to hauling waste, compost, and recyclables. King notes that amount is dwarfed by the savings from energy and water conservation measures. In addition, King reports "an increase in business of at least $10,000 per month. The majority of this comes from corporate accounts, but walk-in business has increased as well" (King, 2008).

CONSTANT JOURNEY TO BECOME EVEN MORE GREEN

While the Boulder Outlook's success in its sustainability efforts rightly serves as an inspiration to other businesses, King continues to strive for even better practices. In the area of guest recycling, for instance, King notes a 60 percent participation rate, attributing what he perceives to be a low rate to lack of commitment on the part of his staff rather than the guests. "The owners launched it before the team had achieved it. Currently, approximately 60% of guests participate in the recycling program. In order to move this number closer to 100%, we will need to improve upon it by having 'The Green Team' develop and implement new processes" (King, 2008). In every area of hotel operations, King relates that the hotel staff "goes as far as it can and is always looking for new, better, or further means by which to maintain and improve upon its zero-waste model."

THE OTHER SIDE OF SUSTAINABILITY— COMMUNITY INVOLVEMENT

The Boulder Outlook does not limit its sustainability efforts to the environment. Through a number of programs, King hopes to contribute to the greater Boulder community. To ensure the development of his staff, King offers English as a second language courses free of charge. The hotel also partners with the Boulder Valley School District, providing on-the-job training in the hotel's restaurant to students with disabilities, and has hired one of the students from this program. As a member of the Boulder Community Foundation, 2 percent of the hotel's profits are donated annually to charity. In addition, nonprofit charitable organizations can use the hotel's executive boardroom for meetings. Through the hotel's Local Artist

Program, the Boulder Outlook supports local artists by displaying their artwork in the hotel's lobby, providing wine and cheese receptions, and selling the artwork without charging a commission. Last, through the hotel's environmental stewardship, working with students from a variety of schools and universities, and speaking at industry conferences, King hopes to spread the word about sustainable business practices.

ADVICE AND SECRETS TO SUCCESS

The Boulder Outlook Hotel and Suites has succeeded in implementing and profiting from its sustainability initiatives through the consistent and committed efforts of every hotel employee. While King shares how success depends on employee involvement and ideas, the staff notes the necessity of having a leader whose passion is infectious, and all agree that King is just that kind of leader. From jumping into a dumpster to sort waste to his constant search for new or innovative ways to achieve zero waste, King's passion and commitment are apparent to, and noticed by, the staff.

When asked for some words of wisdom for those just embarking on the journey toward sustainability, King exclaimed, "What are you waiting for?! You can't just say that you're going to do it and expect it will happen. It is essential to obtain commitment from top to bottom and really work it, revisit it, think about how you're going to do it. You must have a true and unrelenting dedication for sustainability. There is no end in sight, only a journey. There is always room for more improvements. Lastly, the staff must be awarded with the opportunity and flexibility to make positive changes" (King, 2008).

The success of the Boulder Outlook is enviable, and one might assume that King would fear copycat operations. Boulder is certainly a ripe environment for such businesses, and when good deeds are rewarded with profits, competition could pop up quickly, threatening the hotel's unique position in the market. This possibility does not worry King at all. In fact, his response is quite the opposite to what might be expected of a business owner. In his 2007 sustainability report, King stated: "We have been advocates of other businesses adopting environmentally sensitive programs, particularly within the hospitality industry. We have spoken out at industry meetings encouraging other hotels and restaurants to join the Zero Waste movement" (Boulder Outlook Hotel, 2007). He encourages questions from other businesses about what they can do to make their companies sustainable and looks forward to the day that the Boulder hotel community will be entirely waste free and carbon neutral.

LESSONS LEARNED

(1) Building an environmentally friendly operation is a continuous effort.

(2) Employees are crucial partners in implementing and improving operations and procedures that improve sustainability. Involve them, empower them, and use their ideas.

(3) Direct savings from energy and water efficiencies more than pay for the direct costs of zero-waste efforts and environmentally friendly products and cleaning supplies.

(4) Although you have to look for them, you can find suppliers and service providers that also operate as sustainably as possible. Don't limit your efforts to your own operations.

REFERENCES

Boulder Outlook Hotel, *The Boulder Outlook Hotel's 2007 Corporate Sustainability Report,* http://www.boulderoutlookhotel.com/docs/2007CSR.PDF

City of Boulder, Colorado, http://www.bouldercolorado.gov

Ecochem, *Composting Process,* n.d., http://www.ecochem.com/t_compost_faq2.html

Energy Star, *Learn about CFLs,* n.d., http://www.energystar.gov/index.cfm?c=cfls.pr_cfls_about

King, Dan, Video on Boulder Outlook Hotel's sustainability efforts, 2007, http://www.boulderoutlookhotel.com/ecovid.html

King, Dan, Personal interview by Jamie Dandar, January 2008.

OzoneLab™ Instruments, http://www.ozoneservices.com/faq/faq015.htm

RecycleWorks, *Why Buy Recycled?* n.d., http://www.recycleworks.org/paper/paper_wbr.html

U.S. Department of Energy, *Wind Power Today,* April 2009, http://www.nrel.gov/docs/fy09osti/44889.pdf

Waterless Co. Inc., *Water Conservation,* 2009, http://www.waterless.com

PART III

Overall Lessons

FOURTEEN

Overall Sustainability Lesson: Why Small and Medium-Sized Firms Should Invest in Sustainability

Blair Gifford

Most firms are occupied with selling products and meeting payroll and feel they don't have time or aren't all that impassioned about "saving the world." However, ignoring sustainability is not really an option. All businesses have stakeholders to whom they respond. Stakeholders, such as employees, customers, and other businesses, make choices, and their loyalty can be fickle. Maybe a handshake and a nice holiday card will keep a few close stakeholders loyal, but there are many competitive small and medium-sized businesses out there; especially during trying economic times, businesses should not disregard the views of all of these people and firms who do business with them.

The tipping point has occurred. An ever-growing chorus demands and expects firms to fit their views of the world into a paradigm of sustainability. The varied and strong interests of these stakeholders might include:

- Insurance companies that view environmental threats as business risks
- Consumers who wonder what's in the products they buy and whether an organization is adding benefit or taking it away
- Business-to-business customers who demand that suppliers reveal how they make their products and exactly what's in them

- Employees and potential recruits who want to work for an organization that will match their values and passions. After all, no one wants to have the name "Enron" on his or her resume.
- Banks that reinforce all these concerns by factoring environmental risk and other sustainability issues into loan decisions.

These stakeholders and others can have a real effect on a business's fortunes. As a result, a business's relative sustainability can play a role in whether projects are financed, the ease of taking products to market, and whether a company is able to attract and retain customers and employees.

HOW SMALL AND MEDIUM-SIZED FIRMS FIT

Large and small companies are being held responsible for a broader set of social responsibilities than in the past, such as product safety, quality assurance for products and services, ethical business practices, safe and healthy working conditions, fair trade, responsible marketing and communication, stakeholder involvement, transparency, and moral codes of conduct. The weight these sustainability practices are given varies among companies.

Of course, a company's size influences its sustainability initiatives. Virtually every company in the Fortune 1,000 has a sustainability director, and consequently those companies often have well-developed sustainability policies. Smaller firms are less likely to have such a position and so lack similar policies. According to a recent survey in *The Economist* (Economist Intelligence Unit, 2008), four times as many large companies engage in triple bottom line reporting—environment, social, and financial—compared to smaller firms. These differences between big and smaller companies many not reflect dramatic differences in the sustainability outlook, because smaller firms tend to have fewer policies in general and may operate in accordance with sustainability goals without explicit policies.

Regardless of stated policy, the lack of coherent sustainability strategies within small and medium-sized businesses does matter. On specific environmental and social outcomes, larger firms rate their efforts much higher than smaller ones. For example, 38 percent of larger firms rank their efforts on greenhouse gas and waste reduction as being very good, compared with 19 percent of smaller and medium-sized firms. Even more striking, more than twice as many small firms ranked themselves as poor performers for every sustainability action in *The Economist*'s survey.

The reason smaller and medium-sized firms are less likely to adopt sustainability measures may be due to expectations and market pressures. Small and medium-sized firms are under less pressure to deliver sustainability strategies. These firms are generally not the targets of activists, so they don't have to build their defenses. Another factor is that small and medium-sized companies tend to be local.

Whatever the reason for their poorer performance on formal metrics, small and medium-sized businesses need to improve their sustainability. They face the same opportunities and challenges as large, global companies do. And, in many ways, there are niche opportunities that small companies can fill that are often overlooked by large corporations. Further, the performance of small firms has great implications for the aggregate success of sustainability. Some 80 percent of companies worldwide are small. The aggregate of their problematic activities can have a substantial impact. Also, small companies tend to find more innovative ways to meet social needs, and their size often enables them to implement decisions more quickly than large firms, which tend to require multiple levels of approval; there's every reason to believe this is as true for achieving sustainability as it is in other areas of small business.

Finally, many smaller firms are local in orientation. Owners and managers live and work in a chosen location and have a stake in the locale. These location choices are often rooted in emotion rather than economics. Belief in and commitment to a common purpose rooted in the bond entrepreneurs have with their chosen locations drives value for these businesses more than the scale of production does. Thus, sustainability holds real meaning for smaller businesses and delivers both profitability and excellence in behavior as measured by the quality of relationships. In such environments, the idea of work-life balance, as well as sustainable values, is not a mystery.

LEADERSHIP

So who is tasked with leading the charge? There seems to be no consensus about this. Managers want all employees to take the initiative in sustainability, while employees expect corporate leaders to lead the drive. The best course might be to enliven sustainability interests by bringing on people who want to save the world, giving them space to be innovative, and figuring out how to keep sustainability as a core corporate value. As promising as such a grassroots, populist-based approach might be, the responsibility for leadership still falls on management. Employee turnover is a given, but managers are more likely to stay the course. There are four basic strategies that managers should implement to advance a sustainability-based vision for their companies: know the company, see sustainability as an opportunity, integrate, and monitor and report the impact.

Know the Company

Sustainability programs should be based on companies figuring out what they think is right and acting accordingly. The programs should not be based on changing and fickle public demands. A company can't be all things to all people, but it can be a leader on a particular issue or two that are of interest in their markets—both external and internal to the firm. Thus, a well-grounded firm will know when to say no to outside influences.

See Sustainability as an Opportunity

One of the biggest challenges organizations face in addressing sustainability issues is outdated mental models and perspectives on sustainability. Many companies either are oblivious to sustainability issues or just don't know what to do first. At its best, sustainability programs can open the way to new market opportunities and prepare a company for the growing risks in these areas. Sustainability should not be viewed as the latest fad that one has to adopt to be seen as current. Nor should sustainability be seen as a burdensome imposition from the outside. Sustainability is about the relationship of business to other elements of society. Taking account of social and environmental issues can lead to extensive innovation and goodwill that will cut costs in the long run.

Integrate

Sustainability will not work as an add-on. It needs to be integrated into corporate structures and processes and become a core mission. Such change can be hard to manage, but it is a key element of success. Employees need to understand the goals to realize a vision, and they need to be evaluated and rewarded accordingly. These goals can range from new sustainable product development, to conservation, to customer relations. But to merit employee buy-in and ownership, the company's own people need to be part of the goal setting for sustainability.

Monitor and Report the Impact

A company must measure baseline conditions and then analyze the impact of interventions for sustainability to demonstrate program impact and credibility. Moreover, such analysis should include all aspects of the triple bottom line—environment, social, financial and even employment benefits. Of these, companies should not shy away from reporting the employment benefits. After all, maybe *the* primary benefit of doing business sustainably is the creation of wealth and jobs.

KEY STRATEGIES FOR SUSTAINABILITY

Translating the concept of sustainability into practice is highly challenging. Several tools and methods of thinking provide strategic and visionary frameworks for companies that are considering the development of sustainability strategies, such as the triple bottom line of people, prosperity, and planet. What is clear from this list of broader responsibilities is that sustainability issues are not just about the environment but also about the broader notion of relations at the market and local levels, both within the firm and in the community.

Although there may be a combination of reasons, there is usually a primary motive for a firm to go green. It may be for tactical reasons, such as avoiding fines for breach of environmental legislation, costs associated with waste disposal, heavy taxes, or bad publicity. The motive also might be saving money or responding to competitors. There is also the possibility for exploiting the concept, such as utilizing sustainability as a marketing tool to attract further business and to paint a positive image. After all, if only some of the market is environmentally aware or active, perhaps there is an opportunity for market segmentation with those environmentally aware groups. Another motive for wanting to go green may be pressure or influences from various stakeholders, such as customers, government, interest/pressure groups, media investors, financial institutions, and the local community. Some company decision makers have also become aware that there are both internal and external opportunities and benefits to becoming green. Examples of these include cost savings from gained efficiencies and lessened waste, reduced risk, the enhanced ability to enter international markets, and employee recruitment and retention. Finally, there may be altruistic or moral influences, such as concern about the environment and community. Decision makers who feel a genuine sense of responsibility are likely to be more inclined to take a long-term sustainable strategic position.

Also, these decision makers may feel they have to consider green issues because of the nature of their business and its environmental and social impacts.

A primary motivation for going green is revenue generation. An A. T. Kearney report (Environmental Leader, 2009) found that, during the current economic slowdown, companies that have had a true commitment to sustainability have outperformed their industry peers in financial markets. Specifically, the report found that, in 16 of the 18 industries examined, companies recognized as sustainability-focused outperformed their peers and were better protected from value erosion. The companies that were defined as sustainable are included in either the Dow Jones Sustainability Index or the Goldman Sachs SUSTAIN focus list.

Likewise, *The Economist* (Economist Intelligence Unit, 2010) reported in its 2009 survey of sustainability and corporate growth that "sustainability leaders believe that sustainability provides a market advantage: 43 percent say that is important to customers compared with only 16 percent of respondents from other firms in the survey. Similarly, 39 percent of sustainability leaders believe that sustainability can enhance revenue growth a great deal, compared with 26 percent from other firms." For example, sales of General Electric's Ecomagination line of products rose by 21 percent compared with just a 5.8 percent growth for the company overall in 2008. Looking ahead, 80 percent of sustainability leaders see these initiatives as very important to future growth, compared with 40 percent of all others in the survey.

The case studies in this book were chosen as best models across a variety of industries. The goal of the book is to make owners and managers of small and medium-sized businesses aware of the possibilities that sustainability can present to their firms and to help entrepreneurs and managers gain a level of comfort going forward. Given the potential of revenue generation and profitability from sustainability, the next question that small and medium-sized business owners need to ask is: On which sustainability strategy or strategies should we focus? Lack of clarity about how to begin might be due to limited knowledge of similar companies and their sustainability experiences. But it also might be due to an underappreciation of the value proposition of sustainability.

The results of *The Economist* (Economist Intelligence Unit, 2008) survey of "key motivations for sustainability initiatives" provide a structure for analyzing and summarizing the findings presented in the case studies. These motivations include branding and marketing, regulation and cost savings, and creativity and new products. To these three, a fourth motivation—employee relations—is also relevant. Employee relations is particularly important in the more intimate and local setting of small and medium-sized businesses.

Regulation and Cost Reduction

The recent malfeasance in financial services is only the latest in a series of scandals that have eroded public confidence in the economy. Over the past decade, several U.S. corporations came to symbolize betrayals of public trust—Enron, Adelphia, Tyco, HealthSouth, Sunbeam, Worldcom, Waste Management, and Imclone. According to the *Edelman Trust Barometer, 2008,* just 38 percent of the self-described informed adults in the United States trust businesses (Edelman, 2008). This is a decline of 20 percentage points from the previous year, and the lowest level of trust in a decade. As a result, governments are going to take an especially keen interest in how business is managed for the foreseeable future.

Managers in the private sector who have grown accustomed to ducking behind corporate and government-relations professionals will need to develop new mind-sets and skill sets that will enable them to maintain a collaborative rather than adversarial relationship with government entities. Managers should expect a new type of working partnership where governments will offer incentives for desirable business behavior, and executives will work more directly with governmental agencies to tap into those incentives. It's tempting to adhere to the lowest environmental standards for as long as possible. However, it's often smarter to comply with the most stringent rules before they are enforced. To do so may yield substantial first-mover advantages in terms of fostering innovation and scooping market share.

For example, hospitals are notorious for having many compliance issues to address. Realizing the substantial cost savings and cost avoidance that sustainable practices often beget, **Boulder Community Hospital** (BCH) uses sustainability to meet regulatory requirements and as part of its fiscal strategy. BCH has become a leader in using wind energy; promoting alternative transportation; developing green, high-performance, sustainable buildings; and in recycling. The use of green techniques has earned the organization several certifications and awards. BCH began its sustainability efforts out of a sincere concern for the health of the community it serves. Due to its sustainability practices, it was able to save over $500,000 in costs associated with energy consumption through its Leadership in Energy and Environmental Design– (LEED-) certified building and use of renewable energy.

Foreseeing the potential for a company dedicated to proper e-waste disposal, Mike Wright decided to create **Guaranteed Recycling Xperts** (GRX), an electronic waste recycler, for his next business endeavor. Although he did not intend to build a cleantech company or to create a sustainable business model, Wright anticipated there would be a market for this type of service in coming years. As Wright predicted, governments began passing laws regarding e-waste disposal, and consumers began demanding guaranteed destruction to avoid fines, ensure privacy of data, and limit bad publicity. GRX used sustainability to expand its customer base. The company used new laws prohibiting businesses and local governments from disposing of electronics in landfills as an opportunity to market its service to a range of small organizations, therefore increasing the company's revenue. Wright also utilized relationships with like-minded associations to raise awareness about his business and has received ISO 9000 and 14000 accreditation, which give GRX a distinct competitive advantage. Sustainability is a cause that has proven both beneficial to the environment and to GRX, and it continues to be a driving force as Wright grows the business, expanding across the Rocky Mountain region.

Once companies have learned to keep pace with regulation, they become more proactive about environmental issues. At this more evolved level of sustainability, corporations work with suppliers and retailers to develop eco-friendly raw materials and components to reduce waste. As a result, large corporations can be a source of great stress for small and medium-sized businesses, demanding ever-lower prices with no cut in quality or service. Increasingly, they demand information on what's contained in products, where the ingredients and materials are sourced, and how the products are made. In many industries, proof of environmental responsibility has become a requirement for getting major contacts and keeping customers. The sustainability relationship between large companies and smaller suppliers can potentially be more productive and less stressful through increased collaboration.

Walmart is probably the best known big firm for increasing pressure on suppliers in recent years, demanding lower fossil fuel use and reduced packaging and waste. The company has asked all its suppliers to fill out performance scorecards as a way to drive change and improve Walmart's overall record. Walmart has even asked suppliers to calculate the energy use of their products—a cradle-to-grave approach—from raw materials to manufacturing to distribution. This pressure is spreading through the supply chain: Walmart suppliers press their own suppliers, and so on.

Creativity and New Products

Sustainability demands innovative practices that integrate green values into the structures, processes, and incentives that mold behavior inside companies. Social and environmental initiatives should not be something that firms do in addition to their profit-making activities. Instead, sustainability should be a central part of the strategy for a company's prosperity.

Sustainability is not a single process; it doesn't lend itself to straightforward calculation of profit and loss. Sustainability alters how companies approach issues. Any business model variation will have some benefits and some drawbacks, leaving results dependent on execution as much as new ideas. Thus, it is probably best to look at the economic opportunities sustainability provides, rather than overall net financial benefits from adopting sustainable practices.

Green innovations such as those that reduce emissions through energy efficiency and the use of alternate energy sources, natural products, and waste reduction programs have become popular in recent years. Companies with a history in green innovations have reaped the most benefits, and those that continue to make meaningful investments will continue to prosper both in terms of business results and public perception. For example, **The Digital Frontier** did not adopt sustainable practices as a conscious strategy to increase market share and profits. Instead, the company realized the potential value of this business model after winning a bid due to its use of a Heidelberg DI offset printing press, which employs a greener printing process than traditional presses. Only after discussing trends with other exhibitors at an industry trade show did company president Mark Scott fully realize the opportunity sustainability offered.

This insight was the impetus behind a transformation of the company's marketing efforts, emphasizing its eco-friendly practices. Today, this marketing campaign continues to provide momentum toward the company's goal to optimize its sustainability. Unlike some companies that have been able to cut costs through sustainability, The Digital Frontier often incurs greater costs to use greener processes and products, such as soy-based inks and more sustainable equipment. However, the company remains dedicated to reducing its carbon footprint and continues to use sustainability as a primary marketing strategy.

Developing a new product or even a new business model requires exploring alternatives to current ways of doing business as well as understanding how companies can meet customers' needs differently through sustainable approaches. Managers must learn to question existing models and to act entrepreneurially to develop new delivery mechanisms. As companies become more adept at this, the experience will lead them to new products that extend beyond a single market. For example, **Eco-Products** food service suppliers, the brainchild of Kent and Steve Savage, was conceived in 1990 in response to the burgeoning environmental movement. The father-son duo sought to carve out a unique market niche using sustainability as a primary strategy to drive profit through innovation. According to that first business plan, the company's goal was to "capitalize on both the reality and perception among consumers and businesses that it is crucial to both recycle and purchase recycled products."

Throughout its life, Eco-Products has consistently used this core concept—to expand the market for recycled-content products—to inform its actions. This model spurred innovative ideas that continue to help the company capture greater market share and helped to form a culture that encourages creativity and global thinking. For example, the company looked to Asia, where compostable technology is far advanced. As a result, Eco-Products was able to distinguish itself from its competition by building a unique brand, reducing costs, and developing superior products. Using sustainability as its beacon, the company plans to gain even more market share with the spin-off company, Ellie's Eco Home Store, making a wide variety of environmentally friendly products and services available to the general public.

Marketing and Customer Relations

Small and medium-sized businesses are local in orientation. The desire to do the very best for clients, while not always seemingly rational or economic, builds relationships of intrinsic value that promise both resiliency and longevity. Smaller companies just can't afford the damage to reputation and long-term bottom line that accompanies poor workmanship, so they strive to make certain there isn't any. Thus, sustainability holds real meaning for smaller businesses and delivers excellence in behavior as measured by the quality of relationships as much as profitability. Work is embedded in life and a community of interest and sustainable values.

With sustainability at the heart of its operations, the **Denver Machine Shop** reduces costs by allowing very little to go to waste, extending the life of cutting fluids and turning off all compressors and machines each night. Yet, as important as these sustainable best practices are, for Denver Machine Shop, sustainability has and continues to be primarily about customer relations. Denver Machine Shop has used the core value of customer relations to drive profit for nearly 100 years and continues to do so in all its operations. By being active in community matters, and through excellent craftsmanship, it has given something back and instilled loyalty in the community. Practices like these make Denver Machine Shop the most long-lived, sustainable machining company in the area.

Another benefit of sustainability policies is enhanced reputation, which increases brand value and reduces reputational risk. Some expected benefits are the opportunity to attract and retain customers, the ability to manage reputational risk, and the higher perceived value of a brand renowned for its commitment to sustainability. For example, **Forest City,** a large private-sector development firm, added sustainability to its value statement after becoming master developer at Denver's Stapleton community in 1998 and adopting the *Green Book* as Stapleton's sustainability plan. The role sustainability would play in Stapleton developed along with the community. According to Sustainability Director Melissa Knott, sustainability pervades all the company's activities and is used as a strategy to brand the community, attract loyal customers, and ensure positive public relations. With 30 percent of its land dedicated to open space and environmentally friendly services such as park compost areas and a recycling program that helps fund a children's center, Stapleton real estate is in high demand. Consequently, home prices have increased 10 percent every year until the 2008 recession and have maintained their value while many other home prices have declined considerably.

A leading sustainability focus in business is communicating performance to investors and stakeholders. The reputational effects of such a policy certainly exist. At a basic level, good credentials can be essential for a social and sometimes literal license to operate. For example, **Boulder Valley Credit Union**'s (BCVU's) interest in sustainability was partially financially motivated. The cost savings of installing a solar electric system made fiscal sense. The company used sustainability as a strategy to increase return on investment through reduced energy costs. Chief Executive Officer Rick Allen decided to install energy-efficient lighting and windows and a Fat Spaniel monitoring system on the Web site that shows how much electricity the system produces, along with energy savings generated by the new panels. These efforts generated favorable publicity for the credit union and were the driving force behind the use of sustainability as part of the marketing message.

Fueled by the positive feedback from customers and the industry, the Boulder Valley Credit Union's sustainability efforts gained momentum and set it down the path of authentic sustainability rather than the green-washing public relations campaigns that are prevalent across industries. The credit union added additional solar panels, forged partnerships with eco-conscious groups, and began using eco-friendly supplies. This change in direction did not always reduce costs, but it did pay off in the form of awards and certifications, which allowed BVCU to brand itself as an eco-conscious financial institution, giving the company a competitive advantage over other financial institutions in a community that prides itself on sustainability.

Boulder Outlook Hotel from the start had a mission to reflect the values of the Boulder, Colorado, community to maintain a healthy community, to protect the environment, and to offer fun, informal hospitality. Dan King made the decision to be Boulder's first zero-waste hotel and that the costs of being environmentally conscious were costs of doing business that would be absorbed. With new customers and revenues, these costs were more than offset. Boulder Outlook Hotel has had tremendous success attracting environmentally conscious customers.

Employee Relations

Good employees truly can be the competitive edge for a firm's survival. We know that the key intrinsic motivators for employees are the desire for autonomy, mastery, and purpose. Firms that fulfill these needs go a long way toward creating high-performance environments. This is especially pertinent in small and medium-sized businesses. Smaller size puts a spotlight on individual performance. This is amplified by the intimacy and immediacy of relationships, which create a desire not to let one another down, employees and clients alike. A real alignment with employee interests creates an organization that delivers inherent motivation.

When **New Belgium Brewery** outgrew Jeff Lebesch's basement and then its second home, the railroad depot, and moved into its current location in downtown Fort Collins, it did not leave behind its dedication to environmental responsibility or its entrepreneurial and small business feel. In the beginning, Jeff and his wife Kim Jordan created a list of company aspirations regarding social and environmental stewardship that still hold true today. The first company in the United States to get 100 percent of its energy from wind power, New Belgium Brewery did not stop there; the company continues to design more efficient processes that reduce environmental impact and enhance the company's bottom line, such as heat recovery systems, an on-site process water treatment plant, and various automations of the brewing process.

These sustainable ventures make New Belgium Brewery a rewarding place to work, and serve as a great example of how a firm can use sustainability as a strategy to recruit and retain good employees. New Belgium Brewery is also a great example of how a firm that profits and grows from sustainability can still be a fun and creative workplace where employees are committed to their jobs. This holds real meaning for people and delivers excellence in behavior, measured by the quality of relationships and a community orientation.

With **Boulder Outlook Hotel**'s mission to protect the environment and reflect the values of the Boulder, Colorado, community, employees took on the role of environmental leaders as well, meeting every week to see what's the next thing that can be tackled to accomplish goals to be completely waste free in the future. Customers also became part of the community for improving the environment, learning how to personally become waste free, with the hotel providing examples of how to do this.

Values truly are a primary consideration for businesses today. They help companies find business opportunities and motivate both employees and partners. Employees are hungry not just for their paychecks and some creativity in their jobs, but they also want to work for companies that pay attention to worldly and environmental issues. Companies such as **First Affirmative Financial Network** (FAFN) that invest in sustainability in logical ways, have the potential to unleash an emotional commitment in their employees. FAFN shows that the business model of profit as the only bottom line for a company fails, because it is not rooted in any real sense of belief in the purpose of work beyond the instrumental requirement to earn money. It fails because it has no qualitative component of meaning and does not instill in employees a commitment to a common sense of purpose that is rooted in values and place.

Since its inception, FAFN has been focused on socially responsible investing. Throughout its existence, the company has used sustainability to drive profits through innovative product development that focuses on fulfilling the demand from investors who wish to make philanthropic and profitable investments. The company enjoys a distinctive position as one of the few companies operating in this market segment. It has used its dedication to social and environmental sustainability to market itself and build a solid reputation in the industry. Sustainability not only stimulates profits by cornering this specific market, but it has proven to be a valuable recruitment instrument, too. The company's fundamental mission is especially attractive to job seekers, allowing FAFN to choose among the best in the industry, reducing recruitment costs, and increasing productivity.

Table 14.1   Key Drivers for Sustainability Strategies

	Regulation and Cost Reduction	Creativity and New Products	Marketing and Customer Relations	Employee Relations
Eco-Products		Primary	Secondary	
Barrett Studio Architects		Primary	Secondary	Secondary
Forest City		Primary		Secondary
Boulder Community Hospital	Primary		Secondary	Primary
Digital Frontier		Primary	Secondary	
Boulder Valley Credit Union	Primary		Secondary	Secondary
New Belgium Brewing	Secondary			Primary
Guaranteed Recycling Xperts	Primary	Secondary		
Denver Machine Shop	Secondary		Primary	
Boulder Outlook Hotel	Secondary		Primary	
First Affirmative Financial Network		Secondary	Primary	

THE WAY FORWARD FOR SMALL AND MEDIUM-SIZED FIRMS

Regardless of whether a company wants to save the world, there are numerous good reasons for small and medium-sized businesses to proceed with sustainability plans. As described in the preceding chapters and summarized in this chapter, there are four primary strategies of sustainability that bring value and profits to a smaller or medium-sized business: cost reduction from conservation and regulatory compliance illustrated by Boulder Community Hospital and Guaranteed Recycling Xperts; new product creation demonstrated by Eco-Products and The Digital Frontier; the need to match the interests of customers and business clients in behavioral and attitudinal changes they are making toward sustainability showcased by Denver Machine Shop, Forest City, and Boulder Valley Credit Union; and harder-working and top employees seen at New Belgium Brewery and First Affirmative Financial Network.

Our research enabled us to confirm many of the beliefs that we have held about sustainability in business, but we also learned some new things. For instance, we were surprised at the wide range of factors that caused our small companies to embark on a sustainability journey in the first place. As expected, it was often the personal philosophy of the owner or founder to use his or her business not only to make a living but also to contribute to the wider good of the planet, society, and the local community. It is this notion of the local community that often separates the sustainability practices of small and medium-sized businesses from the more formalized sustainability process initiatives undertaken by large non–community-based corporations. In others, the impetus toward a more sustainable business model came from a severe environmental regulatory problem that was threatening the very viability of the enterprise or perhaps the need to break out of a market stalemate by developing new products designed to build a brand image around eco-friendliness or social responsibility. In one case—Boulder Community Hospital—the actions of two midlevel employees (nurses) kicked off a corporatewide drive toward sustainability.

In almost all cases, we found that companies started off with small, typically inexpensive initiatives, achieved some measurable successes, and then moved on to more ambitious steps once they realized the benefits, even for a small business. We also confirmed that sustainability is as much about the preservation of human capital and employee relations as it is about being green. People at all the businesses realized that they could use sustainability as a focus for building a strong, productive environment that engaged the commitment of employees over and above the basic need to earn a paycheck. Further, we found that the leaders of the featured companies were intensely proud of their sustainability efforts, not just because they felt the efforts had helped them to build a more financially successful business, but also because they felt they were making a real contribution to the welfare and well-being of the community and society in which they operate. They were more than willing to share their thoughts and ideas on sustainability in small businesses and have committed to support our continuing educational efforts in the future by making themselves available for teaching and presentations.

In sum, most small and medium-sized businesses are defining sustainability broadly, looking at a range of relevant environmental and social goals. The specific form that sustainability policies take for these firms, however, is inevitably shaped by varying drivers, needs, and values. Fortunately, small and medium-sized businesses rarely need to establish clear new values for themselves. Instead, they need to apply the ones they already have regarding environment, location, employees, and customers. Thus, social and environmental initiatives should not be something that small and medium-sized businesses do in addition to making profits. Instead, they should become a central part of a company's values and strategy for prosperity.

LESSONS LEARNED

(1) "Large and small companies are being held responsible for a broader set of social responsibilities than in the past, such as product safety, quality assurance for products and services, ethical business practices, safe and healthy working conditions, fair trade, responsible marketing and communication, stakeholder involvement, transparency, and moral codes of conduct."

(2) "Belief in and commitment to a common purpose rooted in the bond entrepreneurs have with their chosen locations drives value for these businesses more than the scale of production does. Thus, sustainability holds real meaning for smaller businesses and delivers both profitability and excellence in behavior as measured by the quality of relationships."

(3) "People at all the businesses realized that they could use sustainability as a focus for building a strong, productive environment that engaged the commitment of employees over and above the basic need to earn a paycheck."

(4) "The specific form that sustainability policies takes is inevitably shaped by varying drivers, needs, and values. Fortunately, small and medium-sized businesses rarely need to establish new values for themselves . . . thus, social and environmental initiatives . . . should become a central part of a company's values and strategy for prosperity."

REFERENCES

Economist Intelligence Unit, "Doing Good: Business and the Sustainability Challenge." *The Economist,* 2008, pp. 1–52 (sponsored by A.T. Kearney, Bank of America, Orange, Jones Lang LaSalle, PricewaterhouseCoopers, SAP and ExxonMobil, SunGard), http://a330.g.akamai.net/7/330/25828/20080208191823/graphics.eiu.com/upload/Sustainability_allsponsors.pdf

Economist Intelligence Unit, *EIU Mediadirectory Summary, "The Link between Sustainability and Profits Remains Unclear to Businesses in the Short Term, According to New Research,* February 8, 2010, p. 1, http://www.eiuresources.com/mediadir/default.asp?PR=2010020801

Edelman, *Edelman Trust Barometer, 2008,* http://www.edelman.com/TRUST/2008/TrustBarometer08_FINAL.pdf

Environmental Leader, "Sustainable Companies Outperform Peers during Financial Crisis," *Environmental Leader.Com,* February 11, 2009, p. 1, http://www.environmentalleader.com/2009/02/11/sustainable-companies-outperform-peers-during-financial-crisis/

Glossary

Affordable Living: Developing diverse, affordable housing offerings, including housing that below median income households can afford.

Aspen Institute Beyond Grey Pinstripes: The Aspen Institute is a non-profit institute with the mission to foster values-based leadership and encourage individuals to reflect on ideals, discuss, ideas, and act on critical issues. Beyond Grey Pinstripes encourages social environmental stewardship in the Masters of Business Administration (MBA) graduate school curricula and research of universities. MBA programs are ranked worldwide on their preparation of students for social and environmental stewardship (see http://www.beyondgreypinstripes.org/index.cfm).

Balanced Scorecard: A company report that not only includes how a firm is doing in terms of profits (a financial dimension) but also includes a focus on people (a social dimension) and the firm's effect on the planet (an environmental dimension), at times noted as economic, environmental, and equity dimensions.

Basel Action Network (BAN): A nonprofit charitable, watchdog, and educational organization with the mission to prevent the globalization of the toxic chemical crisis, including the export of toxic waste, technology, and toxic products to developing countries by industrialized nations (see http://www.ban.org).

Biodegradable Products Institute (BPI): A not-for-profit association of key individuals and groups from government, industry, and academia.

BPI promotes the use and recovery of compostable materials through municipal and backyard composting and provides information and resources for finding a composter. BPI has a compostable label program for educating manufacturers, legislators, and consumers about scientifically based standards for biodegradable materials, as well as other services (see http://www.bpiworld.org).

Brownfield Site: An abandoned industrial or commercial facility made available for another use or redevelopment that may necessitate an environmental cleanup before it can be reused.

Carbon Cap and Trade: Trading emissions to reduce pollution, whereby economic incentives are provided. A government or other central authority provides a cap or limitation on the amount of pollutant emissions, and firms are allowed to issue emission permits with the requirement that they must have a sufficient, equivalent number of allowances or credits to be given this right (which cannot be greater than the cap). Firms buy credits from other firms with less pollution if they need to increase their emission allowance, and credits can be traded on carbon exchanges, such as the Chicago Climate Exchange (www.chicagoclimatex.com), and other affiliated exchanges. (See http://en.wikipedia.org/wiki/Emissions_trading for a detailed discussion, including a history of cap and trade and trading systems for different countries, and http://www.exchange-handbook.com for a survey of carbon exchanges.)

Carbon Footprint: A measurement of the impact of activities that a firm or individual has on the environment in terms of the amount of greenhouse gases produced with use of fossil fuels for electricity and transportation, among other uses. A primary carbon footprint shows direct emissions of CO_2 from these activities (referred to as Scope 1 emissions, which are based on firm-controlled or -owned activities). A secondary footprint includes the indirect CO_2 emissions based on the entire lifecycle of products used (referred to as Scope 2 emissions, such as the purchase of electricity from a utility company, and Scope 3 emissions, such as business travel, employee commuting, outsourced activities, and waste disposal).

Carbonfund.org: A nonprofit organization with the mission of moving toward a ZeroCarbon™ world by making it easy and affordable for individuals, businesses, and other organizations to reduce and offset their carbon impact and facilitate the transition to a clean energy future with climate change education, carbon offsets and reductions, carbon calculators and worksheets, small and large business partnerships, and public outreach (see http://carbonfund.org).

Carbon Offsets: A financial instrument whose purpose is to reduce greenhouse gas emissions, with one carbon offset equal to the reduction of one metric ton of carbon dioxide or its equivalent for other greenhouse gases. Two markets exist: a compliance market, where organizations purchase carbon offsets to meet a required regulatory cap on carbon emissions that are allowed, and a smaller voluntary market for purchasing carbon offsets to reduce a firm's greenhouse gas emissions from direct or indirect emissions. Many firms offer carbon offsets for sale (up-sell), and many companies provide services to help firms measure their carbon footprint and purchase offsets, including financial support of projects that reduce greenhouse gas emissions (see http://en.wikipedia.org/wiki/Carbon_offset for a detailed discussion).

Cathode Ray Tubes (CRTs):   Tubes used in computer monitors, televisions, and other technological equipment made of thick glass that contains large amounts of lead to protect users from the hazard of radiation. The lead content makes CRTs difficult to recycle.

Chicago Climate Exchange (CCX):   A financial institution with the objectives to apply financial innovation and incentives to promote social, environmental, and economic goals using the Chicago Climate Exchange and the Chicago Climate Futures Exchange (CCFE). CCX is North America's only cap and trade system for all six greenhouse gases, with global affiliates and projects worldwide. CCFE is a derivatives exchange that offers standardized and cleared futures and options contracts on emission allowances as well as other environmental products (see http://www.chicagoclimatex.com).

Cleantech: Technology developed and used to better utilize the world's resources. Cleantech represents a diversity of products, services, and processes with the purpose of providing superior performance with lower costs while reducing or eliminating the ecological impact and improving both the responsible and productive use of natural resources (see chapter 1 and http://cleantech.com/about/cleantechdefinition.cfm).

Climate Conservancy Assessment: A life-cycle assessment (LCA) by the Climate Conservancy, a group of university, business, and engineering professionals and graduate students that developed its own standards for LCA that concentrates on greenhouse gas emissions (see http://www.climateconservancy.org).

Climate Leaders Small Business Network: A U.S. Environmental Protection Agency–sponsored consortium of small business leaders that measure, set, and achieve goals to reduce their greenhouse gas emissions. The network provides members training, best practices, and the opportunity for public recognition for their accomplishments. A business is considered small if it has annual revenue less than $200 million and uses less than 15 million kilowatt-hours of purchased electricity per year, less than 1 million gallons of transportation fuels per year, and less than 2 million therms of natural gas per year (see http://www.epa.gov/stateply/smallbiz/small biznetwork.html).

Climate Registry: An organization that provides guidelines for measuring and reporting green house gas inventory (www.theclimateregis try.org).

Compact Fluorescent Lightbulb (CFL):   An energy-saving type of lightbulb that uses less power with a longer life. Because CFLs contain mercury, their disposal can be complex.

Connectivity: In the context of designing a housing development, connectivity refers to easy access to and a diversity of various means of transportation (see chapter 4, "Barrett Studio Architects").

CORE: Connected Organizations for a Responsible Economy: A nonprofit business association based in Denver, Colorado, with the mission to help small and medium-sized businesses to understand how they can benefit and achieve competitive advantage through sustainable business strategies.

Corporate Social Responsibility/Sustainability Report: A report to stakeholders (stockholders, employees, customers, regulators, and others) about a firm's activities to protect the environment, reduce any negative environmental or social impacts from its operations, and to benefit society.

DEHP: A softener for polyvinyl chloride used for intravenous bags and tubing (and other hospital uses). Some individuals with certain medical procedures can be exposed to high levels of DEHP (Di(2-ethylhexyl) phthalate), and the compound has produced adverse effects in laboratory animals.

Eco-Cycle: A nonprofit firm in Boulder, Colorado, that provides assistance with and expertise on recycling, zero-waste certification to help business, individuals, and communities become zero-waste entities (see http://www.ecocyle.org).

Eco-Friendly Products: Products that are environmentally responsible—good for people and the environment. Examples are nontoxic, recycled, natural, organic, nonpolluting, and low- or no-waste products that involve little or no damage in their production and use by consumers.

Elegant Density: In architecture, when a variety of sizes of residential and mixed-use buildings exist and form layers of complexity and create a sense of community and diversity. Elegant density allows services and amenities to be provided within a primarily residential community (see chapter 4, "Barrett Studio Architects").

Energy Star: A government-backed program to assist businesses and individuals to reduce their energy consumption and protect the environment by utilizing products with superior energy efficiency (see http://www.energystar.gov). Products are provided ratings based on their energy efficiency. In addition, Energy Star energy performance ratings are often included in some green building standards, such as Leadership in Energy and Environmental Design. The Energy Star program has also developed performance rating systems for several commercial and institutional building types and manufacturing facilities (see a detailed discussion at http://en.wikipedia.org/wiki/Energy_Star#Energy_Performance_Ratings).

Environmental Management System (EMS):   A set of practices and processes used by a firm to reduce its impact on the environment and increase its operating efficiency (see http://www.epa.gov/ems).

Environmental Protection Agency (EPA):   A U.S. government agency with the mission to protect human health and safeguard the natural environment upon which life depends, including administering laws to protect the environment and an educational mission (http://www.epa.gov).

Equator Principles: An agreement among large international banks and financial institutions for environmental standards and principles in lending. The principles include guidelines on social and environmental issues in lending to developing countries and making environmental assessments of major loans.

European Climate Exchange (ECX):   A leading marketplace for trading carbon dioxide emissions in Europe and internationally, with two types of carbon credits traded: EU allowances and certified emission reductions (see http://www.ecx.eu).

E-Waste Disposal: Disposal of electronic products such as computers, monitors, televisions, fax machines, copiers, telephones, and cabling that are difficult to dispose of and contain components that can cause environmental harm if not recycled or disposed of properly.

Global Reporting Initiative (GRI):   Provides general indicators for economic, social, and environmental reporting with protocols to explain each indicator, methodology, the intention for the scope of each indicator, and sector supplements for particular industry sectors (http://www.global reporting.org).

Greenhouse Gas Emissions (GHGs):   Gases that trap heat in the atmosphere. Some GHGs, such as carbon dioxide, are naturally emitted. Others result from human activities and include carbon dioxide as the result of fossil fuel burning, solid waste, and other chemical reactions; methane from the production and transportation of coal, natural gas, and oil; nitrous oxide from agricultural and industrial activities; and fluorinated gases from different industrial processes (see http://www.epa.gov/climate change/emissions/index.html and http://www.greenhousegasemissions. com).

Greenhouse Gas Inventories: An accounting of greenhouse gases created over a year or another specific time interval, providing information on the activities creating emissions and details on the methods used for calculations (see http://www.epa.gov/climatechange/emissions/index.html).

Greenhouse Gas Protocol (GGP):   Provides methods for measuring and reporting greenhouse gas inventory (see http://www.ghgprotocol.org).

Greening the Economy: Creating green-collar jobs that provide benefits to the environment, such as developing new pro-environmental types of energy and new products that reduce waste and promote sustainability. The United Nations Green Economy Initiative assists governments in greening their economies by investing in clean technology, renewable energy, water services, green transportation, waste management, green buildings, and sustainable forests and agriculture; reducing greenhouse gas emissions; using and extracting fewer natural resources; and reducing waste and social disparities (see: http://www.unep.org/greeneconomy).

Greenprint Denver: Part of the U.S. Mayors Climate Protection Agreement, whereby cities provide information and education and take steps in their own governmental operations and communities to reduce their impact on worldwide global warming pollution. The goal is to meet or exceed targets set forth by the United Nation's Kyoto Protocol (see http://www. greenprintdenver.org).

Green Supply Chain: Having suppliers that engage in sustainable practices and meet a firm's green goals. Green supply chain practices include telecommuting, reducing packaging, using recycled products, paper reduction, information technology optimization that results in more efficiency and lower operating costs, transportation management systems to optimize the transport of goods and eliminate less-than-full-truckload deliveries, using efficient heating and cooling mechanisms, and other earth-friendly practices (see http://www.greensupplychain.com).

Greenwashing: Advertising by an organization promoting its pro-environmental reputation versus actually engaging in pro-environmental activities.

Harvesting the Sun: An architectural concept whereby the solar exposure available to all lots on a site is studied to provide protective measures, including thoughtful site planning and solar fences to enable daylighting design features and solar energy (see chapter 4, "Barrett Studio Architects").

Institute of Scrap Recycling Industries (ISRI):   An association of companies that process, broker, and consume scrap commodities, providing sustainable solutions for the balance of environmental stewardship and economic growth (see http://www.isri.org).

International Organization for Standardization (ISO):   Sets environmental management standards and provides certification for companies that meet these standards. The ISO also provides guides to help assess environmental issues based on available information on a product's life cycle.

ISO 14000:   A series of process standards of eco-management and audits for continuous improvement by the International Organization for Standardization (ISO); it has become an international standard for environmental certification (see http://www.iso14000-iso14001-environmental-managemen.com/ for a discussion of the different ISO 14000 standards).

ISO 26000:   A voluntary guide for all types of organizations including small to medium sized firms that provides concepts, definitions, and terms associated with social responsibility, principles and practices, core subjects and issues, and advice on the integration, implementation, and promotion of socially-responsible behavior throughout an organization, issued in November 2010 (see http://www.iso.org for detailed information).

LEED Standards: Building to LEED standards includes consulting costs and working with the U.S. Green Building Council, which often costs more to build but leads to considerable future energy savings. LEED is an internationally recognized green building certification system that provides third-party verification that a building or community used strategies to improve performance across all metrics for energy savings, water efficiency, CO_2 emission reduction, indoor environmental quality, resource stewardship, and impact sensitivity (see http://www.usgbc.org/DisplayPage.aspx?CMSPageID=1988).

Life-Cycle Analysis (LCA): A detailed analysis of the total impact of a product, including consideration of both wholesale and retail operations and the supply chain of materials and transportation used to create the product. LCA involves a measure of the environmental and social impact of a process, allowing managers to analyze the LCA results to identify any opportunities for improvements in a product's design or process to reduce its environmental impact. *Cradle-to-Grave:* The life-cycle analysis on a product from manufacture to the end of a product's life. *Cradle-to-Gate:* The life-cycle analysis on a product from manufacture to distribution. *Cradle-to-Cradle:* The life-cycle analysis on a product expected to be recycled at the end of its useful life. *Gate-to-Gate:* The life cycle analysis for a product that works only on value-added processes. *Well-to-Wheel* is a life-cycle analysis for the transportation of a product (see Chapter 2: Measuring Costs and Benefits).

Light Emitting Diodes (LED): An energy-saving light that uses diodes, which are electronic components that allow electricity to pass in only one direction, emitting visible light with the application of electricity, similar to a lightbulb.

Living Community: A community designed as an interconnected system of built environments, cultivated food-producing plots, and significant tracts of open space (see Chapter 4: Barrett Studio Architects).

Permaculture: The design of systems for agriculture, developments, cities, regions, and other types of human settlements that emulates ecological relationships in nature.

PVC: Polyvinyl chloride plastic used in home furnishings, packaging, toys, auto parts, building materials, and hospital supplies. PVC is the most environmentally damaging of all plastics, contaminates humans and the environment throughout its life cycle, and has toxic properties.

Recycling: Preventing waste of useful materials by converting them into new products; reducing the consumption of raw materials, energy use, and pollution; attempting to lower greenhouse gases.

Reduce, Reuse, and Recycle: A common mantra for helping to reduce the environmental impact of human activities and waste fewer natural resources.

Renewable Choice Energy: A company located in Boulder, Colorado, that partners with firms to calculate total greenhouse gas emissions and to purchase a corresponding number of verified emission reductions, a commodity sold to finance U.S. methane capture projects.

Resource Awareness: A commitment to reduce energy use compared to required energy standards, such as by 50 percent (see chapter 4, "Barrett Studio Architects").

Socially Responsible Investing: Also known as ethical or socially conscious investing, this investment strategy has dual goals of maximizing an investor's return and supporting social good, including stewardship of the environment and other social goals (for a detailed history and discussion, see http://en.wikipedia.org/wiki/Socially_responsible_investing).

Sustainable System: A system that matches present and future needs but does not harm renewable resources and unique human-environmental resources of a site: air, land, water, energy, mineral resources, human ecology, and other (off-site) sustainable systems (see chapter 1, "Introduction").

Sustainability Management System (SMS):   An all-encompassing approach of identifying and organizing efforts, setting up baselines, and defining and creating plans for sustainable actions across an organization (see, for example, a discussion of the Boulder Valley School District at http://www.bvsd.org/green/Pages/sms.aspx).

Three Ps: People, Planet, and Profit (or sometimes referred to as Prosperity), a focus on not only profit, but also reducing a firm's environmental impact to allow the earth to regain its capabilities for self-recovery to allow the global environment to be sustained, and where environmental, social, and economic activities and relationships produce an ideal society (for a detailed definition and efforts, see http://www.ricoh.com/environment/management/earth.html).

TIF: Tax Increment Financing is a type of public financing that provides a subsidy for community or country economic development for socially desirable projects. The public financing entity (such as a municipality, state, or national government) provides the subsidy with the view that once the development is completed, the value of the real estate in the area will increase resulting in increased tax revenues. With tax incremental financing, tax increments are in turn used to repay the debt issued initially to pay for the project (see http://en.wikipedia.org/wiki/Tax_Increment_financing and http://www.lincolninst.edu/pubs/1078_Tax-Increment-Financing for additional details).

U.S. Green Building Council: A nonprofit organization and community of leaders that work to make green buildings available, perform LEED certification, and provide education and resources (see http://www.usgbc.org).

Verified Emission Reductions: A commodity sold to finance U.S. methane capture projects.

Zero Carbon Footprint: Reducing a carbon footprint by managing sustainably (recycling, solar power, composting, and other practices) and offsetting any remaining carbon emissions created by purchasing carbon offsets.

Zero Waste: A concept encouraging the redesign of product life cycles, so there is a reuse of all products (for a detailed discussion, see http://en.wikipedia.org/wiki/Zero_waste).

Index

About the Editors
and Contributors

ABOUT THE EDITORS

FRED ANDREAS, AIA, LEED AP, is a principal architect registered in the state of Colorado; a national certified architect, NCARB LEED AP; and assistant professor at the University of Colorado Denver, with 30 years of experience in ecological, sustainable, and green design throughout the United States.

ELIZABETH S. COOPERMAN is a professor of finance and entrepreneurship and currently serves as the MBA program director for the Business School at the University of Colorado Denver.

BLAIR GIFFORD is an associate professor of international health management in the Business and Public Health Schools at the University of Colorado Denver and a Senior Lecturer in Yale University's Global Health Initiative. He was awarded a New Century Scholar/Fulbright (Haiti) in 2009/10.

GRAHAM RUSSELL was formerly the executive director of Connected Organizations for a Responsible Economy (CORE), a sustainable business association based in Colorado, and is currently a Sustainability Consultant in Denver, Colorado.

ABOUT THE CONTRIBUTORS

STEPHEN R. BERNARD is an environmental engineer and manager with over 20 years of environmental and sustainability experience in the aerospace and telecommunications industries and is currently completing a master of business administration degree focused on sustainability.

KENNETH BETTENHAUSEN is an associate professor of management and currently serves as the management program director for the Business School at the University of Colorado Denver.

ELIZABETH R. BROST is an entrepreneurial consultant and is currently a master of business administration student at the University of Colorado Denver.

CLAY CHASE is a student of architecture at the University of Colorado Denver.

JAMIE M. DANDAR has a master of business administration degree with an entrepreneurial focus from the University of Colorado Denver and is director of business development at Cameron-Cole, LLC, a national consulting firm in sustainability, social responsibility, and climate change/greenhouse gas management.

SHAREN A. DURST-ALDRIDGE is a Christian, mother of four, and a master's degree candidate of architecture in the College of Architecture and Planning at the University of Colorado Denver.

BECKY ENGLISH is a Denver-based sustainability consultant specializing in creating and documenting corporate responsibility initiatives.

NATASHA GLEICHMANN is a master of business administration student at the University of Colorado Denver.

PAMELA GOODRICH-YOHE holds a master of architecture degree from the University of Colorado Denver.

ROBIN GROPPI is a business manager for her project management company, SPACEmatters, and recently received her master's of architecture and urban design from the University of Colorado Denver.

DAVID JACOBS is a student of architecture at the University of Colorado Denver.

ELIZABETH LONG has a master of business administration degree in managing for sustainability from the University of Colorado Denver and is a Sustainability Business Consultant in Denver, Colorado.

LIZ LOWRY is a graduate of the University of Colorado Boulder.

CLINT MCCARVER is a graduate of the University of Colorado Boulder.

K.J. MCCORRY is the owner of eco-officiency, a sustainable consulting company based out of Boulder, Colorado, that works with small and medium-sized businesses to develop sustainability plans. She is the copresident of Connected Organizations for a Responsible Economy and serves as a director of the International Society of Sustainability Professionals.

JENNIFER MICH is a corporate responsibility analyst at ProLogis. She has a master of business administration degree and master of science degree in marketing from the University of Colorado Denver.

MARIBETH NEELIS is a graduate student in the master of business administration health administration program at the University of Colorado Denver.

CARRIE YASEMIN PAYKOC has a bachelor of science degree in biology and a master of business administration degree in health administration and a master of science in managing for sustainability at the University of Colorado Denver. She currently works at Mercury Healthcare and is the incumbent executive director for Global Health Connections.

MARIA ELENA PRICE is a graduate of the University of Colorado Boulder.

ALAN ROMERO is a graduate of the master of business administration degree in health administration at the University of Colorado Denver.

SARAH E. THOMPSON has a master of business administration degree in managing for sustainability and a master of science degree in management, both from the University of Colorado Denver, and teaches wilderness survival and hiking skills in Colorado.

CHRISTOPHER THORP, ASSOC. AIA, LEED AP, is a graduate of the University of Colorado College of Architecture and Planning with a master of architecture degree and is currently an associate at Arcadea Architecture in Boulder, Colorado.